from Michael +
Paul October
2017

The Love of Impermanent Things

The

LOVE

of

IMPERMANENT

THINGS

A Threshold Ecology

MARY ROSE
O'REILLEY

MILKWEED EDITIONS

Published 2006 by Milkweed Editions
Printed in Canada
Cover design by Kristina Kachele Design, llc
Cover illustration by Albrecht Dürer, used by permission of the Albertina, Vienna.
Author photo by Robin Fox
Interior design by Brad Norr Design
The text of this book is set in Goudy.
06 07 08 09 10   5 4 3 2 1
First Edition

Milkweed Editions, a nonprofit publisher, gratefully acknowledges sustaining support from Emilie and Henry Buchwald; Bush Foundation; Patrick and Aimee Butler Family Foundation; Cargill Value Investment; Timothy and Tara Clark Family Charitable Fund; Dougherty Family Foundation; Ecolab Foundation; General Mills Foundation; Greystone Foundation; Institute for Scholarship in the Liberal Arts, College of Arts and Sciences, University of Notre Dame; Constance B. Kunin; Marshall Field's Gives; McKnight Foundation; a grant from the Minnesota State Arts Board, through an appropriation by the Minnesota State Legislature, a grant from the National Endowment for the Arts, and private funders; an award from the National Endowment for the Arts, which believes that a great nation deserves great art; Navarre Corporation; Debbie Reynolds; St. Paul Travelers Foundation; Ellen and Sheldon Sturgis; Target Foundation; Gertrude Sexton Thompson Charitable Trust (George R. A. Johnson, Trustee); James R. Thorpe Foundation; Toro Foundation; Serene and Christopher Warren; W. M. Foundation; and Xcel Energy Foundation.

Library of Congress Cataloging-in-Publication Data

O'Reilley, Mary Rose.
   The love of impermanent things : a threshold ecology / Mary Rose O'Reilley.— 1st ed.
      p. cm.
   ISBN-13: 978-1-57131-283-9 (alk. paper)
   ISBN-10: 1-57131-283-8 (alk. paper)
   1. O'Reilley, Mary Rose. 2. Poets, American—20th century—Biography. 3. English teachers—Minnesota—Biography. 4. St. Paul (Minn.)—Biography. I. Title.
   PS3615.R456Z46 2006
   813'.6—dc22

For Peter Crysdale

The Love of Impermanent Things

Prologue
Family Recipes

As I'm making dinner, the blender stops blending and begins to go *thunk thunk thunk*. Damn, what's wrong with it now? My daughter Julian, home for vacation, is experimenting with a vegan diet. She gets in the way of my cooking, reads the label on everything I put in the soup; no dairy product must pass her lips. Before she got to analyzing the contents of the stockpot, I slid it into the blender. *Thunk thunk*.

I pour a stream of puree back into the soup kettle, more steamed potatoes into the blender. *Thunk*.

"Julian, taste this." She pokes around in the puree, adds soymilk. I taste it, add some dill.

"It's a weird color."

"That's just the carrots." We go to the table, hold hands, and pray over the soup. Julian opens her eyes and says, "There's a tail in my soup.

"It's just a piece of basil stalk that got missed in the blades."

But then I notice, even with my weak eyes, the circular epidermal contours on . . . the . . . tail . . . in my soup.

We are now jumping up and down in the living room, and screaming, though without commitment. Neither of us is particularly bothered by mice, nor even by the possibility of ingesting them. We ate hot dogs for many years: what do you think is in those? *Eeee-eee-eee!* we scream, a mother-daughter bonding thing. This amuses us for a while. *Eee-eee.* I stick an experimental fork into my soup and

1

engage a tail of my own. My piece has a tiny foot attached. *Eeeeeeee!*

We speculate for some time about how the mice got into our soup and decide, finally, that they must have fallen into the blender some months ago, starved, and mummified. This is the least disturbing scenario we can come up with, and we cling to it. Then we go out for Thai. Tofu in coconut milk. Very white, very clean.

If you want to know something about the life of any family, begin with a sentence about *eating*. Begin at the dinner table, begin with the word *food* . . .

I love old cook pots, the ones that remind me of my Grandma Rose's cooking and even my mother's, which is odd, because neither of them was known for her great hand in the kitchen. Nor am I. Last week in a thrift shop I happened onto a treasure trove of copper-bottomed pans from the 1950s with a full kit of steamer contraptions and double boilers and cauldrons. So now I am cooking turnips. Rare is the steamer you can let simmer for twenty minutes without its boiling dry, but this deep old pot will do the trick.

When my grown children come home to visit, I make them tour my Griswold frying pans and chicken cookers: "Some day this will all be yours." Lately I have begun to beg them, "Take this, will you? It belonged to your great-grandmother." I'm afraid that I'm going to forget which of the old, black pans belonged to Rose O'Reilley and which came from yard sales and the Goodwill. But it was from Rose O'Reilley, that simple cook, that I got my love of the iron skillets in which she cooked her wondrous, comforting eggs.

"I cannot replicate the eggs," my sister tells me. "Even with the iron frying pan." Peggy is the master cook that Rose was not. She would be too conscientious to slather in lard or bacon grease, which was the secret ingredient in our grandmother's rolls or fry bread. Fry bread is ubiquitous in all the cuisines of poverty. My Grandma Rose told me how, when she would come home from school, "My mother had the bread rising and nothing else to eat in the house, so she would nip a pinch of the half-risen bread and deep-fry it in the pan for us."

My mouth would water. Oh, to be poor. To live on fry bread and a bit of sugar. Sometimes Grandma would make fry bread for us, but more often the treat was scrambled eggs. She'd begin with a pat of butter or bacon grease in the iron pan, then stir in eggs whipped a little with Carnation's evaporated milk and salt. She'd stop when the eggs were yellow and a little wet.

Grandma could also produce anything in the root vegetable line, potatoes, turnips, sweet potatoes, carrots—your heavy-lifting vegetables—or all of this combined in a "boiled dinner." I think of this as the cuisine of Ireland, though I may be wrong. I'm told they also have salmon, but perhaps only for the landlord.

I'm steaming these turnips for my mother. They are a beautiful saffron color. I don't like turnips, but they are one of my mother's favorite foods. If I bring them out to her house, she will be happy for a little while, and I will ease for myself the guilt that gnaws at me because I can so seldom please her.

These are the things my mother was good at cooking: Swiss steak simmered for hours in a thin tomato gravy, served with new potatoes, green salad with "California" dressing or "Ranch": it all came to the same thing, Miracle Whip with a few tablespoons of catsup in it. My mother loved to cook with all the canned and bottled and boxed things that came on the market after the war. Miracle Whip went into most things, into the canned string beans, into a kind of tartar sauce she made by chopping up bottled pickles into the Miracle, onto peanut butter on white bread, the kind that builds strong bodies eight ways.

Bottles and bottles and cans of stuff came into our house, straining the grocery bags week after week. A fussy eater, I mashed the canned peas to mush with the tines of my fork and spread them around the huge plates with their design of apple blossoms—"the Franciscan,"

Mom always called it, brand names everywhere, as though remembering to carry the smooth coins of popular culture ranked with memorizing the succession of English kings.

Soon I was learning to cook, which in our house was accompanied by a kind of carnival flair. We would make, for example, angel food cake with a little package of colored candies that came in the box, called "confetti angel food." At the last alchemical moment, you would toss in the candies to melt into the white flesh of the cake. Once, in 4-H, I got a blue ribbon for a cake I'd made, and then was disqualified when the judges asked for my family recipe. I was dumbfounded. The idea that cake came from any family but Pillsbury was beyond me. Mom said she could dimly remember one of her aunts cracking dozens of eggs to make angel food cake, but this she considered primitive behavior, something you might do in Albania. "It tastes the same, anyway," she said, and argued this point with the judges, who let me keep my ribbon.

"Your mother can talk like a Philadelphia lawyer," Grandma Rose would say darkly.

I wish I had been able to pick up some crumb of charm from my mother's feistiness, but instead I learned to button down, because she embarrassed me with her strident assertion. As I stand here stewing these turnips of which she is inordinately fond, I try to retrieve memories of her kindness. I remember her cooking fried cornmeal. Nowadays they call it *polenta* and charge $4.98 for a little bag of the stuff. When I used to make cornmeal mush for my children, we called it our "Little House on the Prairie" dinner. No wonder they grew up to be vegans. Leftover cornmeal mush can be sliced into steaks and fried; my mother would put the fried cornmeal ceremoniously before my old great-uncle Boo, who lived with us until he died. Tears would come to his eyes when she served it. "I didn't think I'd live to eat this again," he'd inevitably say, pouring maple syrup onto the comfort food of his childhood.

Boo would sit by the hour in the picture window with one of our cocker spaniels on his lap. All his life—because railroad engineers weren't allowed to smoke—he chewed tobacco. Next to his chair my mother would put a red coffee can for him to spit into, and several times a day he'd knock it over onto the carpet. Nobody minded. We all loved him profoundly, my mother most of all. Her own father had died young—one of the traumas that defined her life—and her mother, my Grandma Josie, was violently psychotic. Thus, it was Uncle Boo and his "maiden sisters," Mamie and Sadie, who nurtured my mother through the crises of life and love. They made sure she had a bunny-fur wrap for the senior prom and money for college. She returned this devotion to them as long as they lived, and when they died, she couldn't recover. She incurred Grandma Rose's indignation for the things she got up to, and alienated many of those she might have depended on. If now, in her old age, I mention to her the name of any relative or friend, I loose from her a torrent of vituperation and spite. Each one, she tells me, has methodically insulted her. Since my father died she has become reclusive, holing up in her house with an incontinent, snappy dog and the carton after carton of cigarettes my sister dutifully brings her. Stopping off for those hated cigarettes week after week is one of the bravest acts of my sister's conscientious life as a nursing professor: "What if one of my students sees me?" she frets.

This morning I read in the *Tao Te Ching*:

> When a truly kind man does something, he leaves nothing undone.
> When a just man does something, he leaves much to be done.
> . . . .
> Therefore the truly great man dwells on what is real and not what is on the surface.

To her old relatives, my mother did kindness. She left nothing undone. I can only do justice, and steam turnips. I phone her, as I do most every day. "How are you?"—and she is off on one of her spiteful narrations. I always feel scalded when I hang up. My sister and I keep trying to have a relationship with her, to understand her, but we don't have the compassion or the skills, I'm not sure which.

At the heart of the labyrinth, we recognize our mother's motherlessness.

There was an old photograph of her, leaning over a pool of water in a sort of Maxfield Parrish pose. Bending over the water, she stares into her own brown eyes; her skin is the shade of expensive paper; her smile is the smile called "pert" in the stories read by women under the hairdryers, "plucky." She looks into her reflected face, seeing her own image, I guess, in something of the way a mother sees the child at her breast, the child she cannot get enough of seeing, the visitor from its foreign cloud. Her own mirrored gaze seems to mesmerize her, just as the infant stares back into the eyes of the mother, all the world, too shortsighted and disoriented to see anything beyond the mother. Here the fundamental orientation is established, crystal north of the soul. This elemental gaze is not merely a *look* but a cementing of subject and object, on which the child, object, begins to grow and thrive. A seeing-into and a being-seen that changes the neurological structure of mother and child, a new tarot flung down from quick hands, a fate: *see me, know me.*

In my mother's case, all haywire.

If the mother does not return the gaze, as crazy Grandma Josie most certainly did not, the child must learn to stare into her own eyes. It's a matter of survival. The eyes of my mother's mother were shuttered against her, her mother's mind closed to her. Therefore she began searching, caught finally the image in shallow water. *Love me, love me*—crooning into the brown eyes, auburn lashed—*return my gaze so that my sight can focus, quiet the hunger with which a baby comes into the world.*

Many people who know about such things have taken a tour around my mother and pronounced her "narcissistic": in recalling this old photograph I have unconsciously tied her into the story about the beautiful boy who fell in love with his own reflection and was changed into a flower for his vanity. That's not the worst punishment I can think of, and, anyway, narcissi are sacred lilies to the Chinese. The old myth seems to recognize how unpredictable can be our progress toward compassionate involvement with the human community, how easily something like a hereditary crimp in the soul can leave us stranded in self. The story of Narcissus condemns us benevolently: *be a flower forever.*

But, in fact, my mother had little vanity. She was, if botany can image her, a lotus, hallowed for its ability to spring out of the muck (the teeming fourplex our extended family inhabited together; her pathological mother; the secrets my cousins hint at about alcoholism, teenage pregnancy, incest)—*plucky.* Dysfunction and environmental stress simply caused my mother to shoot up, triumphant, through her green fuse. It was not an easy performance to be with, but it had its exemplary quality. Her life must be evaluated in terms of her own proud boast: "I never had a single nervous breakdown."

However, our mother required attention, and my sister and I learned to give it. We both entered the "helping professions." In middle age, I for one, am learning to *withhold.* I'm not particularly proud of this; many women learn to define themselves as "givers," and without this identity, who are we? I suppose I could find a pool to gaze into, searching for an answer.

Pools and looking glasses are sacred to Celtic mythology. But it's not *yourself* you're supposed to come up with, scrying that way: rather, the future or the past. All the mirrors in my house are old and cloudy. At the top of the stairs I often meet strangers, lately, my Mormon great-grandmother in that beveled frame, her hair slicked back, her little round spectacles.

"What do you write about?" my mother asks one day.

"Oh, just my life."

"Who'd want to know about that?"

"Well, just *life,* then."

Mom likes Regency romances, a taste I find odd, but what do we know about our parents, after all? "Why don't you write about me?" she goes on.

"Why don't *you* write about you?" I respond.

"I'm not such a narcissist," she says. Nudge, nudge.

"Well, it's a sacred flower to the Chinese."

It's dim in my kitchen, where I sit on the phone, steam turnips, and talk with Mom. My end of the conversation is usually "Uh huh, uh huh." How many hours of life have I given up to this phony talk, or worse, phony listening? The calculation is staggering. Phony listening is not a skill one should train oneself in. Sometimes I sit there reading George Eliot or cereal packages, anything to keep from being vulcanized by the anger that pours out of her: long narratives about how this or that relative has wronged or abandoned her, friends who do not call or, calling, say the wrong thing. I keep from her any detail of my life or hopes or aspirations. Neither my sister nor I have ever said an unkind word to my mother, and very few true ones. In trying to maintain civility, we have delivered a certain "justice." But, *"The great man dwells on what is real . . ."*

Today, in hindsight, I see what I might have done and failed to do as she grew old in her fury: set some gentle limits, for example. "Mom," I could have said, "I really want to be close to you, but when you yell at me and talk nineteen-to-the-dozen about how you hate all our relatives—whom I'm fond of, by the way—it silences me . . ." I could have initiated a real conversation with my mother.

This is Minnesota, this is impossible.

But it is not impossible. My niece, Ella, has developed a gift for dwelling on the real. She helps Mom out several afternoons a week; they argue. *Argue*. This is amazing to me. Ella yells at her and Mom yells back. So healthy for both of them. Better than turnips. I wonder if they still make that confetti angel food cake from a box.

"Mom, I'm bringing you over some dinner."

"Oh, that'll be nice."

The knot in my stomach relaxes. Sometimes I ask my mother about her childhood or something that happened in the long past. Rarely will she respond, though she hints at Gothic scenarios. There have been times when—for medical reasons, even—I've wanted to

know what was wrong with Grandma Josie. My mother will say
nothing except what a child would say, because it is as a child that
she inhabits that scene; she could not grow beyond it: *she would
not feed me,* is all my mother will say. *I learned to cook when I was
seven years old.*

If you want to understand something about the life of any family,
just begin with a sentence about food. That will give you something
like a sample plot, as field biologists call it; student ecologists and
naturalists often undertake the study of one square foot of earth,
pondering the relationships among its many species. Before my eyes
as I write is a reproduction of Albrecht Dürer's watercolor *The Great
Piece of Turf.* It represents with botanical accuracy a sample plot of
the artist's world: layers of soil at the bottom, above, dandelions, at
a particularly unattractive stage in the life cycle, mullein, common
grasses and seed in heads. I'm drawn to the painting's plain, almost
monochromatic beauty. Here are the most ordinary things in nature,
the greens we step on every day, raised up for us to look at so that
we will never be able to ignore them again.

It is in Dürer's spirit that I write. What follows is not a collection
of essays, still less a memoir. Please do not read this book with any
expectation of rising action or falling action, epiphanies and revelations. If I ponder a mystery, do not anticipate its unraveling. My job
is simply to sketch and honor ephemeral things.

If this were a story about my life, instead of a story about *life,* I
would tell more about what went on. I would know more, I would
have done research. Someone might be able to tell me why my dad
quit flying for the airlines, the facts behind my mother's crazy anec-
dote; surely the records exist on Grandma Josie's long incarceration
in the state hospital. If this were a story about my life, I would try to
establish a chronology and a balance among the facts. What passes
for facts in this book are like Dürer's grasses, mullein, soil. It would

seem dishonest, at least to my purposes, to manipulate them toward some conclusion of my own. You will find things out here not by an analytical process, but by following a logic of images.

Why should one want to do that? Because it's a different, softer way of knowing, and one in which most people in our culture are unpracticed. We are a pragmatic folk, and we like the clean-edged analytical statement. I started out in college as a philosophy major, and the elegance of syllogistic reasoning delights me like ballet. Or the Ice Follies. But I switched to literature because poetry offered at least the other half of what I needed to learn, a way of talking about the inwardness of things, the paradoxical, that which resists closure. If we have no vocabulary, no process, for such exploration, we will not address the issues of spirit—family life is one of these—and our souls will starve. The analytical part of my brain, for example, wants a diagnosis for Grandma Josie and would pin one on my mother if it dared. Poet-mind, however, is less violent. It can hold the picture, today of one flower, tomorrow of another, and wait awhile to label ephemeral things. Like Dürer, it will honor the data of the world, but it will paint a *watercolor.*

How does one follow a logic of images? I invite you not to work but to rest. Stare and ponder. What you find out, I hope, will not be the story of my life, but of your own.

Let me suggest another way of framing the contemplative action we are taking on, together, here. Now that my mother is leaving the world—she died four months ago, as I write this, but I think of her death as a journey I am still on—I sort through box after box of her family photos, egg-tempera studies from the 1860s, black-and-white snapshots taken with an old Brownie. "Black-and-white photos are so much more arresting," says my friend, the painter Karl Pilato, "because they have already crossed over and become images."

Photography and cinema, perhaps better than the verbal arts, reflect the workings of the human mind. Why does one scene rise and not another? The mind is full of random shots; or, if motion pictures are your point of reference, it fast-forwards, segues in and out between real life and mental play; flashbacks comment on the current action: the vision behind our eyes obscures the vision in front of them.

"But, Karl," I will say months after our conversation, "I can make a good case for the symbolic potency of color slides." Before my sister and I put most of our parents' things into a garage sale, I dutifully went through some fifty cartridges of slides, sorting out the scenery from the family groups, which got saved or sent to distant cousins. Then, when I went to sleep, those color transparencies would super-impose themselves on the night. I would live my life in reverse from bedtime to dawn. I would dream my parents' dreams.

When I say that this is a book about life—perhaps merely about consciousness—I simply mean that the person who is writing, and her story, are not as significant as the *perception* we all, as humans, share. I study the picture of my Mormon great-grandmother, this plain woman I so much resemble. It vexes me that I possess a like-ness, but no sense of the visions that lay behind her eyes. "Likeness" itself is an odd word. A photograph is "like," but it is not the person. What would it mean to inhabit the mind of a woman crossing the prairie before the Civil War? I wish she had written this book; that's why I'm writing it. The texture, so precious, of any given day, is the texture of perception. Anyone's will do.

PART ONE

Bloodroot

How Should I Live the Life That I Am?

"HOW SHOULD I LIVE THE LIFE that I am?" writes Rabbi Abraham Joshua Heschel. I hear it as a cry. I see a man shaking his fist at the creator. Respectfully.

Because I was born in an Army-Air Force base hospital, it may be that the B-52s and B-17s flying over every day warped my soul to querulous upstretch, gave me a petulant longing for transcendence. Most every pilot's child is taught, literally, to reach for the sky; we were reinforced by the scream of Dad's engines, a dip of the wings. I love songs about flying; I love the old hymns about having a home "on high." And, like Rabbi Heschel, I expect some response, dammit, from an authority whose name I do not presume even to spell. At least a dip of the wings.

Our family traveled for years, from Pampa, Texas, to Florida to Kansas, an Air Force family adrift like so many others with parents just out of their teens. Surely these young cadets talked about "home" every day over dinner. After my mother died, I found among her things an old photograph of my parents and their friends in the officers' mess hall—kids the age of my university students—leaning over their dinners in earnest conversation; I can see each mouth forming the syllable of "home." I sometimes look around at what seems to me the driven loneliness of much contemporary *lifestyle*—to use a word I dislike—and think how dislocating the experience of World War II must have been for young people, starting out marriage and family life in dormitories, far from the constraints and comforts of the old neighborhoods.

When we came "home" to Minnesota, it did not seem to me to be exactly the right place, the place the soul remembers. I'm sure it

15

did not feel like home to my parents, either: a generation cut off from their roots, what mere neighborhood could nourish them? I believe now that children are not finished at eighteen or twenty; they need sustenance and the support of a loving community well into their child-rearing years. Yet it was unthinkable for these particular young people, with the war experience behind them, to settle back into urban parishes, the Saturday night roast beef at Grandma's house. My father had had what service people call "a good war," missing out on combat because he was an unusually competent flight instructor, but we returned to a neighborhood psychically bombed out. One uncle had died of meningitis in the navy; another, who had lied about his age to fight through the terrible landings at places like Tarawa, was suffering from undiagnosed post-traumatic stress. My mother's mother, Grandma Josie, always unstable, had evolved into the madwoman in the attic.

At first, we all lived together—three generations, including cousins—in one apartment of a fourplex on the east side of St. Paul, on Case Street in St. Patrick's Parish, where both my parents' families had settled as immigrants from Ireland and Germany. The east side is one of those mythic St. Paul neighborhoods—every city has one—that swells with wave after wave of poor immigrants. There were no lawns; we played in the dirt and in the landfill with its treasures, learned to hit and bite and scratch in defense of our family stories. Every now and then Grandma Josie broke out in rambunctious insanity. Children, I venture, enjoy this sort of environment, though they do not necessarily thrive on it. It runs by a kind of kid rulebook, primitive as Hammurabi's; still, it creates a core of anxiety at the center of the personality. My responsible parents, all too afraid themselves, migrated as quickly as possible to the suburbs. We moved north, where east-siders aspire to go, to Roseville. As the old hymn puts it:

This world, I cried, is not my home
I seek a place on high.

A country far from mortal cares,
A home prepared for me.

But Roseville, with its Levittown houses, never seemed to match the mental picture I had somehow formed in my mind, as a toddler hanging onto the legs of all those young pilots, trying to decode the concept of "home." Roseville landscaping ran to tarmac or sod laid over the memory of truck gardens. Beyond the picture window my mother loved to bask in—what a pleasure it must have been to her after the dark days on Case Street—we could see an old man plowing with horses. For a little while we could see him. His wife kept an orchard. Then Roseville passed some ordinance and that property, too, was leveled. We visited the old man once where he had gone to live: the county poor farm. I remember, for some reason, his skinny knees jutting through shiny pants, I remember the fuzzy, white hair around his bald spot, the look of longing with which he stared across the fields that were not his.

Some bright morning, when this world is over,
I'll fly away.
To my home on God's celestial shore
I'll fly away.

As much as I had wanted to fly, I turned to *burrowing*. Children seem to have the necessary instincts to heal themselves of petulant longing. Years later when pop psychologists talked about "feeling grounded," I puzzled about what they might mean. Oh, I get it. You know you can't fly, that's a dream; what you can do is dig in the earth. The earth is all we are given, what we have. My grandfather told me that if you could dig a hole deep enough, you would reach China. Since I believed this to be true—and craved multicultural experience—I worked hard at burrowing. Children know what they need. As a child, one of my favorite toys was a big, yellow Tonka truck with a plow on the front. Later I took up gardening, pottery, work with animals: went *to ground.*

Much of what I write—it comes to me now in my middle years—has to do with this process of seeking the heart's true home—which may be as elemental as landscape. There are mountain people, with mountain minds, who find it hard to understand the plains dweller. Years ago, when I spent a winter in the New England woods, I pined until the train, returning to Minnesota, broke through into prairie light, a space my coastal friends find tedious and flat. Or it may be we are looking for our people. Academics, as I learned late in a teaching career, are not necessarily mine; being a hands-on person, I'm more at ease among farmers, police officers, and petty criminals. Above all, we seek the place where our gifts intersect with the available options for community. Few of us magically live where we need to be. Surely, I'm not the only one trying to form the word "home" on a stuttering tongue. I'm not an alienated artist. I'm just a woman at midlife, when the need becomes imperative.

Henry David Thoreau tossed off a comment in the midst of his essay "Solitude" that takes for granted we know what we're doing, that we have an inner compass that will point us to what we need:

What do we most want to dwell near to? Not to many men, surely, the depot, the post-office . . . but to the perennial source of our life, whence in all our experience we have found that to issue, as the willow stands near the water and sends out its roots in that direction. This will vary with different natures . . .

This will vary with different natures. It would be easy if we could all live according to the same plan. But between the lines of Thoreau's essay we may trace a brave quest for self-knowledge. You have to know what kind of tree you are, he suggests; you must find the ecosystem in which you can thrive. The needs of a Scotch pine are different from those of a willow. *How should I live the life that I am?* Why are you drowning your roots by a watercourse, wilting and sighing through the night, if you are an oak, and need to be on a savannah or a sand plain? What is the perennial source of *your* life?

My mother was an actress, a teacher of high school English and what they used to call "dramatic arts"; therefore, much of my childhood was spent backstage or doing my homework between the plush folding seats of some high school auditorium while she rehearsed the *The Man Who Came to Dinner* or *Our Town*. Growing up this way gave me an odd perspective on reality. In my mother's plays, things were always happening behind the scenes, in front of the scrims, behind the scrims, on the catwalk. Katherine Anne Porter, in her short story, "The Grave," crystallizes a woman's experience of life in a sentence about how the past superimposes itself on the present: "She halted, suddenly staring, the scene before her eyes dimmed by the vision back of them."

Like Miranda, Porter's heroine, I frequently halt and stare as I make my way through the middle of my life. Things are as they are in the present because other things happened in the past. We see what's before our eyes through a scrim, a gauze, of the past. At midlife, I am trying to compose my life with attention to these gauzy curtains that foreground and background the central actions of life. I do not want to leave them out of an account of my time on this planet—these tag ends of memory and dream. Yet I have to laugh at the pretentiousness of such an agenda. The theater of my childhood was full of bad actors. It was an amateur production. People spoke their lines badly; they didn't know what the words meant. The floor was dusty, and there was chewing gum under the seats.

Yet I sense that we must recover the past into the present, make a wholeness of it, if we are to play out our lives with integrity. This is as true for the humble person as for one who has a dramatic role to play in history.

How can I live the life that I am? Thomas Merton, the Trappist monk and poet, often wrote about how difficult it was for him to live the religious life with the spiritual equipment of the artist. My friend and fellow Quaker, Parker Palmer, signs on to Merton's iconoclastic agenda in words that I could borrow for my own: "I value spontaneity more than predictability, exuberance more than order, inner freedom more than the authority of tradition, the challenge of dialogue more than the guidance of a rule, eccentricity more than staying on dead center." Perhaps because people like Thomas Merton and Parker Palmer have done their work, it is possible now for me to conceive of spirituality as, in fact, a species of *artistic perception*. I could not make this leap as a young person, even when I became a novice in a Catholic order of nuns. But my failure was not the fault of the sisters. When I was young, what imaginative gifts I had were so undisciplined and unschooled that they obscured as much as they clarified. When it came to organized religion, in particular, my instincts were always at an oblique angle from what the community preached. Lacking whatever combination of arrogance, wisdom, and folly would have been necessary for me to follow my intuitions—lacking it, fortunately, because my instincts were fragile and wouldn't have supported the flight of a gnat—I tried, with great reserves of good will and terror, to conform myself to the prevailing ethos of family, church, and neighborhood.

Such internal dissonance wrought suffering and even a kind of internal deformity not only to me but to many others, and it grew out of larger patterns in the community, unknown to us then. Little in our lives watered the barren spaces of the soul; I grew out of Texas in the dust bowl, then found myself transplanted to a treeless Minnesota suburb. In high school English, I wrote fanciful stories about life in medieval England. My ornery and beloved teacher, Sister Carmena, would write in the margin, in the way of high school teachers from time immemorial, "Write about what you know." *Roseville?* My father was building a fallout shelter in the basement of our tract house, in case the Communists invaded. He was trying to teach me to shoot a pistol; he was telling me that we might have to fire upon the widow next door and her son, Michael, the companion of my tomboy childhood, and at the Protestants behind the fence with their Protestant names, Diane and Gloria, if they tried to get into our basement when the bombs fell. I instinctively recoiled from what I knew, and I didn't want to write about it. Perhaps I didn't "know" it; I could not penetrate it imaginatively; I had no compassion for it; it was empty of spirit.

To grow in compassion for one's own life is the great task of the middle years, and it requires that, first, one must embrace with love and pity a whole reception line of relatives, then move on to the politicians. It helps to have a comic vision. Dante and Shakespeare, younger than I, understood that comedy establishes a cosmic perspective and reconciles forces that, viewed up close, grate dangerously against each other in the social world.

I hope I am not making a big deal out of it, which Minnesota would rebuke, if I suggest that my life has been comic in this way: Roseville, the fifties, the bomb shelter, my family, and my sturdy little self—indeed, all life, if you can get to better, higher ground, is comic. The comedy of a life seems essentially tied to its holiness, the holiness of any life, even one as arid and imaginatively barren as America imposed on its children in the postwar years. Both the comic and the transcendent are showstoppers. They turn the world upside down for a moment and put the meaning up for grabs, a glorious effect. Our mouths drop open and we applaud. Georges Poulet wrote that "The comic is the perception of an ephemeral and local fracture in the middle of a durable and normal world." This could also serve as a definition of mystical vision, if you grant my suspicion that "mysticism" is integral to the world as it is, durable and normal, the world experienced by dogs and sphinx moths and the ephemeral chickadee who swings above me on the bend of a Scotch pine, *today.* I spent years in Buddhist practice, trying to live as simply in the moment as any animal naturally does.

Why ponder the past? To forgive? To attain insight? Forgiveness, in hindsight, is an act of great simplicity. "Insights," looked at over the shoulder, are so dead obvious I have to put the word in quotes. Yet the laws of the universe do not allow us to skip the struggle— unless you are a dog like my old Shep, who would retrieve sticks by stealing them from another dog who had taken the trouble to go into the water she hated.

"So, it's sticks you want," Shep would say to God.

Wrong, God would say. *Get in that river.*

The Corseteer

WE ARE GOING DOWNTOWN *on the Grand Avenue car to buy Grandma Rose's new corsets at Schuneman's* . . .

"We are going to visit Miss Dellaney, my corseteer": my grandmother's promise has summoned Miss Dellaney's pink face to us at the breakfast table. Miss Dellaney wears abundant rolls of red hair bound over each ear, stuck with combs, and cantilevered into a bun at the back. She has attended our yearly visits to Lingerie for at least as long as I have lived on earth and ridden the Grand Avenue car.

The streetcar seats are upholstered in blonde raffia, stiff in winter and scratchy in the summer heat. The raffia matting is worn away in places, popping cotton, and stained a little, but not much. In those days before plastic, people were careful about spills because you had to live with the results a long time. We caught the car across from Wilwersheid's mortuary, where the German Catholics buried from. We were O'Halloran's people ourselves, and Grandma always gave Wilwersheid's a little sniff in passing, a dog that would get no treat from her.

Ching-ching! The conductor pulled the bell. The streetcar ran along a sparking suspension line, connected below to a system of tracks that ran down the middle of the street. Automobiles were always getting stuck in these tracks, ladies turned their heels, and the days of the streetcars were numbered. Soon they would disappear in a coup financed by the automobile companies. *Ching-ching!*

Ladies didn't go shopping in those days, as ladies do now, without a precise goal in mind. We entered the cathedral vaults of places like Schuneman's only with solemn purpose: the fitting of

23

undergarments, the purchase of ugly school oxfords—you could hop on and off an X-ray machine that showed you the white bones of your mortal feet—for the yearly requisitioning of items on Grandma Josie's list at the asylum—three seersucker housedresses, two cotton slips—and for the festive, thrilling, yearly attainment of Easter hats. There were Miss Dellaney's attending each revolution in the liturgical year of commerce: ladies to fit shoes, three or four millinery ladies—always the same ones—to coo over hats. Only Grandma Josie's errands were accomplished anonymously, in the bargain basement. Into the booth and out again; my mother would pin the seersucker dresses to me. I was skinny like Grandma Josie, a handy mannequin for madness.

"This'll fit her, she has no bust. Let's go." My mother hated to shop.

Family folklore assigned to my mother's mother, Grandma Josie, the role of demonic outsider. No one could ever tell me where she came from or how she fit into the family line. She seems to have appeared among us just as she enters the family photograph album, smiling on the arm of my innocent-looking grandfather McManus, her high-boned aristocratic face giving no hint of whatever craziness sprouted behind that gaze. She was, according to the family narrative, tall and beautiful and bad. By contrast, Grandma Rose, my dad's mother, won the part of good fairy. Short and beatle-browed, obviously born to plant potatoes, she came on the scene too late to undo the bad fairy's spells but in plenty of time to mitigate them. She was the force for logic and order in our family, the formidable matriarch, who handled the practical, civilizing details of life, among them the exhausting task of keeping Grandma Josie under control.

Family stories, the sitcoms of a preliterate culture, love simple dichotomies. Surely the reality of my grandmothers' lives was more complex than the assignments of "sinner" and "saint" we gave them in collective memory. Some day, with a more nuanced understanding of mental illness than was available to my forebears, I'd like to research Grandma Josie's life, pencil her into the space from which the family erased her. There are many inconsistencies in the little that was said. Given my family's disdain for undisciplined artiness, I'd always assumed that Grandma Josie must have been some kind of poet. Yet my mother mentioned, in a rare reference to Josie, that she had had training in higher math, and was well known in the neighborhood for a kind of scientific brilliance. I regret that I must abandon so rare and strange a life to the reductive role it played in my subconscious: the witch who carried a knife, who threw children down the stairs. Surely she had her story, and it was knocked out of her with shock therapy in the state asylum. *Therapy, asylum:* the diction of healing, the geography of safe space. Lies I learned to deconstruct, though the truth eludes me.

Nor was Grandma Rose the simple, efficient saint most people took her to be. She was rigid as well as good, and puritanical. She considered madness to be a moral failure and a form of slovenliness. Her overbearing righteousness cast my mother's innocent worldliness in a darker light than it deserved. Yet, instinctively, I wanted to be with her as she processed around town in her black coat with the gray, mouton shawl collar, with her capacious pocketbook. She had nothing fashionable and nothing shabby about her, because things were hung up properly in her house, or tucked away in tissue paper at the end of the day. This plain rectitude was, for me, the very soul of trust. *Therapy, asylum.*

Schuneman's was dark and redolent of polished wood, like St. Luke's church. I half expected to see the image of Christ Pantocrater materialize over the elevators, eyes that followed you wherever you strayed, that hieratic hand raised to bless or slap you good and hard in Housewares. We took the escalator, with its toothy steps. I could never get on fast enough. A virus in babyhood had left me with a weak leg, which made all my relatives furious when it manifested. They suspected I had had polio and, if word got out, it would spoil my chances to make a good marriage or be hired into the telephone company, which represented their pinnacle of aspiration.

Nobody in my family was allowed to have tuberculosis, cancer, or polio. It was forbidden to be insane or get drunk or marry a protestant. My Grandma Rose, with the crisp articulation of convent school, had a way of simply erasing people with an Irish formula of *Kaddish*: "We will not mention their names."

At my parents' house in Roseville, we had just gotten our grainy first TV. Grandma Rose, whose force extended effortlessly into the suburbs, disapproved of the "platinum blondes" with low-cut dresses and hips that swayed when they walked. She disapproved of the June Taylor Dancers. I am only allowed to watch the news and the Army-McCarthy Hearings. All summer long I have been sitting in my sweaty pinafore, riveted with heat and boredom to shifty images of men with slick hair *naming names* far away. Or, more understandably, *not naming names*. "I refuse to answer on the grounds that it might incriminate me": this amusing mantra has passed into the jump-rope jingles of our neighborhood. Refusal-to-speak has grown delicious inside of me, an entity claiming its own space. Societal repression conjoins with family reticence, a bigger animal, which so many women of my generation will categorize in friendly generalizations about the elephant in the living room. My grandmother seemed to carry a wedge of secrets inside her mouton shawl, a pocketbook full of chastened ghosts. This capacity to bear the dead, the demented, and the stories of the race I am learning to associate with being a mature woman, in full sail through Schuneman's.

Snicking their way along, the escalator steps ascended out of some hell under the floor. My grandmother had propelled me on with a sharp shoulder jerk. Left to myself, I would stall in front of the mechanism, pondering things. In my mind's eye, I would watch myself stumble and cut my face on the metal stairs, my hands splayed out and caught in the mechanism.

But, *jerk!* "Don't hold the rail, you don't know who's been here before you."

It embarrassed me to cling to my grandma's hand; I was too old. I schooled my face to immobility, like one of the newsreaders on TV.

Christ Pantocrator, impervious like Edward R. Murrow, looked at me with approval from the yellow wall over the second-floor landing, ladies' lingerie, hose, and housedresses. *He was crucified, died, and was buried. On the third day, he ascended into heaven.* Getting off the escalator was another moment that required supreme concentration and focus, because you could fall and your whole body be shredded into inch-wide strips in the elevator mechanism, like the Jesuit Martyrs of the Iroquois Nation, your blood rain down upon the wild, pig-faced men in chains who turned a turnstile in the basement of the store, fur on their backs. *Jerk!*

On the other hand, if you focused too hard and watched too long the place where the moving steps collapsed and fell into hell, you could tumble forward dizzily onto the thick, rose carpet of Lingerie. Or worse, you might careen backward upon the frail, elderly ladies in lavender downtown suits, their swollen joints and bones like the material of wrens, and down the stairs onto the chic salesgirls who wore their glasses on chains, whose hair was not platinum blonde, who were, Grandma said admiringly, Norwegian and therefore *natural* blondes, who would dependably break your fall. *Jerk!*

"Oh, for heaven's sake, Mary Rose, just step," for I would be clinging to the filthy, black rubber rail, no matter who had been there before, boys, Methodists, driving my short nails into the rubber as it led on and on and horribly curved and disappeared into the maw of the machine and the lair of the pig-faced—"*Step!*"

Lingerie—light and frivolous, a flaglike word inappropriate to describe the heavy pink or cream-colored webbing that looked like Ace bandages laid out in the display cases of Schuneman's, as if the swollen and dangerous female form required first aid. The walls were painted the color of Pepto-Bismol, the color of beauty schools where you might go to get your hair cut cheaply. Female color. Miss Dellaney, in her dual-exhaust sausage rolls of hair, emerged from the backroom, a tape measure around her neck, as though she had been sitting there since our last visit. She and my grandmother nodded to each other with hauteur. They had a history together, delicate allies in this country of blondes, barbarians, and floozies: flesh and binder of flesh. My grandmother, besides, had great respect for "professional women," having apprenticed in a law office at fourteen. She had married late, and unwillingly, as she proudly told me; then "it was all over." The only hope for a woman—my grandmother drove this point home whenever she got the chance—was education. She wanted better things for me than even the telephone company.

I was made to sit on a Chippendale chair, contemplating education upon a cushion of gray watered silk, whilst examining the bandaged forms of the display models. Miss Dellaney led my grandmother into a cubicle. My mind retreated from the unveiling and measuring, the wilderness of snaps. My grandmother, who had taught me to dress in the morning *under* my flannel nightgown, did not hold with nakedness. Yet hers was the female body I knew, the body I often slept beside and cuddled with. I alone knew the ripple of her flesh when she turned over in undefended sleep. Ten minutes out of bed, she was slickly encased; she despised the "slovenly." Clinging to her by day, I was rather like the baby monkey in the famous psychology experiment, trying to get its nails into something it could get a purchase on. But I knew there was flesh at the core of her.

My grandma always referred to her "corsets" in the plural, as though several layers, at least, of gusseting were essential to the status of a lady. She only left them off when she slept or went swimming. Life is a difficult business, and each of us needs a structure to cling to, or to cling to us.

Years after she died, an old neighbor man told me, "Your grandma was tougher than hide." He was an elderly alcoholic who had been scolded regularly at our kitchen table and sent home with a loaf of homemade bread under his arm. "She could bounce bullets off her."

I thought about Wonder Woman, with her magic bracelets, the forbidden comic I could get hold of in Diane and Gloria's house. It was the *corsets*, I could have told him.

Grandma Rose and my mother disliked each other. The McManuses—my mother's people—and the O'Reilleys—my dad's—regarded each other with hereditary suspicion, trading the dreaded "shanty" epithet behind each other's backs. Black Irish and Red, they had dumped their shadow material onto each other for generations. How could my parents not marry, the Capulets and Montagues of St. Patrick's parish? But Grandma Rose disapproved.

My mother held on to a certain clip of memory—I know, because she often told the story: she is eighteen, but three-quarters of the way through college already and engaged to my dad. She hops out of the car, her curly auburn hair flying out of its bobby pins, the car she drives herself, perhaps owns: *spoiled*, my grandmother will always say, by her indulgent aunts and uncles, an orphan, for all practical purposes, who runs her own life like a boxcar child; "If I had had her education . . ." my grandmother will go on—my mother hops out of the Packard to greet her mother-in-law-to-be and show off the engagement ring. She's wearing shorts and a middy blouse that bares her waist.

I said that my mother told the story, but, as I think harder, I remember that my grandmother told it. It's just that, even as a child, I saw it from my mother's point-of-view, knew how it unspooled behind her eyes and dimmed the vision in front of them. "I went right up to her," my grandmother would brag, "grabbed those shorts and pulled them up to her bodice. She got in that car of hers and came back dressed."

When my grandmother told this story, I laughed as she wanted me to, allying myself shamelessly—or shamefastedly—with the forces of Jansenistic repression. But children naturally inhabit the space of paradox; children know that—in the words of the old country song, "We live in a two story house/ She has her story and I have mine." My grandmother and my mother envied each other, fighting for my soul between them, and perhaps for my father's soul before I came along. I think my mother won the battle for my dad, lost the later one. But at least I could see her side. My mother was the weaker antagonist, and—to use a word which has fallen on bad times for its trace of condescension—I *pitied* her. I felt for both of them—"love" would not be the right word here.

More than clannish antagonism lay behind their enmity. The O'Reilleys were tough little survivors of the coffin ships, with peasant suspicion of any moral complexity. The McManuses belonged to an earlier, eighteenth-century Scotch-Irish emigration, intermarried with—Grandma Rose would have scolded—*who knows who?* I can tell you, *French* people, native people; my great-great-grandfather, on my mother's side of the family, had been a sea captain, converted to Mormonism by Joseph Smith. Grandma O'Reilley's primitive eugenics dictated that the McManuses had "bad blood," which meant Protestant blood, mixed blood, and a strain of hereditary madness. Bad blood would account for the long-legged, dangerous beauty my mother displayed so freely, hopping out of her little car into the 1940s, which would cut her no slack. Grandma Rose, plain among her own lovely sisters, was always conscious of beauty, talent, and intelligence and could anatomize like a postmodern critic the qualities of each she discovered in those she knew; she excelled at what the old theology called "discernment of gifts." But physical attractiveness made her both worshipful and wary.

It's not bad for a child to grow up with such complex antagonisms on the map of family life. It forms a backdrop to the clear lines of latitude and longitude that would otherwise deceive us that the world is a predictable place.

It's odd that my mind should cast up a recollection of my grandmother and me going shopping, which we did rarely, if ceremoniously, to wind up at last colluding over strawberry sodas at The Lexington—or that to this burr of memory is attached my understanding of the enmity between mother and grandmother. The strawberry sodas make me think that memory is like a well-reinforced puppy, which extends a paw or rolls over when treats are

in sight. Why this scene and not another: why shopping at
Schuneman's and not traipsing off to mass as my grandmother and
I did almost every morning? Why the conflation of the two? The
mystery of what's remembered and what's forgotten seems either
portentous or random. Which is it? I turn over a potsherd here, a
fragment there—the archaeology of memory—trying to make a
single ancient pot that will hold together and tell me who I am,
who anyone is.

During the winter, my grandparents lived in a one-room studio
apartment on Grand Avenue, and in the summer they lived in a
one-room cabin with a sleeping porch on a lake in Wisconsin. Much
of the time I stayed with them. In my early childhood, I would
frequently go to bed in my parents' fourplex in St. Patrick's parish
and wake up in my grandparents' studio in St. Luke's. (Catholic
families tended to locate themselves by parish as much as by street
address.) I suspect that these removals coincided with stress in the
Case Street house.

I could never write much about those chaotic days on Case
Street until, one day, I remembered the angels. It began with a
casual question that rose in my mind one summer day, a few years
ago, while I was thinning the carrots in the garden of my durable
and normal world: why was our Case Street apartment always so full
of people? My parents and I—who had moved there after the war,
into a space that my mother technically owned—were never alone.
Besides Grandma Josie and my uncle and all the cousins who lived
downstairs—whom I loved dearly—the walls were circled about
with *beings of light.*

Okay. They were not real angels. They were relatives. They were
my maiden aunts, Mamie and Sadie, and their pudgy old soft-hearted
maiden brother, Boo. They were Uncle Jack, and Aunt Laura, who,
in her eighties, would drive herself around in a black Cadillac with
a huge Alsatian dog in the passenger seat. Grandma Rose would be
on the scene, directing the chorus. Grandpa would be mending the
guardrails on the porch. All of these people, the intermingled clans

of McManus and O'Reilley, had known each other in Ireland and Canada and Red Wing, Minnesota. They had their eyes on each other. They knew what people could get up to, and they hung around like a crowd of social workers, ready to move the children away to St. Luke's: *beings of light.*

My son said to me last summer, "Why don't you tell the whole story?"

As if it were the Army-McCarthy Hearings.

The Dalai Lama says we must always err on the side of kindness; I am going to put the best face on this I can. Besides, I mistrust my memory.

I remember, for example, that there was an image of Jesus's head, crowned with thorns and dripping blood, etched on the glass above the door of our water closet in the Case Street fourplex. I'm calling it a water closet without pretension but with, I think, accuracy. It was one of those old bathrooms with a drum of water suspended over the toilet. You pulled a chain and the water cascaded down with a roar and a crash. I'm sure of that roar and crash, and sure about the image of Jesus, except that of course *Jesus could not have been there,* etched on the glass of a working-class family bathroom.

When I first read Latin American novels in the magic realist tradition, I experienced no surprise, no dislocation. So attuned are the Irish Catholic and the Hispanic sensibilities that I knew exactly where those writers were coming from: from a childhood in which everything was constantly turning into something else, in which reality was permeable by neutrinos of wonder. If you are required to sign on to the Incarnation, the Virgin Birth, and Transubstantiation, you develop elastic notions of the real.

"Besides," as my mother would later say, "Grandma Rose was a religious fanatic." Well, she never let a moment pass without noting its position in some great moral allegory. I'm sure that Grandma Rose would wash my face in that bathroom and tell me stories about Veronica wiping the face of Jesus, the sixth station of the Way of the Cross—because that is the sort of story she would tell if confronted with a simple flannel towel or a washcloth—and from that data my imagination etched the Shroud of Turin over the toilet.

As a graduate student, I was accosted by a famous professor whose first words to me were, "You're a Catholic, what else is wrong with your thinking?" Goodness, I don't know. Lots. Pre-Vatican II Catholicism was incongruent with *thinking*, actually, as most liberally educated Westerners understand the word. One inhabited, rather than dissected truth, navigating by metaphor rather than by syllogism, aware that at any moment the world could be turned inside out by incarnation. It's hard for me, given this background, not to see grace exploding all over the place, even in politics. Why give up sacramental vision for mere *thought?*

So I dutifully bite on each memory like an old woman with a fist full of suspicious coins. Of course I cannot trust them. I remember the clock in the apartment on Grand Avenue, I remember green stiff plush on the ottoman Grandpa rested his feet on, and how the ottoman opened and how, inside, there were Tinkertoys and a few books, the Montgomery Ward catalog naming and spelling: *truss, brassiere*. All the mysterious paraphernalia of a world I had never entered, but the existence of which I believed in; as my grandparents' apartment exists in parallel space (*credo*) before I enter and after I leave, after I walk down the hall, its carpet smelling faintly of dust and feet, past the lever that opens the incinerator shaft into which I am sometimes permitted to throw garbage now that I am big enough to be invulnerable should a long arm reach up out of the fire and try to suck me down; the garbage, wrapped in a wet newspaper and tied with string, going down with a sucking, satisfying *whoosh*. It is always a very small bundle, because nothing is wasted in that set of rooms, not gizzard, not bone nor vegetable peel.

The rooms were crowded, oppressive; winter seemed always to be pushing against the panes. Damp, coal-darkened snow, the radiators hissing and banging, too much heat and a sleepy feeling, patterns on the Turkish carpet under the tiddlywinks and pick-up sticks. The living room held one sofa and grandpa's green chair with its matching ottoman, and a small desk with a top that folded down. Grandpa had made all the furniture, though it looked as fine as anything that came from Montgomery Ward. Imagine a man who could make a sofa, a chair, an ottoman, a desk, as well as the intricately inlaid sewing box and folding tea table that had won so many prizes at various craft shows. At one end of the room was a long closet, out of which the Murphy bed folded at night. There was a dining nook set next to the adjoining kitchen and beyond that a bathroom and large closet, big enough to contain a rollaway bed. At night, Grandpa slept on the rollaway while Grandma and I took over the Murphy bed. Nobody could get up at night without having to make their way across a tray of sleepers.

Atop the desk was a clock that gave out the hours with chimes and the quarters with whirrs and clicks. It woke everybody up, but nobody thought of silencing it. Grandma and Grandpa both snored loudly but complained of insomnia. Grandma, when awake, prayed out loud, her fingers moving over beads in the night.

I was always gasping for air in that room, tormented with a rocking dizziness that afflicted me whenever I closed my eyes in bed, although I loved being with my grandparents. I suffered from night terrors that had become habitual, and a strong imperative to creep away and sleep in closets where I felt safe.

I don't remember what was in Grandpa's ottoman besides the tiddlywinks, or perhaps the tiddlywinks, lovely colored plastic discs, with their white ceramic cup, were not there either. Maybe they were in the drawer of the desk. I do not remember much about what Grandma cooked, but I looked forward to eating it very much. The center of the grapefruit on Easter morning would be a maraschino cherry, its juice exotically dyeing the sour fruit and promising more than it delivered of taste. I do not remember what we wore or when we shopped for food. I remember *suspension*: absolutely nothing happening except a game of tiddlywinks or pick-up sticks that went on forever. In the breakfast nook, Grandma and Grandpa would be playing cribbage and Grandma would be chanting, "Fifteen-two, fifteen-four, and a pair is six," incomprehensible as the mantras of arithmetic class.

In the countryside my grandmother's parents came from, around the turn of the twentieth century, a family of villagers got together and burned a young woman to death in her own fireplace because they thought she was a fairy changeling. They believed the poor woman would come back at the full moon, riding a white horse at the head of a troop of fairies; it was not murder in their eyes, they thought were doing her a favor. They would be required to pull her from her horse and wrestle her down as she changed into terrifying shapes, a snake, a panther—creatures never seen in Ireland except when fairies were on the scene. The villagers had all girded themselves up for a difficult job-of-work before the gardai got there on their bicycles and took them to task for dismembering the changeling bride and committing her to a shallow grave.

The press got hold of the story and in Britain, advocates for home rule for Ireland had a hard time explaining how these superstitious and violent people could be depended upon to govern themselves. If this had been the only case of changeling murder instead of just a particularly dramatic one, little might have been said. But the reporters, on another set of bicycles, quickly turned up case after case of, in particular, child murder. It seemed to be the custom of the rural Irish to do away with those we would now call "differently abled" under the rubrics for dealing with fairy changelings. The priests turned a blind eye, patiently using their skills to build up the local churches—I mean the physical buildings—in order to get religion out of the little turf-smelling cottages where it got mixed up and stewed with the black old ways and the drink. By suppressing Catholic worship during penal times in Ireland, the British had unwittingly driven religion back to the hearth, where it festered. The priests were powerless to preach against the old wives and fairy doctors—those individuals skilled at communing with the race of fairies underground. They took on instead the long-term task of attracting villagers back to a clean, bright public space with its rival liturgy and exorcism. They seldom preached against the fairy scene. Even the priests knew that was bad luck.

I think about this story of my grandmother's home county whenever my feminist friends romanticize the old household religions. Isn't it amazing how Hollywood managed to turn Irish lore into something cute and candy colored, with tame leprechauns and pots of gold? Bing Crosby has a lot to answer for. There was nothing cute about it.

Every night my grandmother came to my bed and made the sign of the cross on my forehead repeating the ancient charm, "Cross of Jesus Christ be about her soul and body and make her a good girl and spare her to Daddy and Mommy and may the souls of the faithful departed through the mercy of God rest in peace. Amen." Owing to that blessing, I was not taken by the bad fairies; ghosts stayed in my grandmother's handbag, wrapped in tissue paper, deep in the closet.

A Week Until Christmas

> Here for her it had been a pat little lifetime without moments,
> an existence among tables and chairs, without raptures or
> mystery, grace, or danger.
> —Elizabeth Bowen, *The Heat of the Day*

PERHAPS LEAVING HOME TO FIGHT a war before they were old enough
to vote used up my parents' store of courage forever. Remembering
my early days, I understand what I could not grasp at the time,
though I felt it all too keenly in my bones: fear was the dominant
emotion of our lives; fear was methodically taught to the young. At
first I was slow to catch on, as bold children are. Then I made up for
lost time. Any spider might be a black widow, any stranger a child
molester, any political liberal a Communist. So many fearsome
things threatened the stability of what was itself so pathetically
vulnerable, the *nuclear family*—ironically named in resonance with
the worst threat of all—as though it were a toss-up whether our
suburb—or the whole planet—would blow up. Pussyfooting above
our bomb shelter, my family mistrusted everything beyond the
nearest Catholic church or strip mall. I'm sure that, by 1955 or so,
my parents felt that the worst was behind them. Never mind the
war, they had managed to escape the old neighborhood, they had
accomplished the soul-draining task of getting Grandma Josie committed to the state institution, they had achieved their suburban
box with its raw planes and angles. Life, after that, progressed
through cycles of smothering ennui.

I am eight years old; I am bored. It will be two weeks till Christmas, a week till school lets out. It will be four months of cold, runny noses, and playground teasing until spring. Leaving Case Street got us away from the peril of Grandma Josie, and put even Grandma Rose at a degree or two of psychic remove, but it sucked the drama out of my life, all the danger and passion. I think my mother felt, too, the lack of any adequate focus for her histrionic powers and had to settle for domestic intrigue. My father, I'm sure, felt only the warrior's relief at having gotten his family into a safe shelter—which we had the audacity to find tedious.

I am lying on the rug, which smells slightly of dog, some dog, one of the five or six short-lived cocker spaniels, all named Heidi, who followed each other across that rug. I feel queasy. Dog hairs tickle my nose. I crawl across the rug and plug in the Christmas lights. This is my job. Dad gets furious if he comes home to a dark house. I don't know why. I would love to come home to a dark house. At least I would have been away, I would have been *somewhere.* Not here, the fibers of the rug scratching my cheek, the smell of Heidis. The red, blue, and green lights on the tree glow with their furious inner demons, refracted over and over by the pierced aluminum stars behind each bulb. These stars had been brought over from Austria and handed down in my grandfather's line. Christmas was a serious business in Austria, and nobody came home to a dark house.

Maybe I am trying to watch TV. I am deeply invested in *The Mickey Mouse Club,* though it only makes me more miserable. Somewhere—in this small, boxy world—black-and-white children with giant mouse ears attached to their heads are having a good time. *Annette! Bobby! Doreen!* each one cries, leaping from the stage. Friends who would love me and share their ponies and curlers and California sunshine with me if they could. I know they would. *Cubbie! M-I-C—See ya real soon!—K-E-Y—Why? Because we like you!*

Oh, God! *Mickey Mouse* is over. Dad's not home. Santa's not coming. Dinner's not ready. I try to read the newspaper, which

I have done every night since I learned to read, including the editorials and Dr. Brady's health tips. I comb the TV schedule minutely, although no one in those days let children choose what the family would sit down on the vinyl-covered sofa to watch together. Marlon Perkins's *Zoo Parade*. Sid Caesar. To my infinite revulsion, they will make me watch Sid Caesar. TV is new to us and still honored for its educational value. Anything that flies through the airwaves beyond the prairie, no doubt including Santa Claus, is educational, according to my family. Watching the ball drop in Times Square is educational. Why are my parents so excited by this?

I was not bored because I was waiting for my life to begin. Rather, I was dreading that it would begin any minute, and it would look like a skit with Imogene Coca. It would be pratfalls and a laugh track; it would be school all over. Except for the happy mouse children—who remind me of my lost cousins on the east side— frankly I prefer the newspaper. Its violence mirrors my sense of reality, developed amongst neighborhood toughs and family chaos, which Roseville seems set upon denying.

I read the St. Paul *Pioneer Press* laid out on the floor, kneeling over it, and it has turned my elbows dirty. Dad, who has a fetish about cleanliness, will yell at me. I get up, go into the bathroom, and scrub my elbows. The green tile butting the pink walls is ugly, the soap smells bad, and we will have Swiss steak for supper. Dad will say to Mom, "How was your day?" That will be her cue to talk through the whole meal about her life as a high school teacher. First hour, second hour, third hour will be dramatized; the "kids" will say this and that. The male teachers, all known by their last names, will rush on stage and say their lines, Minicleer, the principal, Kirkeby, the assistant principal; the women teachers, who have first names, Zarm and Hildie, will have wittier lines, like the teachers on *Our Miss Brooks*, an educational TV program about high school teaching, that comes on some other night. As my mother talks through meat, potatoes, salad, and dessert, my dad will stare at the big, flashy fruit designs on the tablecloth, saying nothing, with an expression I would now call desperate, but for which then I had no name. Sometimes Mom will ask about his day and he will shrug, as though he does not have days.

Minicleer, Chanticleer, Doreen, Bobby, I am so—is it *bored,* exactly? The world seems yellow and dusty. I try to practice Dr. Brady's tips on "belly breathing," a pre-Zen exercise which, oddly enough, relieves the sick tension in my stomach. In my mother's relentless telling, I visualize the data of the world she sometimes takes me to, the high school with its linoleum corridors and blonde wood. It smells of cigarette smoke. The teachers all smoked back then. In this haze, my mother, her red hair, her beautiful green velvets, would be a spot of brightness, like one of Marlon Perkins's doomed birds. In my father's not-telling, I visit also his musty space behind stacks of boxes where he works as a buyer for a department store. In consequence of a bizarre series of events my mother will only recount in the last year of her life, my father has lost his job flying for the airlines. The sign on his desk at the department store reads:

Count that day lost whose low-descending sun
Finds profit shot to hell and business run for fun.

Perhaps that's why he cannot say how his day was; it was lost. As for the poem, I like reciting it. I know that my dad loves poetry, perhaps that's why he keeps this one on his desk; he has read to me every night since I learned to listen, the *Song of Hiawatha, Evangeline,* the tragic poems of Edgar Allan Poe:

It was many and many a year ago, in a kingdom by the sea,
That a maiden there lived whom you may know by the name of Anabel Lee.

I know Anabel Lee better than Cubby or Annette, but I am never sure on what terms all these people inhabit the same planet.

Anabel in her tomb by the sounding sea, Doreen the sun-streaked, Gene Autry, Mario Lanza, Santa, Minicleer. With so much going on, somewhere, why is my life so tedious? I long for my six cousins, whom I will never see again, and the dangerous and exciting Case Street house, bordering a city dump full of fascinating horrors.

Poems are the most exciting places I'm allowed to enter. Even jump-rope jingles are tangled up in mystery. Who was the lady with the alligator purse? I see her easily in my mind's eye: the school health officer in a mannish navy suit and *chignon*—a word I love. Grandma Rose calls my mother's hairstyle a *chignon*. We are all up on the language of fashion because my father is in the fashion business. However desperate, however lost the day, he loves fabric and color. He explains to me over and over what a Chanel suit looks like, why it is always appropriate, and why I will likely wear one some day. No doubt I will carry an alligator purse *(or, with luck, I imagine, an alligator . . .)*.

What you do not speak of does not exist, my parents believed; to drive an incident from conversation is to eradicate it. In my family I learned to vaporize whole worlds of reality in a poof, the way Grandma Rose would eradicate spiders with a shot of mist from her silver can of DDT. Wandering down a college corridor one day recently, I overheard a colleague lecturing on Augustine's *Confessions.* "What Augustine calls *memory,* we would now refer to as the *subconscious,*" I heard the philosopher tell his students. I reached out a hand to steady myself in the hallway, the vision before my eyes dimmed by the vision in back of them. Of course.

I study, with an odd detachment, my dad's profile in the driver's seat of the Packard, his hat pulled low on his brow, as it always is when he's angry. I am standing on the running board of the car, clinging to the car door, trying to hold onto everything as it is. If the lady with the alligator purse would get here, all would be well. She is one of the people who emerge from a vale of safety and boredom far from Case Street: women with dark suits, plain faces, chignons.

I remember with perfect clarity the months when "we"—but that means, of course, the grownups—were going through the terrible process of getting Grandma Josie out of the house and into the hospital. I feel in my bones the terror not only of her behavior—she had become hysterically violent and given to attacking the children—but also of the agonizing decision to drag one's own relative off to a state institution, for it came to that, over the running board of the Packard. Even my sister, five years younger, remembers those days, though she was a toddler when Grandma Josie threw her down the long wooden stairway from the second floor of the old house.

Yet *memory*—I hear my colleague go on—is coextensive with the *subconscious:* a trunk full of old clothing and scraps of jewelry and the scary pelts of the little animals that ladies used to fasten around their necks, the poet's storehouse of images, each one a kind of holograph for an experience or an emotion to be recollected; or the place from which dreams arise, including my sister's nightmare of falling head over heels. My sister, so attractive and cheerful as a child that everyone called her "pretty pink Peggy," suffered from stomach upsets that kept her in the house for weeks at a time.

"It wasn't a dream," I told my sister, years after. "It happened. That was just before we (to use the family vernacular) put her away." *We.* I implicate myself, a child hovering near the Age of Reason, as moral theology called the magic birthday when you could begin to be considered a sinner. Culpability, unstated, unmentionable, pervaded the family. This is no doubt why, at the end of my mother's life, I will suffer such acute guilt at not being able to help her, dithering fatally over the necessity to "put her in the hospital," contravening her own will and agency.

Fear and shame, often conflated. The alternative: boredom, as I was learning to call it. Adults teach us to name our feelings, and often the names do not match the inchoate things we feel. This sets us up for a lot of confusion in later life. When I was a child, adults often told me I was bored—in school, for example—but in later life I began, as we ought to, a true naming. A better word for that feeling came to me when, as a sophomore in college, I read the existentialist philosophers: *nausea*.

Suburban life walled out the big feelings. This is one of the ways our culture deals with fear. We have the money to get away with it, and TV is a handy substitute for participating in the fierce plots of human life. For love and sex, we can domesticate sentimentality, fury can be filtered down to petty bickering; creativity? Well, Dad can build airplanes in the basement out of balsa wood. Yet the tract house was a refuge to my mother. In the last few years of her life, she would refuse to leave that living room, that television set, where boredom had pinned me to the carpet.

Existentialist *nausea* presented a physical image of a precise and particular horror: *that there is no meaning*. When you wall out the big feelings—out of exhaustion or desensitization or denial—you are left with the trivial, or, to use another existentialist counter, the *absurd*. It can turn a child's stomach.

Mouse ears—did someone say?—we're going to have them wear *big, plastic mouse ears! Won't that be fun?*

The House of Memory

BACK WHEN I WAS JOB HUNTING, college English departments used
to advertise for what they called "generalists." I liked the idea of
teaching a little Shakespeare, a little rhetoric; I did not favor the
model presented to me by one of my graduate school profs, who
stood most of each day at a huge collating machine that superimposed seventeenth-century texts on top of each other. The machine
would expose minute alterations in punctuation or the deletion of
an adjective, which he would then meticulously comment upon in
a footnote. I didn't think I had the temperament for that kind of
work, so instead I navigated back to teaching at the sort of college
I myself had attended.

Generalists are blessed with flexible lives, and perhaps they are
people who, by temperament, need to change directions now and
again. I can write out of my life, for years at a time, the fact that I'm
a college professor—I've traveled on a visa that identified me as an
agricultural worker, for example, because that was the reality of the
moment—but I need to stop at this moment in my narrative and
reconfigure myself. What we think of as "self" is anything but
univocal. Not only am I often of two—or three—minds about something, but I passionately engage with other vocations—musician,
potter, for example—that are too central to my identity to be sub-
sumed under the demeaning word "hobby." Periodically you will
find me working hard at my volunteer occupation as a wildlife rehabilitator. I sing with a performing group called Prairie Harmony, play
the violin. Several years ago, I completed a two-year certification
program in spiritual direction—an emerging aspect of ministry—at

the Shalem Institute in Bethesda, Maryland. We are all so much more than our professions or careers, and a friend who knows one on the job may know only a single member of—let's call it—the committee-of-the-person.

Perhaps we try too hard to present a coherent image to the outside world. We stifle the new identities within who are crying to be born, fearful perhaps that they will rend with childish willfulness the fabric of identity we have put together with such care, mostly to please the neighbors—though, in fairness to my old neighborhood, I have to add "to keep out of jail or the asylum." The stakes, in blue-collar culture, were heavily weighted toward conformity.

But, just now, I have to call upon the training of the college professor and the spiritual director to explain to myself what I am trying to do as I play with threads of narrative and scrims of memory. I've thought a lot about how narratives convey whatever truth it is they convey. How does the truth-claim of historical writing differ from that of poetry, for example? We tend to read nonfiction as we might journalism, looking for "facts." Facts are important. To the best of my ability, I stick to them. Our prairie ancestors, whose diaries tell us that "fifty quarts of beans were canned today," and that "Abe sold the heifer," convey a certain kind of truth about life, though it is not quite the truth I crave. What dreams, I want to know, flowed behind my great-grandmother's eyes while she canned beans and worried about Abe? What does it mean to be alive?— remembering the past, expecting the future, gnawed at by half-buried fears and longing, sometimes at peace?—and how can we put that meaning into words? A steady narrative, leaning on the familiar structures of rhetorical exposition, do not allow me to create an image of consciousness.

Consciousness *weights* things. It cares less about your college degrees than about what was in your mother's pantry. The good storyteller—my Grandma Rose was one—must give sufficient data and chronology to allow the listener to make sense of her life and choices. As a result of my grandmother's respect for history, I can tell you where our family stood in relation to the Great Famine and the building of the railroad, and I think that any child who doesn't know these kinds of things about family is impoverished. The facts must bear a structure, a kind of house, that the listener can enter. Having entered that house, however, I want to get into the pantry and rummage.

It's harder to explain why I perceive this task of recollection as a spiritual one—though what I've written about memory and consciousness may recall to many readers what Augustine said in the *Confessions* about his search for God. It's dawned on me slowly that to write about the heart's true home is to articulate a kind of vernacular theology. To graduate from the Shalem Institute as what's quaintly called a "spiritual director" is to commit to listening to people's stories of religious struggle and search. In the old days, spiritual direction involved a contract between a priest (usually) and a seeker determined upon a life of holiness. Today, in the model pioneered by Shalem, it honors the relationship of two people—or a group of people—determined to be contemplatives together, one of whom has formal training. When I call the outcome of this deep listening process "vernacular theology" I'm suggesting that it frees itself pretty quickly from the dialects of traditional religious systems.

Let me give you a homely example. When I first began this ministry of spiritual direction, it surprised me that people wanted to sit and tell me about their pets. There is no space for dogs in Thomas Aquinas. Yet people's experience with animals is often central to their spiritual search. Being gay or straight is not a traditional theological category, either; in fact, sex rarely enters in except in the dissection of sin. So the work of spiritual companioning—as I prefer to call it, being of an egalitarian mind—is likely to take you outside the gates of orthodoxy.

This kind of ministry—as I see it—is nourished by religious tradition and tends to discover its truths in new forms, but in the time of deep listening you have to lay traditional wisdom to the side. You try to create a contemplative space for the holy to manifest itself, and if that force has good spiritual credentials, you can be sure it will surprise you.

It's kind of like laying out treats at the feeder for a very exotic bird.

If I use my own life as the focus of a narrative about spiritual search, then, it's not because my life is important or interesting. It's just a demo life. Perhaps I explore with sophomoric seriousness such a variety of roles—teacher, counselor, caretaker of animals, musician, potter—in order that many different kinds of people can try on my life. I've spared the reader, at least, my high school ventures in shoplifting.

Any life story is a labyrinth; you enter at one place, get lost, come out at another. The intellectual journeys that served me in youth now interest me less and less; I'm obsessed, at this stage, with art and landscape: words are beginning to sink in my taxonomy of useful adaptations to this planet. Mary Caroline Richards, who was a poet, potter, and lapsed English teacher, believed that "All teachers should, as part of their class preparation, practice an art." Pottery, she goes on, engages a dialogue between inner and outer space: "I have come to feel that we live in a universe of spirit, which materializes and dematerializes grandly; all things seem to me to live, and all acts to contain meaning deeper than matter-of-fact; and the things we do with deepest love and interest compel us by the spiritual forces which dwell in them. This seems to me to be a dialogue of the visible and the invisible to which our ears are attuned."

I believe her statement without reservation. The potter's craft—any craft—can become an instrument of inquiry; raising sheep will do as well, or gardening, or playing the alto sax.

When I walked away from collating seventeenth-century texts, an elderly academic called me into his office to say, "You are making the worst mistake of your life." When I dropped the beginnings of a writing career in Baltimore to come back to Minnesota, my editor sneered, "Nobody will ever hear your name again." Their judgments, though, had to do with a path of privilege and prestige;

my grandmother and my academic mentors, according to what light they had, also wanted for me a kind of worldly success—or simply survival. But in recommending a path in life, our teachers inevitably lack one critical piece of information: how the defining forces of life—political, environmental, social, even culinary—will change (Jacobean drama, regrettably, having fallen off the academic agenda).

Therefore, all we really have to guide us is the response of joy and reverence we feel in the presence of what seems to us beautiful, good, and holy. "Love calls us to the things of this world," Augustine wrote. He read a lot, but not all the time.

Mercy

WHEN I WAS STUDYING THE MINISTRY of spiritual direction at Shalem, my class went on retreat with Tilden Edwards, the Episcopalian priest who was one of the Institute's founders. After two days of silence, we had a service together in which Tilden asked us to break the retreat by singing out—together, in whatever kind of harmony we could muster, or concord of discord—the word for God that came most naturally to us.

How would you respond to such an exercise? Please stop and think about it. Try not to get hung up on scary expectations, like making music or doing theology.

For the last few years it's been my blessing to live among the more unfashionable animals—sheep with their needy bleat, rabbits, ducklings, white-footed mice—which I began to do as an agriculture student and continued later as an apprentice in wildlife rehabilitation. Living so much among animals, I am learning to forget the great and complicated names. "Mercy," I sang. As we get older, perhaps, we shed ideas and concepts until only a few simple words remain. "Mercy" remains. The church-of-the-wildlife-rehabilitation-clinic where I work—this abandoned corner of the universe, with its filth and cockroaches—has become my cloud of unknowing.

"We save everything we can. . . ." I explain to a group of friends, gathered for an afternoon music rehearsal, who have asked about my life as a wild animal rehabilitator.

They are thinking, I soon realize, of *prestigious* wildlife, the sort our governor occasionally releases to great fanfare on state occasions:

49

the hawk, the eagle, the peregrine falcon: *manly* birds, if I may put it that way. These animals are tended at a beautiful, well-funded facility, the Raptor Center, across the street from where I work. But in our underfunded world of wildlife rehabilitation, a "release" may mean packing up a crate of Eastern cottontails, driving them into the country and watching their panicky break for freedom. No television crews show up for that.

When I tell my friends about the squirrels with neurological damage, crows needing their feathers reseeded, they are astonished. "You save *everything?*"

We try. My job last evening was to carefully tuck a mash of fruit and "zoo biscuit" behind the broken teeth of a woodchuck who had been hit by a car. Intubating Canada geese—a four-handed job—chucking pills past the serrated bills of mallards: these are the jobs of an apprentice wildlife rehabilitator. Mice are not beneath our notice.

Back in the human world, I gather with my friends on Sunday afternoons to sing the old gospel repertoire of shape-note music, the texts of Isaac Watts, Charles Wesley, and their company. We are always crying, in four-part a cappella harmony, for that mercy.

> Beneath the sacred throne of God
> I saw a river rise;
> The streams of peace and pard'ning love
> Descended from the skies.

I wail the alto. I think about how I've learned to read the pain of animals, often a shrinking that the brain commands, though the body cannot obey. The caged woodchuck, incisors broken, jaws misaligned, is denied the pleasure of bite. He fears me; in a certain sense he "hates" me—or thus I interpret the white, terrible shriek he lets out when a few calories hit his nervous system and he gathers himself to let me know what he thinks of suburban life, automobiles, and me. I'm a teacher, so I relate the cockeyed wisdom of this animal to the actions of students I've encountered now and again. In her book *Basic Needs*, which I'm reading at the moment, Julie Landsman tells of her work with thrown-away kids in the inner city: "I think that perhaps the kids I teach are doing what they need to do to protect themselves, using blind instinct, trying to heal their hurts. Yet they seem to be making such awful mistakes. Carol drinks. Linda curls into a ball . . . And Jackie, in her tight pink pants and white T-shirt, is calling to men, walking down Chicago Avenue at 2 a.m."

As I feed the woodchuck, a couple of the vet students who direct my work gather around, trying to decide how much suffering is too much, whether the animal is beyond help or too crippled to survive in the wild. "Rehabilitate and release" is the ethic I've been taught. Sometimes we can place a hopelessly damaged animal—one who is deaf or blind, for example—in a zoo or wildlife sanctuary, but, typically, space is at a premium for "common" animals.

"But we can't save everything, really," I tell my music friends. Sadly, this is what stressed-out teachers say to each other, along with shelter workers, social workers, ministers, nurses, and every other caregiver whose working conditions make it impossible, logistically, to care in proportion to the magnitude of the need.

The fawn, about the size of a two-year-old child, but lighter, rests in my arms. Its weight leans confidently into my flesh. I can only say it *snuggles*, out of fear, however, rather than comfort. I know it will not be able to live. A young woman, sobbing hysterically, had thrust the animal, wrapped in a bloody blanket, at me as I came out the front door for a break. As I fold back the blanket I see that the deer's foreleg hangs by a thread.

"Someone hit it with a haymower," she sobs. "Can you help it?"

If only I could offer her a cup of tea. She is pale and as shocky as the fawn. "Why don't you sit down and in a minute I'll bring you some paperwork, but now I'll take the deer back to the doctors."

Jim, a vet student, responds to my soft call: "This animal is badly hurt," I tell him.

"What's wrong?"

"Leg amputation."

"He won't make it then. Why don't you sit back there with him while I find Mark." Mark is our supervising vet.

I hold the placid fawn and try to memorize it, as the Navaho teach their children to do. At the clinic, we have been trained, like monks, in custody of the eyes, in silence, never to startle or disturb the animals. "I love the wild not less than the good," Henry David Thoreau wrote of the woodchuck that crossed his path. Yet it seems fair to make an exception and ponder this beautiful animal. In my other life, studying ceramic sculpture, I am experimenting with a wash of glazes in brown, deep red, black, and sand: the background against which all life but our own hides and rests from the human explosions of color and noise. *Be still and know that I am God.*

At the ceramic studio where I go in my off-hours, the woman at the next wheel is a university professor also. She throws pots every Thursday from eight to five.

"It's great that you're taking time for your art," I've told her.

"This is the only life I have," she snaps.

After a few weeks, she's no longer snapping. Years ago, when I spent a sabbatical at Pendle Hill, a Quaker community for study and contemplation, I did nothing useful, though there were many good classes offered and people to talk to. I just played with clay in the basement. One of my elderly friends, a great favorite in the community, told me, "When I came here, I had a lot of trouble on my mind. I went down to the basement and worked with clay for a year— didn't talk to anybody, didn't do therapy—and when I came up, it had all lifted."

Mark, the head veterinarian, materializes and lifts the fawn from my arms. As he unwraps the blanket, the deer's leg comes away. I've worked in hospitals and homeless shelters, where there is always a lot of fuss and exclamation from staff and client alike, as though the duty of humankind were to comment and keep up a running analysis. But here we learn our discipline from the silence of animals. My daughter said to me recently, "I must be getting deaf. I can't hear you when you talk any more." We speak as a little as possible at the clinic, and we take the cues of green heron, coyote, and terrapin. Cradling the deer, Mark carries it to the gas tanks in the corner and slips a mask over its face. The deer looks puzzled and sleepy as its spirit slips under: its spirit, "the deerness"—Thomas Merton wrote of a wild encounter—"that sums up everything." I go back to the woman in the outer office, busy with forms. "Will it be okay?" she wants to know.

"The vet is with him now," is my evasion.

"Can't a deer live with three legs?" one of the new volunteers wants to know.

"Hoofed stock"—Jim begins formally—"put so much pressure on the digital phalanges that the bones of the remaining feet would begin to protrude above the hoofs and it would be very painful. Sheep can do well on three feet, but deer cannot."

Come thou fount of ev'ry blessing
Tune my heart to sing thy grace;
Streams of mercy never ceasing . . .

We sing. Several years ago, when I was raising sheep, all of us workers, most of them, unlike me, Evangelical Lutherans, used to ponder the imagery of the Good Shepherd. Farm kids, you'd think they'd have had enough of Psalm 23, but it remained an icon and a puzzle to us. In the Buddhist tradition, the Bodhisattva of Compassion is often imaged with a nest of rabbits at her feet. The same year I raised sheep, I studied under Thich Nhat Hanh at the Mahayana Buddhist monastery, Plum Village, where I was given the dharma name "Tending of the Source"—a koan offered to me to think about forever, in recognition of and challenge to my shepherd's work. "May all beings be brought to enlightenment," Buddhists pray.

We try to save everything. Even the unfashionable animals. Streams of mercy, never failing.

Pure intelligence, framed in a silver triangle: predators have to be smart, wildlife biology teaches me, and I reflect on this fact as I peer into the gray fox's cardboard lair. She has already trained us to put dog food in front of her, no mice, thanks. The fat rodents we fed her yesterday remain in her dish, and I remove from the right like a good servant. This fox came to us after jumping off the sixth floor of a parking ramp downtown, pursued by an animal control officer. The fall, or flight, did her little apparent harm—in fact, she is pregnant—and she will soon go back to her native habitat. But where might that be? Sixth and Wabasha in downtown St. Paul? The rules of our shelter dictate that animals be replaced where they were found if possible, so they can reconnoiter with family groups. But where is her den? I imagine her traveling by night, past the public library, Mickey's Diner, a shadow making it up the river bottoms from points East, where Jackie, in her tight pants, is calling to men.

If predators are pure intelligence, prey gets to be foolish. I tent the rabbit's thin flesh with thumb and second finger and inject her with steroids. She gives me the rabbit's perennial red-eyed multiplex stare. Rabbits have almost 360 degrees of vision, the better to anticipate trouble from all directions—as you have to do if you are at the absolute bottom of the food chain. Next to me, a clinic worker with blond braids is feeding grubs to a nighthawk, which she has wrapped up in a soft washcloth. We call these "nighthawk burritos." My own next task will be feeding infant bats. It's hard to remember that these intricate little demons are, in fact, mammals, and we feed them formula through a tiny flexible tube which they suck greedily.

First, I have to exercise the opossum. How does one exercise an opossum, you may wonder. The same way as the universe, in its cosmic wisdom, exercises me: by putting my food dish at the north end of the corridor and me at the south. This possum is a sweet animal, with the affect of a sleepy two-year-old, and a tendency to get bored and curl up for a nap.

We have a new administrator at the clinic; therefore the place has been cleaned up and bushy plants put around for the animals to admire. New protocols have been put in place; tonight, some of our best volunteers have been sent home for failure to complete their rabies series. The series costs five hundred dollars and the workers have long been on a list to get cheaper shots at the student health center. But the list has vanished under some pile of trash, and there is a rumor around that the health center will no longer offer shots. Next week, a memo will go out that workers may continue on their shifts so long as they *intend* to get a rabies series, an interesting piece of Jesuitical reasoning. But tonight, shorthanded and overtired, we snipe at each other, change only the top layer of paper in the cages, and start blaming the animals.

This is reminding me a lot of teaching. Lazy old possum, get a move on. I have twenty-six bats to feed.

"Bats?" my music friends question. Some confess to hitting them with tennis rackets. In the dark neighborhoods around us, robins bounce off the hoods of cars, squirrels turn to leather under our wheels. What's a bat, a rabbit, in a nation that's recently finished bombing, just then, Yugoslavia? In a city where runaway teens look after each other in the cold river caves?

"Mercy, O thou Son of David!"
Thus poor blind Bartimeus prayed.
"Others by thy grace are saved.
Now to me afford thine aid."

People speak of the "problem of suffering": how could a good God permit the conundrums of violence? By contrast, I am obsessed with the unfathomable problem of mercy: how could a fallen world unspool this golden thread? In dark alleys of our city, people hurt and maim, while in our clinic, people line up to save things. Thomas Merton, in his last journals, struggles with the relentless dialogue between action and contemplation, retreating deeper into solitude to find, often, God, often, a migrating flock of pine siskins. He senses "total kinship with them as if they and I were of the same nature and as if that nature were nothing but love. And what else but love keeps us all together in being?" A tattooed biker comes into the clinic with eight mallard chicks he's retrieved from a millrace. He fills out the paperwork with barely literate concentration and buys a T-shirt. A yuppie lawyer brings in a half-dead fledgling, donates fifty dollars, and demands a full report in the mail: his eye, too, is on the sparrow. Here is a young girl with the face of a born saver. She does not want to relinquish a newborn bunny she has gotten away from a cat. I explain to her about the impossibility of aiding it without extensive equipment, about the dangers of tularemia, and finally, regretfully, I tell her that it's against the law to raise wild things without a license. Along with her paperwork, I give her sign-up forms to volunteer. "You'll have to have a series of rabies shots . . ."

She'll be there at 8 a.m.

"We try to save everything."

She nods.

"What else but love keeps us altogether in being?"

What do you mean by *love?*

People hate it when I ask this question, but I can't stop. Mark is euthanizing a crow. The crow's talon holds my attention with the vitality of its blackness, made of alien skin, not "leather" but some dark-adapted collagen that looks tried in the fire. It puts me in mind of Mimbres pottery. The crow's talon is clenched and useless, rapidly becoming more useless. Not rapidly enough, for Mark is injecting the badly damaged bird with euthanasia fluid, and it is not progressing in a way that suits the vet. For human doctors, death is the enemy; for animal doctors, suffering is the enemy. "He's becoming psychotic now," Mark says, reading the crow's mental screen perhaps, for the bird is lying still and calm. "But he's not dying. Ah, there, he's gone."

I'm sorry to see this splendid creature go into the green plastic bag and then into the freezer. He will be sent eventually to the

Department of Natural Resources, which keeps tabs on all the animals that come through rehabilitation.

We would give the crow, if we could, a Viking funeral, to suit his pagan otherness, his warrior spirit.

Homes and Gardens

FOR ONE DAY ONLY AT THE BEGINNING of summer, the peonies are
gathered into a drama that outweighs any container I possess. Their
heads are too big for their support system. Like blowsy intellectuals,
they miss their moment and lean forward into a slow dissolve. Storm
after storm has passed through lately. Three weeks ago, the chimney
pot came off and took a line of guttering. I had just finished paying
for it when it flew off again in the next storm. I got a tiny insurance
check over my two hundred fifty dollar deductible. A third storm
came through; this time there were bricks all over the yard from a
missing chimney, nudged down by my neighbor's untended elm.
Twelve hundred dollars, I estimate, slick as an Allstate agent. My
neighbor, always on the run, tells me it was not his tree that did it
but the wind. I'll give that a big *Whatever*. It's not worth arguing
about.

Two boards rotted through under the boot of the gutter inspec-
tor. Everywhere in the garden, things are growing, missing their
moment and sliding down. The house over my head is practicing to
become a ruin.

Robin, companion of my life, hates peonies. When we were
courting, some twenty years ago, I brought him a bouquet from my
garden and he looked at them with the honest contempt he would
never dream of concealing—this transparency being, of course, his
great blessing and curse. "What are they? Something *horticultural?*"
Robin is, by training, a plant ecologist, and he hates—or hated
then—anything hybridized, overblown, cultivated, and not native.
Our long years together have brought me to an appreciation of his

cherished spring ephemerals—the kind of wildflowers that bloom only a couple of days, half buried in humus: trout lilies, hepatica. For his part, Robin is planning an English country border. Things change, as Josef Stalin liked to say.

How should I live the life that I am?—being accountable not only to myself, but to a network of relationships? Other lives interpenetrate mine, all of us struggling for enlightenment and integrity. Robin and I, though firmly paired, do not share a house. We have many excuses for this negligence. For example, we have not found the right one. "Houses," wrote Leonard Woolf, "make everything possible or impossible." I repeat this quotation to Robin frequently, when we are looking for houses, looking for farms. Recently we bought nursing-home insurance together.

"Does this mean we'll get to live together when we're old?" Robin wants to know.

"Will they make us?" I respond. "We'd better check the Medicare guidelines."

I doubt my ability to live patiently with another.

I was married for fifteen years, and neither my husband nor I could find a way, in that construction, to live the life we were. If he had not surprised me by asking for a divorce—which was, in the end, a kindness—I would have wasted away, I'm sure; a willow on an oak savannah pining for its river.

I decline to plunge back into the crucible of marriage, having not yet mastered solitude. I temporize, like Penelope in the *Odyssey*, who wouldn't accept a proposal until she had finished weaving her tapestry. Secretly, she tore out the threads by night. Perhaps this weaving and unweaving is a metaphor for the work each of us must do alone in order to make a sustaining web out of the past.

My family believed in exorcising history by erasing its data from conversation, if not from consciousness. Once I visited an old church in Yorkshire, in which the dead were buried under the floorboards where the living knelt in prayer. I had to flee. It made me think of Case Street.

"Why dredge all that up?" my mother always demanded when I asked her about the difficulty of her childhood with a mother who suffered from dramatic and dangerous episodes of mental illness. Buddhist wisdom is *Have a cup of tea with the ghosts. They are lonely and hungry.* My mother would have none of this. It was a great achievement for her to get my grandmother incarcerated, as I now realize, but one that almost destroyed her courage for any further endeavor. The horror of it. That ghost is not coming to tea.

One day I was working on some needlework with Grandma Rose and Susie, my dearest girlfriend of late childhood. I had cobbled together a few doll clothes before, but I didn't much care for hemming the dishtowels that had been assigned to me that hot July day. Grandma always lamented her own lack of ability at sewing, so why was she scolding me, as if it mattered, for my long, careless stitches? Susie said traitorously, "I don't take such big stitches even when I'm basting."

Basting? Hell, what's *basting?* Not only was there something I could not do, but it was something I had never heard of doing; yet Susie had heard of it, and that roused my competitive nature. Susie's ample mother was inevitably busy about something womanly, she always had a rosy baby under one arm.

It dawned on me at this precise moment, as it seems to me in recollection, that there was a world of fertility and womanly competence our family had no part in. My mother, for example, was the only woman I had ever seen wearing slacks, one of the rare mothers who drove a car, and certainly the only woman who worked, as we now say, "outside the home." Her example made it possible for my sister and me to take the fast train to feminism, but as children we wondered why the neighbors gossiped about us.

Grandma Rose was always finding fault with herself for not being able to sew or cook or arrange the house like grandpa's sisters. These sisters collected, for example, glass trays of china shoes while she, Rose, studied in a law office. None of the O'Reilley girls could cook, sew, or collect shoes. Rose O'Reilley went to work for a lawyer, right out of eighth grade. She was ready to take the bar exam by twenty-two, but *something held her back.* Her sister, Florence, got four more years of school and won a full scholarship to college, which she declined. *Something held her back.* Aunt Florence once told me that their mother had odd ideas about the education of women, the mother, herself, having gone all the way through the Convent of the Sacred Heart. "You'll only marry a farmer and be unhappy all your life," she told her smart, ambitious, but fatally conflicted girls. "If only I'd gone into the convent," Grandma Rose used to say. Her older sister had escaped that way, gotten an education, and learned to baste a hem in the bargain. But the rest of the girls were stuck between worlds, lost to the old ways, unable to find the new, and given to staring balefully at husbands who took away the keys to their roadsters.

Worse, they were not very fertile. Both my parents came from two-child families, and our own little unit, my sister and me five years apart, were a matter of inquiry in our sprawling Catholic parish. Families in our neighborhood were in the reproductive sweepstakes: the Stireks and the Walpoles were both tied at ten— who would make it to eleven? The O'Learys passed them slyly by producing triplets. Mr. and Mrs. O'Leary were both red haired, white-faced, and weak-eyed. Each of their children was pale, freckled, carroty, and bespectacled. They filled a couple of pews at Sunday mass and lived in a tiny suburban tract house like the rest of us, except that its seams on a winter night seemed to heave and sway apart, casting interior light onto the snow.

What did those disheveled lines of Catholic children think of us? We were (at least on Sunday) cleaned up, white gloved, strawhatted, anklets turned down a precise inch-and-a-quarter—for those were my father's standards. They thought people like us were *pathetic,* as I know from later marrying into a family of twelve; I could not grasp the rules of touch football. Having lots of children, in the Catholicism of those days, was a sign of election, like having lots of money in the Calvinist dispensation.

My parents tried hard to fit in. My dad exercised a benign but totally autocratic control over the studied construction of our lives: the flat box of a house, the perfect lawn ringed with its hybrid tea roses. His taste in art, music, clothing, and behavior was all predicated on keeping nature at bay. Lawn maintenance required constant infusions of pesticide; our clothing stung and melted under a hot iron. In espousing this esthetic, he set himself in opposition to the chaos of the busy apartment we had vacated on Case Street. In our suburb, there would be nothing crazy, nothing loud, nothing confusing: no angels. Every month he read *Better Homes and Gardens* from cover to cover. But one thing he could not control: we "lost children." That was the phrase. As though the world were a perilous supermarket. My mother, like my Grandma Rose, suffered multiple miscarriages and stillbirths.

Grandma Rose, who was said to have the gift of seeing the dead, could sit at the kitchen table after breakfast and make the room dance with spirit-children. She had even lost her own twin, she told us. She was three or four years old at the time, living in Canada. In the dark of night, relatives bundled her out of her cot and took her to a neighboring cookhouse. But her twin, a boy, found his way to the window. She ran to let him in, then saw he was floating several feet off the ground, like Peter Pan. "I've come to say good-bye, Rose. Good-bye! Good-bye!" Her aunt found her by the window. "Don't be silly, Rose, Pat's asleep in the cot."

"No, he's gone to God." And so he had.

She would follow up with horrific stories of her own experiences in childbirth, bringing my father and his brother (who died young) into the world. "Catholics, you know, believe that if you can save only one, the mother or child, it's the child you must save. But your grandfather, there in the delivery room, got in a fistfight with my brother the priest and my brother the doctor. Meanwhile the nurse took a knife and slashed me like a melon–"

"A melon?" my sister and I would gaze at her with horror, our girlish parts contracted.

"A *melon*. And the child came, your father. Your grandfather fainted dead away on the floor."

My grandmother would come to my bed and pray over me every night, lest the pull of the night air should suck me through the window. The dead girl she often saw playing beside me was her own Angelica. "It was in the ninth month of that pregnancy that I saw the angel of death come into my bedroom. He leaned over me in the bed, his face a hanging skull, and he bent over my womb and like *that*"—

Grandma Rose leaned forward and made a sound like the blowing out of a match, *poof!* I would jump, no matter how many times she told the story. "—And like *that* the baby died."

Surrounded by the robust, teeming families of Roseville, we knew ourselves to be odd: arid, white-gloved, turned-out, without. When we went to visit relatives at Thanksgiving, over the river and through the woods, it would be to visit our lonely aunt and uncle on the farm, whose daughter had died one winter of a burst appendix in the family sleigh, whose son had been killed in Korea. With nothing better to occupy their time, the women in our family went crazy, turned to drink, or flung themselves whole hog into religion.

Because none of us could sew, we all stood staring with horror at the packet of tissue-paper patterns that had arrived in our kitchen one day in June, a week after I graduated from high school. Just as high school graduates today wait for the fat envelopes from Eastern colleges that signify acceptance, girls like me waited in farm kitchens and in elm-shaded Victorian city houses and in suburban ranch homes to hear that we had been accepted as postulants in some religious order. And that we would have to spend the summer sewing these strange medieval garments. We would do this as generations of Catholic girls had done before us, not knowing we were among the last who would bend our necks to this particular yoke with this particular innocence. As soon as we felt its weight, most of us would bolt. Of the thirty-some women who entered the novitiate with me, only five or six brave women remain.

If your older sister or cousin was a nun, as was so often the case in those big Catholic families that knelt down to say the Rosary together every night, the clothing patterns held no mystery. Besides, girls from big families could sew. It was only a couple of long, black half-slips and some ankle-length aprons; my father brought to the problem at least some comprehension of blueprints as he laid them out on the table, but his practical approach would have unfortunate consequences. "The patterns say the slips are supposed to have pockets," he told us. "Surely this is, a mistake." Also he noted that the aprons had a square bib, but no straps to hold the bib to the body. "Skip all that," he ordered the seamstress he found to take over these tissues of absurdity. "And skip the pockets. They don't make sense."

My Roseville family was, compared to our relatives in the old neighborhood, rational about religion, though my father was a sincere and faithful Catholic. (My mother had no time for any of it, but she kept that opinion to herself.) Neither of them understood why I had come up with the idea of entering a convent. Nor did I; I had a set of reasons at the time, but they certainly were not the real reasons. Today I see quite clearly what a perfect intuitive step it was for me; if nothing else, it made my mother mad, which for most teenagers is sufficient reason for any course of action.

The poor woman had to stand there, smoking Marlboros in her velvet capri pants, among her avocado appliances, trying to decipher a pattern for medieval underwear. My mother boasted of her family's religious eclecticism, as Mormon and Episcopalian as it was Catholic, but she hadn't much to hold onto spiritually; her family had produced such a line of miscreants, crazy people, and riverboat gamblers. In marrying my father, as she often told us, she sought stability, taking on, I fear, his caution and conservatism without being able to fathom his spiritual tenderness.

My little imperiled family had no stable identity, no authority or sense of itself from which to critique any aspect of the culture we drifted in. We just tore into packages as best we could and tried to put things together. To insiders around the parish, we sometimes looked like radicals or rebels, perhaps "interesting," perhaps threatening, but really we were just outsiders, trying to read a pattern for which we had no context and no skill. It was not because I was a rebel, but because I was clueless, that I entered the convent without bibs on my aprons (which were supposed to be pinned, I soon learned, under our capes) and without pockets in my slips.

As I watched the other young women unpack their things, I realized I had problems. They were plugged into some folk knowledge that had gone right by me. For example, under the tutelage of those loving cousins or sister-friends, they had produced aprons in subdued patterns of gingham checks, with embroidered borders a foot above the hems or a little discreet smocking. Most rural grandmothers could have confidently fabricated these, the outfits of their own girlhood. But my grandmother, who had worn flapper costumes to the law office, had not been able to offer guidance. I pulled up at the novitiate with brightly flowered calico aprons on backgrounds of blue, yellow, and hot pink, immediately branding myself an extroverted show-off.

The opposite was true. I had never gone shopping in my life. Because he worked for a department store, my dad bought all our clothes—he loved fashion—and his women just put them on. My high school friends told me in later years that everyone envied my clothes, but my sister and I hardly noticed them. We had no full-length mirrors; I don't think my mother, or my sister, Peggy, or I had anything that would nowadays be called a "body image." My taste, in consequence, remained at the level of a six-year-old with a crayon box, and with that esthetic in place I had gone to the strip mall and picked out my apron fabric. When I wandered in off the lawn of the novitiate where we said good-bye to our parents, the sisters discreetly commented, "We'll know what laundry box to put your clothing in."

Nuns require pockets on their slips because their medieval dresses were designed in the days before purses. The "habits," as they were called, had slits on the sides to allow access to deep pockets. Old-time nuns carried an astonishing volume of handy stuff: handkerchiefs and chalk, books, pins—always pins—third-degree relics of martyred saints. When, as a Catholic child, did one ever express a need or require a course correction (smack with a ruler? handcuffs? sutures?) that Sister couldn't answer to right there on the playground?

Because I had bolted from home without pockets in my slip, an elderly nun supplied me with an even stranger medieval item: a set of detachable saddlebags that fastened around the waist and hung down on each side. Suddenly the old nursery rhyme made sense, "Lucy Lockett lost her pocket." I was always losing my saddlebags. The snaps gave as I genuflected in chapel or served at table, and all my wares would be laid out on the floor.

Becoming a nun happened to be a terrific solution to problems I didn't know I had: naïveté, incompetence, inexperience in community life, undisciplined academic skills, an uncertain eye for beauty, and poor musical taste. Young girls enter religious life for the same reasons young girls get married, because they think they are in love. Love is likely to be an illusion in both cases, but with luck you can learn something in the process of being flayed away from your erroneous notions. The soul gravitates to the lessons it needs to learn and it never makes mistakes.

Sacred Space

THIS IS HOW THE STORIES GET STARTED: some threshold space at the back of the garden leaks infinity. The traveler falls down a well in a holy grove and wakes up in the secret world where myths form. For my part, I was trimming the relentless vines at the back of the garden that spend their infinitely renewable life cycles trying to climb the Scotch pines. There is a place in the garden I reserve for the *devas*. Hindu mythology asks us to leave a wild space for the garden spirits; but human hands need to get in there occasionally to root around, for example, to deliver these serene evergreens from the stifling love of vines. I worked an hour, then fell into an old green and white plastic garden recliner that's abandoned back there for *devas* to nap in. That chair commands a secret world; before my eyes the pine boughs bend down to the ground, the garden fence encloses another two sides, and a pergola covered in climbing roses forms the third. It's one of those wonderful burrows that both invites and manifests inwardness of spirit.

I rested and then, *tap tap tap*, a downy woodpecker went to work a yard from my head. Next, the red lacing of a cardinal's flight slid across my visual field; he and his green mate landed at my feet. Two small yellow warblers on their migration lit by my left hand, and, as I turned to look, a shaking in the air became a hummingbird. I sat very still. A few minutes passed as though time had turned inside out like a big wool sock. Then they were gone. I started breathing again. My neighbor's little cat insinuated herself into the miracle, and she was not unwelcome. I needed to move; rational humans try to pull down the curtain on miracles—"*an ephemeral and local fracture in the middle of a durable and normal world"*—as quickly as they can.

Such things happen, and the stories people subsequently tell are often miracle stories. Our categories may not be elastic enough to properly file these incidents; they seem miraculous—and if miraculous, then vexing—because we are rarely awake to the nature of reality. We need to look harder and longer. "*Mira*, Mary Rose!" one of my Spanish girlfriends would cry. "Look!" Wonder does not require a suspension of the natural law, but simply the ability to slow down and see what's available.

What was going on in that sacred scrap of garden, *deva* territory? Some eccentric truce obtained for a moment between worlds, a door opened. My grandfather used to look at the globe of a full moon rising and say, "It looks like a door, doesn't it, that you could fly through."

When I was in the novitiate, an old nun called Sister Anselm taught us novices church history and the daily calendar of the saints. She was a severe rationalist, banging on the doors of the holy with dates and numbers, addresses and quadratic equations. That was her way of loving. And we were modern, educated young women. I had gone to an excellent Catholic high school in the city, and, at seventeen, the superstitious, frilly piety of my grade school days and my grandmother's house seemed far away. Any one of us novices could prove the existence of God in five mathematical steps. We understood the historical context that had produced such bloody and bizarre devotions as the Sacred Heart, weird as an Aztec blood eagle. We had a taste for lean, modern religious art. We came to class on October 4, the Feast of St. Francis of Assisi, eager to hear what assault Sister Anselm would make on the giddiness of this excessive saint. Francis was the one who, disenchanted with men, preached to the birds, until they settled on his outstretched arms. Sister Anselm, how could this be?

But Sister Anselm was not in a deconstructive mood that particular day. "*He had allowed himself to be healed,*" she snapped, and had no more to say. I wrote down her words where I could ponder them for thirty-five years, and there, on a green plastic chair in the back garden, I began to understand. Life becomes sacred when we soften to it. It is not, in the technical sense, miraculous. It just is. To be healed of our separation, there is nothing we can *assert*. There is no syllabus but to surrender and *permit*.

The Islamic poet, Hafiz, wrote these lines, which I scratched on a plaque of wood and hung up in my garden, where I rarely pay it the least scrap of attention, so busy am I weeding and moving bricks.

> Just sit there right now
> Don't do a thing
> Just rest.
>
> For your separation from God,
> From love,
>
> Is the hardest work
> In this
> World.

"But I have this idea"—I was saying to my sister—"that I'm being led by God, call it God." The word Rabbi Heschel would not spell.

"Things don't happen unless you make them happen," my sister responded. Imagine us in a kind of Italian opera, where two people relentlessly sing opposing arguments in harmony. This particular opera was about some little decision that affected us both. Peggy wanted me to make up my mind about whatever it was, but I didn't feel sufficiently "led" (as Quakers so annoyingly say) to engage with it yet. My sister and I have different ideas about how decisions should get made; but things happen to us both, good and bad, ready or not.

The scent of broccoli, chopped fine, carrots heating on the radiator, brings Easter into the room, or the weeks before Easter anyway, when bulbs are lined up and made to work hard. Here in the lamplight on a chilly day, we're nursing a young Eastern cottontail. For five days I fed him sugar water with an eyedropper every hour and a half around the clock, trying hard to find the small comma of his mouth, not feed a nostril instead. Then it was kitten formula, carefully maintained at body heat. Now, having achieved three ounces, he lies in my flannel shirt and stands on my bra and begs bits of desiccated vegetable out of my fingers, which smell always of some rabbit snack.

"*Wabush*," my colleague Heid Erdrich calls him, the Ojibwa name for rabbit. "And besides, a trickster figure in our mythology."

He came into my ken like a trickster. I'd been teaching a freshman honors class, which included a reading from the *Fioretti*, a selection of stories about Francis of Assisi, called "Francis and the Wolf of Gubbio." I had included this story in my syllabus because I was developing a theme about the relationship of "man" to nature, with special emphasis on what various religious traditions have contributed to this dialogue. In Catholic hagiography, St. Francis is always depicted in the thick of numerous relationships with animals—one of them being the Wolf of Gubbio. The wolf makes a dandy villain, mercilessly lunching his way across the Umbrian landscape like the rogue animals of Russian folklore. Francis walks out after him, they have a conversation, and the wolf agrees to come in and be domesticated.

I love the old fable for its delicate poise. On the one hand, Francis is a mystical intermediary between human and nonhuman modes of consciousness; on the other, it's possible to see him as an emissary of colonial power and hierarchical urban values. Would he drive an SUV, do you think?

Although I teach in a Catholic university, none of my students knew anything about Francis and his iconography. Since they had no articulate constructions, there was little for me to deconstruct. In fact, these young readers of the *Fioretti* were immediately charmed by Francis and held me after class with questions: did he *really* speak the language of the birds? Did the wolf *really* put a paw in his hand? Only one young girl—a high school student on the postsecondary program—was ready to critique the domestication of the wolf and to lament how he passed off stage, slinking from hearth to hearth like a dog. This girl was the sort who painted her fingernails black and wanted me to write her a recommendation for the admissions committee at Brown.

"But *did it really happen?*" the others wanted to know.

I finally snapped, "No, of course not, it's a folk tale." I carried on with a lecture about how the story polarizes the walled medieval city against the imagery of a wolf-haunted wilderness . . .

When issues like this arise in class, I usually introduce students to what I call the "Simone Weil Doubting/Believing Game." Simone Weil, the great twentieth- century French philosopher and mystic, taught that, given any statement, we should go through the following mental process: "Suppose this is *not true:* list the consequences." All French school children cut their teeth on this Cartesian methodology. But Weil went a step further: "Suppose this is *true;* list the consequences." Such good mental discipline.

I went through all these intellectual moves with my class and then closed the book, a little piqued, I must say. These modern students are so credulous. They watch too much TV. They tell me there's a whole network devoted to animal miracles.

But now why are my students so dejected? Sometimes I think they come to college—especially small, denominational colleges—longing to have their childish versions of reality validated. They would be happy, I think, if I reinforced their belief in Santa Claus. Thus I was fuming on my moody walk across campus. It was an inner debate I had hosted many times in the past—I'm sure every responsible teacher struggles with the duty, on the one hand, to inculcate responsible, analytical habits of mind, the rules for the verification of an hypothesis, and so on. This is even more important nowadays when popular culture is so rife with "documentaries" about everything from alien babies to past-life regression. On the other hand, a teacher must support the timorous learner, whose psyche may be organized and integrated around some set of fairy tales that he or she takes to be "real." My colleagues in the theology department must have a hard time with this, as they try to introduce their classes to more nuanced ideas about religion, without pulling a string that holds the whole personality together, and in turn the family relationships.

On one level it unnerved me that my students wanted to hold onto their wonder years. I'm a person who withheld from my own children the person of Santa Claus, because I didn't want to destroy my credibility; the jolly old elf did not set foot on our roof. But then, as I fumed along that day, I began to feel guilty about the classroom exchange. After all, what did I really know about Francis's adventures with the animal kingdom? I come from a line of people who had fairly unusual relationships with animal familiars. *Sister Anselm, how can this be?*

I began to feel that in my snappish response I had been unfaithful to my deepest knowing: which is that phenomena simply are and our job is to describe them as faithfully and truthfully as we can. One should be reluctant to dismiss any story out of hand; there are many things to wonder about.

One of them was about to befall me as I crossed campus.

A young woman was waving her arms and shouting to me beside a drainage ditch that runs along one of the campus buildings. There had been a torrential rain in the night, and I recalled seeing a spilled nest of rabbits over there, two or three little drowned pelts, on my way to class earlier. It was October 4, late for rabbits to bear young—in fact, *it was the Feast of St. Francis.* Not that I retain the old calendar of feast days by heart; it's just that the Feast of St. Francis, like Valentine's Day or St. Patrick's Day, has a little shine to it: on October 4 we have a big party for the animals at our house and let them eat on the picnic table—which they hate, by the way; it upsets their training. I probably had had the date in mind when I put the *Fioretti* on the syllabus, a private joke set up for myself, which went right by me in the autumn press of business.

The young woman was hailing me about a tiny living creature, the size of a frog, who had survived the flood. *Why are you calling me? Do I look like a rabbit rescuer?* Yes, apparently I do. The cottontail was about as big as the thumb of my glove, where I immediately tucked him.

Reader! Don't try this at home. Now that I am a trained wildlife rehabilitator, it's my job to tell you that you must leave abandoned baby animals right where they are—although swimming around in a flooded drainpipe is not the best place for newborn rabbits. Usually their mothers come back for them. Cottontails, in particular, appear to abandon their nests, but in fact return to nurse at sunrise and sunset. It's not likely this particular bunny would have survived its hypothermia, of course, until the mother's return, but it's my responsibility to tell you what the law says.

I didn't know about the law then. People in my family were always raising wild critters turned up under a farmer's plow or in the roots of a downed tree. Neighbors brought such survivors to my grandfather who often had a line of shoeboxes on hot water bottles in his carpentry shop, mice the size of Vienna sausages, or feral kittens whose mother had been shot, usually by him. It's not that we were a sentimental family, it's just that we had a kind of Marshall Plan with the wilderness. One of my young friends raised a nest of robins in his bed, a messy deal but a successful one. So it never occurred to me not to take over the rearing of this tiny rabbit. The only questions I had were about nutrition and feeding schedules, and I got all the information I needed in a call to a retired veterinarian. He also gave me syringes to feed with, and the wisdom, "Brace yourself. He hasn't got a snowball's chance in hell."

Thus began a peculiar obsession. A maternal frenzy came over me; I was gentle and relentless at that tiny rabbit mouth. Wherever I went, I carried a picnic cooler hooked up to a heating pad. "Excuse me," I might say to the professor at a neighboring college where I would be delivering a guest lecture, "do you have an outlet where I can plug this in?"

The wabush taught me his ways. He permitted the medicine dropper to be slipped into his mouth, then the eyes would close and resistance or contemplation ensue. Ten seconds might pass. The nose would twitch, and then I'd clock a tentative swallow, motion in the fragile cording of the neck, barely perceptible. At first it was a victory when he would take a full dropper. Then, suddenly, he was taking a tablespoon and, later, feeding on scraps from my hand, eating all day if he could manage it.

We named the rabbit Alyosha, after the gentlest Brother Karamazov. He quickly became "Yoshi." Soon he graduated to an open cage on the floor of my study; before that he was in an aquarium in my daughter's old bedroom. At first he refused to come out of his huge cage, made for a medium-sized dog, but then he began running around, urinating on my academic magazines and bestowing his little pellets everywhere. I put down a copy of The Chronicle of Higher Education in the corner and soon he became paper trained.

Next, he began to use the litter box in his cage. Previously, he had slept in it. It seemed he had been thinking less of his cage as home, more as outhouse. He moved nests a lot, spent a spell behind the radiator, another vacation behind the poetry books on my lowest shelf, a week in one of the children's discarded Easter baskets (that's how those stories get started). Then he took to lolling in a big wicker picnic basket next to the radiator, with his nose between his front paws and his great hindquarters, a good half the length of the rest, spread out behind him.

One seldom sees a wild rabbit at rest; so much panic attends their way through the world. One seldom sees them in the posture depicted by Albrecht Dürer, who must have lived more intimately with creatures than it's possible for us to do. When Yoshi half rests, his small body contrives a circle, his fur fluffed, his gullet puffed. In full rest, the circle collapses and everything spreads out like a sigh. It's impossible to photograph him this way. He can be at peace with me in the room, if I have been quiet a long time, but he cannot rest with my camera and me. The clicking box rouses him to instant attention.

"I don't believe in any normal God," I am saying to my sister, "but I believe we are led and kept of *something*." This small creature has had a revolutionary effect on my life and teaching.

That October, I was missing animals terribly. I had developed arthritic problems that made the hard work of farming—which had occupied the previous two, happy years—impossible; besides, I needed my teaching job. I had committed myself to the dream of starting a farm retreat center, but the vision was receding like a mirage. Land prices seemed to be going up hourly, as people moved out to telecommute in their pajamas. For the moment I, with my day job at the university, needed the opposite, the simplicity of falling out the back door on a winter day and hiking to my classroom five blocks away.

Along came Yoshi. In learning how to keep him alive, I discovered the vocation of wildlife rehabilitation and came under the tutelage of the veterinarians and volunteers who taught me a new way of being with the world.

The effect he had on my classroom was even more transformative. "It's like kindergarten around here," one of my colleagues, not at all unkindly, remarked. A rabbit in a beer cooler changes the dynamics of a college class. A rabbit in an aquarium above the computer in your office changes the kind of meetings and conferences you have. Yoshi's presence lent my office an air of wacky misrule from which it has not recovered. On April 1 in medieval times, which used to be a more serious feast of foolishness than it's become, it was customary to let a trickster figure ape the gestures of the priest at mass and the king at court. Medieval people seemed to recognize the need for these inversions of hierarchy and holiness to signal the presence of an even deeper mystery. In my classroom, as we debated environmental issues, the animal world began to look at us with the authority of Rilke's bust of Apollo: "You must change."

When I Was a Boy

ROBIN AND I HAVE LATELY BEEN WORKING on the Friday night treatment crew at the wildlife rehabilitation center. Last night we dealt mostly with birds. We learned to give injections and oral medications, taking care not to pop a pill into the laryngeal opening. We learned to feel for the "keel" of a bird, a bony prominence in the center of the chest, and how to slip a needle into the muscles on either side. I worked with a flicker who had hit a window and suffered neurological damage. I had to uncage several mallards and supervise their swim in a bathtub while I cleaned their cages. Mallards are rather nasty—if birds can be held accountable to moral standards—aggressive wife beaters whose idea of copulation often results in injury to the female. We had a lot of juvenile rock pigeons to mind, now that it's gutter-cleaning season. People toss them out of this habitat with the dead leaves. Our job was to palpate their crops and check for sufficient nourishment. If they weren't eating, we hand-fed them.

My last job was to assist Jim, our vet-student supervisor, with a necropsy on a mallard. He slit the skin over the bird's breast with a scissors, peeled it back, and laid open the dark red slabs of muscle that give it the possibility of flight. Mallards are simple-winged balloons, hollow even in the bones. Especially in the bones. Breathing goes on everywhere in the bird body. They are beings of breath. Air sacs even down the gullet. "Rise my soul and haste away," I hum under my breath. No wonder we humans have no lift. Our dialogue with gravity is so different, such a no-contest.

Mark's needle injects euthanasia fluid into a fetal bird-form two inches long, a sparrow chick fallen from the nest without feathers, eyes sealed. There is not the remotest hope for its survival. In another room full of cages we turn a Canada goose onto the floor hoping her shattered leg has healed in something like a position that will allow her to survive. Otherwise she, too, will go on the euthanasia list. If an animal can't be returned to its habitat or placed in an educational facility, it must be put down.

"You're all scratched and bitten," comments my young neighbor friend when I come home from my shift. She traces the line of a scar across the top of my hand, a rake from the talons of a sora rail. There's another scrape from the serrated bill of a mallard, a slash from muskrat claws when I had to dive for him behind the water pipe. "I don't mind being scratched and bitten," I reply. "When I was a boy"—we burst out laughing—"I mean, when I was a girl . . ."

When I was a girl I was a boy. "Nobody is born a woman," wrote Simone Weil, and Gloria Steinem put it even more succinctly, "A lot of female impersonators are women." Being scratched and bitten, in my asexual preadolescent world, was a mark of honor. It meant you were bold and adventurous, not that we would have characterized each other that way; we didn't put people in categories anymore than fish characterize each other as "gnat catcher," "swims well with others." We just got up on summer mornings ready to pelt off on our bikes down the dirt roads that led from suburb to farm. We'd chase cows and make them run, climb apple trees and steal the fruit, get hold of feral cats and try to make pets of them. My girl (boy) friend Carmen and I made a life one year breaking into a line of half-built houses near us, where we played a frenetic, inverted version of *house*: house *breaker*. Carmen and I clawed each other when we got mad, pulled hair, boxed, and practiced elaborate tripping skills as if we were made of leather and ball bearings. Cuts and bruises interested rather than horrified us, the bloodier the better. You got points for deep lacerations, honor for stitches. The back of my head is still flat from a boyish crack-up I got flipping into a quarry pit while "sledding" on ice—at that point we had no sleds, but rather card-board boxes found in the dump.

I assume, though I may be wrong, that most of the women who retrieved feminism for my generation began as fierce girls like this. I may be wrong; how would I know? It's not the kind of thing college professors talk about while peeling off their panty hose in the gym locker: "Melanie, do you know how to give somebody an Indian burn?" Modern girls do not grow up with as much freedom as we had; the world has become too dangerous and they must stay inside playing wholesome games of *Doom* with their brothers, similarly confined.

I remember the first time I saw a grown girl cry—she was a first grader. She had fallen in the schoolyard and ground cinders into her knee. I watched in fascination as tears ran down her face, her huffy sobs. It wasn't that Carmen and I repressed our feelings, we simply didn't have many. No doubt, by modern standards we were socio-pathic. Also, we mostly ran with the (real) boys, especially two bruisers named Mike and (this was Minnesota) Birgir. Mike grew up to be a fireman; I lost touch with Birgir. In this company, to cry was to lose the fistfight. Criers might be seen abroad in the world, but they were an alien species to Carmen and me—sighted now and again on their way home to the sanctuary of Mom, the open door, and the injunction to "stay away from those rough girls." Vis-à-vis Roseville, east side kids were streetwise and mean.

My home was not a sanctuary and my mom was not in it. She taught school. Carmen's mom was right off a farm and it never occurred to her to confine her daughter. In those days there were outside kids and inside kids, the way cats may be subdivided these days.

We outside cats came to despise the girly girls when we became aware of them as a species, and we learned that the detestation was mutual. My own awakening came in May of first grade. In spring, in a Catholic neighborhood, the big deal was "May altars," shrines we built in each classroom to honor the Blessed Mother. Much artistic excess was spent on these projects, flowers, candles, the works. At our school, an eighth grader was appointed Queen of the May according to some standard of beauty and goodness Carmen and I were never privy to. The May Queen got to put a wreath of flowers atop the statue of Mary in church, which would have been carted out to the front steps for that occasion. It was quite the event. The queen and her court wore prom dresses; there was delirious singing, incense, and general frenzy. We processed around the neighborhood, giving testimony to our faith on the streets of the Protestants and Jews.

Where this all impinged on Carmen and me, as first graders in the flush of boyhood, was that the eighth-grade girls chose "pages" from amongst the lower graders, and the pages all got to dress up and be up in front of the crush.

This eminence appealed to me, and I expected to be chosen as soon as I got wind of the election campaign. My grandparents and doting old Mamie, Sadie, and Boo expected me to win every competition, every spelling bee—why not this? At recess, the tall goddess eighth graders would walk around checking out page material, pouncing now and again on a child, carrying her off with delight to be dressed, curled, and fawned over for her cuteness. In my hubris, I could imagine no reason why I would not be chosen *first,* and by the *queen herself.* I was the best fighter, biggest mouth, second to Carmen the best runner. Scarred and bitten, possessor of several semiwild animals, trickster, baiter of nuns, I waited, as though for a train that never came.

Sandra Schultz was chosen first. I could not fathom this. She had curly black hair and pink cheeks. She came to school in black patent-leather shoes. Patent leather *for school,* carefully vasolined. Carmen and I and another girl, Cherry Donovan, who had pierced ears and snapped gum all day, were among the losers. The total losers. Nobody chose us at all.

Our boy-buddies didn't care. We tore off to the woods where a stream, soon to be dammed up for a housing project, still ran, where the wild cherry trees were in flower and it was irreligiously, antisocially, May.

I have been remembering Carmen and our boyhood because almost fifty years have passed; I am losing my edge, my speed, and, by increments, my life and my chance to understand it. A couple of years ago when I was managing sheep, I had to stop because I began to have fits of paralysis in my hips. Now the disability fairy has touched her wand to my upper body. One day I woke unable to move my arm above shoulder level. Some kind of rotator cuff problem, the doctor said. I thought that was something that happened to automobiles. I couldn't play the violin for six months, or do my share on the Treatment Crew. Like being a shepherd, managing wildlife is one of those wordless team efforts I love. But you have to depend on the competency of every other member of the team, so you don't get your finger bitten off in the midst of a crucial maneuver. You can't be thinking about the twinge in your rocker-arm assembly mechanism.

On the road ahead of me, my mother is failing faster than I am and just as crankily. Last night I had a nightmare about trying to drive her to the doctor. It was winter; the freeway was slippery and crowded. I was trying to find a suburb I had never been to. Mom was doing one of the weird things we do in our family. Suddenly a voice in the car was asking me if I was Born Again. *Maybe*, I said. I always repeat the magic words with the preachers when I land on an evangelical radio station. You have to cover your bases.

I have been reading Thomas Merton's recently published journals, which tell about his years in the monastery after publishing *The Seven Storey Mountain*. The journals are full of obscure literary analysis and fulminations against the institutional church in five languages. What interests me is the thread of reflection on the major issue of Merton's life: his strange, compelling desire to move away from his brother-monks and become a hermit in the monastery woods. Hermitages appeal to me, too, for reasons I cannot explain, and I recognize it as a longing felt in my residual boy-mind. It's harder for girls to live alone in the woods, though there are some who make a notable success of it. I'm fascinated, too, by the process of heeding a "call," no matter how cockeyed and illogical. It seems to me that we humans are wired for this curious pilgrimage, even if we aren't overtly religious. Yet it's not something we have a way of talking about in contemporary culture; Merton's abbot certainly didn't want to hear it, and the two men struggled year after year to impose their respective wills on each other. As I trace this monastic game—*mate, checkmate*—through the journals, it's like watching one of those microcosmic conflicts that seem to structure life on this mysterious planet: it's like watching two ants fight all morning to control a crumb of sugar, thinking, as you watch: *if I can understand this, I will know why I was sent here and what I should do with my time on earth.*

Reading along this morning, I was stunned to attention at the section where the abbot finally allows Merton to go and live in a hermitage, fulfilling his lifelong obsession. What's exciting is not the final *checkmate*, but rather the way the text suddenly comes alive. Merton has, at this point, only a few years to live—he died in his early fifties while attending one of the first international meetings of Christian and Buddhist monastics. Here, close to the end of his relatively short life, his narrative breaks through into a space of light and peace. He is in touch with his nature at last; he has found his heart's desire.

The last few months have passed for me in an odd dialogue between superficial happiness and an underlying feeling of dissolution. How did I wind up facing my old age alone? And why do I *like* to be alone so much? What did I in my foolish naïveté do differently from other people, who are apparently all holding hands and singing *Ba-hoo Do-ray*? Can I please have another chance? Another job? Another incarnation? Yet despite this counterpoint of inquiry, I am happy in my creative work, my teaching, and my time, limited as it is, with Robin. I can't discern whether the conflicted voices come from the culture outside, or from a deeper level of wisdom. They seem to say, "You *shouldn't* be happy. Solitary women should be sad and anxious. Your life is not on track."

If my life were on track, what track would that be? Would I be securely married, like Sandy Schultz, like the girls in the Clearasil ads? Well, if I listen carefully, that sounds like a Hollywood voice-over. It seems to me that at the age of fifteen or so—a summer I spent in Central America—I made some intuitive decision to stifle that voice, to take a mountain road instead of the one to Peaceful Valley. But America still calls me on the phone: get a life, get a TV, get some lipstick. It takes so much time to patiently interrogate these voices—which I call to order as members of my inner commit-tee—and to evaluate their authority. The old spiritual vocabulary called this process "discernment of spirits." No wonder I long for a hermitage, someplace without a fax machine. I need some quiet. Merton writes in midlife, "It is enough that there is the same mixture of anguish and certitude, the same sense of walking on water, as when I first came to the monastery." By those standards I am on track.

Quoting Kierkegaard, Merton goes on, "It is through error that the individual is given access to the highest, if he courageously drinks it." This reminds me of something E. M. Forster wrote in *Howards End*: "The business man who assumes that that this life is everything, and the mystic who asserts that it is nothing, fail, on this side and on that, to hit the truth." But truth is not, as the compla-cent tell us, somewhere "halfway between . . . No; truth, being alive, was not halfway between anything. It was only to be found by con-tinuous excursions into either realm, and though proportion is the final secret, to espouse it at the outset is to insure sterility." "Continuous excursion into either realm" insures missteps and crack-ups, the error that Kierkegaard recommends. I love Forster's contention that we must earn the middle way. "Don't *begin* with proportion," one of his characters says early in the book, "Only prigs do that." My life has been full of error, heresy, and bolting: perhaps that has been its gift.

This inquiry is, for me, to some extent what academics would call *gendered*. I haven't lived the proper life for a *woman* of my generation. And I want more, not less, of what men take for granted. I don't mean a corner office, I mean the physical freedom Carmen and I cherished in our boyhood. Curiously enough, women at midlife have a chance to recapture their wildness, because stalkers get bored with you and, in fact, nobody is watching anymore. Thus I ponder the eccentricity of my choices, feeling abashed, yet, at the same moment wishing they had been *more* eccentric. Maybe I still have time.

Yoshi, the Eastern cottontail, has been living on the deck for a month now in the huge cage we built for him, and I must begin to leave his door open from time to time, to let him try to make a life outdoors if he can. This is not a perfect solution for him. Although I have resolutely tried not to tame him, he has, in a sense, tamed himself, expecting his daily ration of lettuce and rabbit biscuit. Alternatively, left in that drainpipe he would not have survived. Taken to the wildlife sanctuary—which I now realize would have been the correct and legal course of action—he would have been euthanized because he was below the triage weight. So many rabbits in the world. Instead, he is my illegal resident alien. He has spent a year eating poetry and running circles around a little bungalow and a university classroom, an incarnation as crazy as my own.

Parallel Universes

AWAKENING IN MY BEDROOM LOFT, I see a beautiful day beyond my skylight—rain at dawn had been steamed up by the sun, but the day is nothing like hot. Squirrels run in pursuit of squirrel business.

My mind continues to run with the temptation of making wild, interesting choices. Could I move to Bhutan? To a solitary refuge in the Boundary Waters? Join the circus? Yesterday one of my gentle, quiet friends told me he is quitting his job of twenty years, marrying a woman he met on the Internet, and emigrating to northern Canada. Further, this is not a precipitate action, but something he has been carefully planning for two years. All his boxes are packed, his ducks in a row—not that in my experience of wildlife ducks stay in a row very long. Whatever happens, it will push open the portholes of his soul. Never in my whole life have I considered anything so bold.

This morning I opened Yoshi's cage and he walked right out, took a few turns around the deck, and then launched himself with a joyful bound into the nasturtiums. In ten minutes I found him in his most beautiful relaxed Dürer posture under the roses, then I saw him no more today.

What did he find out there in that parallel universe that runs alongside ours, intersecting so seldom that you can entirely miss it? Sometimes—in the midst of reading Thoreau—I send my students outside to sit in nature for half an hour, just watching, then write about what they notice. Most of them have never done anything like this, except perhaps in a duck blind. One girl reported last year—having seen her first squirrel nests—"I notice that students seem to have been dumping bags of leaves in the trees."

Well, it's an observation, at least.

I'm fascinated at the moment by green herons, last month by nighthawks. My preoccupations represent migration patterns, I guess. Or personal affinity. Green herons, like me, have an unruly crop of feathery stuff on their heads. And stab with that fine bill.

Robin and I just got back from a Shape Note singing convention, where, somewhat unexpectedly, one of the Southern singers got up to preach—this is not something that usually happens in a secular context. "There are three things we know about heaven," he said. "We shall see God, we will know each other, and we will sing." Talk about heaven embarrasses me. Perhaps I've had bad experiences with eschatological theology. The concept of heaven has turned out to be a poor solace for grief and no substitute for engagement with this fragile world; yet I love to sing about it. Released by music from relentless logic, I can sing confidently about how, "with our songs on our lips, and our harps in our hands" we can "meet one another again." Words about heaven promise the possibility that the existing structure can be radically reorganized.

"Do you think it could be literally *true?*" I cornered one of my priest friends.

He backed up into deconstruction, "We know each other now, we sing. We see God in creation."

That was worth mulling over. But, I whined, "I want to see my dad. I want to see my dog, Heidi. I want to know that I'll be able to continue taking care of my children."

At the wildlife clinic, Robin and I intubate, inoculate, slit frozen mice for the ravens, slit frozen crows for the fox, and while rustling up these frozen entrées, clean cages, and act as lifeguards for the mergansers on their therapeutic swims. Meanwhile I learn to pay attention to the orders of creation that are likely to slit me, or stab at the eyes.

Last night's shift at the wildlife clinic didn't start too well because I was tired from sitting through a long series of university meetings. Occasionally my several lives conflict with each other. When I got to the clinic, the new VIC (volunteer-in-charge) started arguing with me, in the way of VICs (or deans), about who had dibs on the wading pool. Was I going to swim my tundra swan or he his coot? We got the tundra into the pool and the coot into the bathtub.

Free at last of the university world, I spent a long, quiet hour settling into real things—no, physical things—because the life of the mind and collegial discussion is *real,* of course—but, but—I'm trying to be fair—why does the word *unreal* come so readily when I think about academic life? Instead of critiquing that system, I should just observe that I, at this particular time of my life, prefer to be engaged with physical, palpable realities.

My principal task of the evening was to patiently untape our raven's wing, which had gotten a load of buckshot, so it could be reset; then I helped the vet student perform surgery to place an external fixator to hold the bones in place. On the way to X-ray, we taped the raven's beak closed, so none of his "Nevermore!" shit, and he gave us intelligent looks as we worked on him. Jim says ravens are so smart they can be said to operate at the level of higher primates. This particular raven is a long-term guest of ours, so it's particularly difficult not to let him get tame. They pick up language like two-year-olds and want to start answering the clinic phone.

Then I fed bats, which is a congenial task if the little demons are eating. You have to warm them up on a heating pad. We have lots of bats in for "disturbed hibernation," all lined up in aquariums in a private room. Bat species are somewhat prone to rabies so you have to be careful with them. If one bites, our protocol is that it has to be put down, so we are especially careful for the animals' sake. Everyone who works in the bat room has had a rabies series, of course, but we would have to get another if bitten.

We are sad about losing a beautiful tundra swan we've been nursing along for months. Mark, the head veterinarian, let us watch her necropsy. The spores of aspergillus throughout her body, which had killed her, looked exactly as they might growing in my refrigerator. Implicate order decrees that things damaging to an organism look ugly, even to the rankest novice. We students, huddling around Mark's dissecting table, were not used to rummaging in the bodies of swans, yet to none of us did the shiny liver look ugly or the air sacs gross. The aspergillus, by contrast, looked every bit the destroying angel it was; it had killed our fine bird with respiratory infection and progressive systems failure.

Tundras, like loons, are difficult to nurture in captivity because they are especially prone to aspergillus when their immune systems are compromised. This bird's source of stress had been a bullet in the head. She was shot by a hunter who mistook her for a goose. Fortunately, that particular hunter had been caught and booked by the game warden. By Minnesota law, the hunter will be responsible for all rehabilitation fees the bird incurs. As we necropsied our beloved bird, we spent a good deal of time in mental arithmetic, calculating the bill for the services of one vet and four students. Each student had several advanced degrees, and one was a lawyer. We saw the potential for plenty of billable hours.

"Don't forget to add in the wading pool," said the VIC. "It cost $10.98."

PART TWO

Born Into Time

The Luckiest People

BARBRA STREISAND COMES ON THE CAR RADIO singing, "People who need people are the luckiest people in the world," a musical phrase I find, at the moment, annoying. I wish popular culture would quit playing around with the holy complexities of love.

My mind returns to a day when I visited a couple in southern France, Richard and Joe, who have been together—and friends of mine—since I was in graduate school. At the time of my last visit, Joe, my beloved mentor and teacher, had gotten old and crippled. He would only live a few more years. As Richard was putting up with Joe's moody childishness, changing his diapers and cooking food to his fussy taste, I said something banal about how much they must love each other. Richard gave me a straight look and said, "It has nothing to do with love." I think he was telling me that *love*, that poor tacky word, just didn't cover it. Nobody writes ballads about changing the diapers of elderly men.

Robin and I meet regularly with a couple enrichment group in our Quaker meeting. Two members of the group brought a provocative question to our discussion recently. They asked us to list our fears and what we thought our partners' fears might be. Then we shared our lists and talked about how our fears affected the relationship.

There were no great surprises in this for Robin and me, as we know each other's hopes and fears pretty well, though not always how to deal with them. Robin said he thought we had the *same* fears. At first I disagreed, but then I saw that we had constructed micro and macro versions of the same list. He was afraid of rejection, of anger, of being perceived as cold. I had the micro list: afraid of being encircled by strangers, of being controlled by others, of hurting or disconnecting from those I care about. Then, as I chewed my pencil, another significant issue emerged: I am afraid of being trapped without solitude, at the mercy of others' noise and behavior. It is this particular constellation of fears that, within a year, will make my mother's illness and death so horrifying to me; these are the humiliations she herself will suffer, these are the insults from which Richard saved his old friend.

Though articulations might differ, Robin and I both fear, on the one hand, losing our selfhood in the crowd and, on the other, losing community in defense of self. Both of us, when pressed, will choose the island of the self over the communal voices; though that choice sometimes presents a difficult prospect.

"Self" has been, for me, so hard-won. Catholic children of the fifties were taught "unselfishness" until they barely knew who inhabited their skins. Therefore, at this point in my life, I think of self-abnegation as a semisuicidal impulse. I've been reading a book called *Proverbs of Ashes* by Rita Nakashima Brock and Rebecca Parker, in which these two feminist scholars discuss their awakening—as pastors and professors of theology—to the way the story of Jesus has been used to justify the brutal suppression of an individual's true vocation, especially a woman's sense of call. Parker writes, "Christian theology represents Jesus as the model of self-sacrificing love. . . . We are tied to the virtue of self-sacrifice often by hidden threats of social punishment . . . we allow our lives to be consumed by the trivial and by our preoccupations with others. We never claim our lives as our own. We live as though we were not present in our own bodies."

Self—I would argue, along with Brock and Parker—is too precious to be conjoined with *sacrifice*. *Selfhood* is a kind of mysterious extraterrestrial jewel one is entrusted with. Human beings are born with an imperative to defend this treasure. I know that this is what God, call it God, desires of me: that my spirit flower into this being—however peculiar—just as a baby's limbs, freed from the constriction of the womb, expand in the five seconds after birth with blood and nerve impulses and individuality. Our spirits, like our bodies, must be born into time. I value the specificity and personalism of this vocation as the Judeo-Christian tradition records it: "From your mother's womb I have known you and called you by name." But religious culture—as opposed to religion itself—has tended to exclude women from the journey of identity, imprisoning them in the handmaid's role, or the martyr's. Brock and Parker have named the injustice well.

It was so hard for me to learn to value my own vocation—it's still my basic instinct to spill over for anyone who asks—and now, in midlife, I am not going to give up what I know.

This ingrained self-sacrificing impulse, which I link with psychic suicide, is not only a woman's issue; I have known gentle male pastors and priests who have been deformed by such perfidious training. I used to worry about Mr. Rogers. But self-immolation is one of those impulses which tempts *most* women and only a *few* men. Hurray for my contemporary nun-friends, who don't even bother to agitate for change—they simply become it.

Someone in couples' group asked whether our behavior with our partner in any way mirrors our behavior with God. Oh, yes! When I deal with God and when I deal with any man I have ever loved, the relationships are haunted by specters of "the good Catholic girl" or "the dutiful wife." Why is it so difficult and frightening to follow our inner spirit, our *daimona*, as Socrates recommended? With such a breath of relief, one can say instead, *Oh, thank heaven, I just have to be a good Catholic girl.* I just have to remember what the nuns taught me in grade school. I can offer myself to be burned at the stake or have bamboo splinters driven under my fingernails by the heathen Communists we were warned about in parochial school. Martyrdom is easy; to cherish the opal of the inner life is hard.

Religious culture, at worst—along with many other kinds of socialization—encourages a kind of spineless surrender, but our own laziness co-opts us further. Virginia Woolf wrote about how she had to kill "the angel in the house"—the image of womanliness she had inherited—before she could do her own work. The work was difficult, and it would have been easier, perhaps, to preside daintily at the tea table.

Do you think God is honored because you abase yourself? I wrote this question—a variation on something Nelson Mandela said—on a card inside my violin case. One of my violin teachers used to yell at me as I played, *Attack! Attack!* But often I slither along the strings, making a bashful, uncommitted sound.

Not that you get to be a pig. One of my counselors once warned me, "Don't give up being neurotic for being a sociopath."

Barbra Streisand, mooning about love, and my friend Richard, patiently caring for an ornery old man, represent opposite ends of a continuum of understanding for me. I sense nothing of pitiful self-abnegation in Richard's service and perhaps that is why he refused the facile cultural analysis. "It has nothing to do with love. It has to do with who I am," I think he would say.

The *Bardo* of Winter

I DON'T THINK IT REGULARLY SNOWS in Bethlehem, but this is how I picture the Little Town: mounds covered in deep snow lit by an inner light, the everlasting light so widely advertised, or perhaps by the full solstice moon. The small round houses of Bethlehem look like the winter burrows of animals, and over it all hangs the deep peace of rural Minnesota winter. O Little Town of Brooten or Wadena.

I think of God these days as do, perhaps, women whose husbands are long missing in action. For quite a while, I can imagine such a woman keeps vigil, looking out the accustomed windows. Then—

I do not much like to hear talk about the supernatural these days, because it reminds me of how cut off we are from what's simply *natural*. Many things that people categorize as "supernatural" are the subtle and mighty actions of nature. We are always scanned by that eye, as though by a rabbit in the grass or by a deer in the green space off the freeway, as though by God.

I dislike religious words. There is a mystery to creation that fixates me to passionate attention, but traditional spiritual language annoys me. I want every spiritual word to be new, minted that second. Or else I want silence. I'm waddling toward silence at the moment like a fat bear heading for her winter cave. Silence, music, beauty, clearing out space and giving things away: a good Christmas agenda.

This is the Christmas I found out I didn't have breast cancer. On mammogram day I had been unnerved by the sympathy of the technician, who seemed to be a little overheated from the office

Christmas party. Instead of yelling down the hall after she looked at my X-rays, as she did with the other girls shivering in their cubicles, she knocked, looked soulfully into my eyes, and gripped my shoulder. "It's okay to go now," she said. I suspected I was toast.

Then came messages on my answering machine, one at home, one at work: *please call the radiology lab.* Usually you get a card in the mail several weeks after the exam, letting you and the postal service know you are in good health.

I get back to "Beatrice, extension 47." She says, "Oh yes," and "I'll get that file." I know she is merely breathing and preparing her little speech. I would. She has no file, I'm sure, but a list of thirty-two phone numbers to call, all with the same disingenuous message: the radiologist would like to do a few more scans of the right, the left, nothing to worry about: two of you will be dead by this time next year, a bunch more will have a bad year, and a couple of you—your technicians had too much punch at the party. Come in Friday, no we'd rather not wait until next month. What a karma for Beatrice, extension 47.

I called Robin after talking to Bea. I said I was scared, and I heard my voice breaking up like static from the Planet Mongo. He said, "Don't be afraid. There's nothing to be afraid of." Then I felt ashamed of my fear. But I wanted to hide, maybe out in the woods next to a good old sleeping bear.

It turned out okay—it turned out to have been the kind of mammogram you get the afternoon of the office Christmas party.

Robin says, "There will always be these knocks on the door."

"Right, and I am never going to be good at them. I am going to be fearful and dependent. You are going to hear a lot of whining."

"But you don't show it. You show bravado. I am learning to hear the words under the words."

It's about time. Suffering in silence is futile if nobody knows you're suffering. It's humiliating how scared and lonely I've felt the last thirty-six hours. Hopefully it will help me to be more compassionate. Probably it won't.

I was so happy not to have cancer that I bought a velvet blouse, deep burgundy, along with a beautiful sweater from Iceland, gray and black with silver clasps down the front. This was the Christmas I threw out all my denim cotton dresses, giving up Quaker simplicity just when it's getting popular and somebody invented a magazine about it. This is the Christmas I bought a Wonderbra, perfectly wired for young rabbits to stand on. I've tried to be a good Quaker for so long and now it's "Where is my finery?"

"You see, God is watching over you," one of my religious friends told me when we chatted about the mammogram.

But then is God not watching over the two women who will be dead by this time next year, or the healthy woman I read about this week who had a double mastectomy because the pathologist made a mistake? I think God, call it God, is watching over us all right, but his love is so different from ours that I can't imagine we even belong to the same phylum. And that may be a good thing.

There will always be these knocks on the door . . .

Shortly after acquiring all this velvet and underpinning, I feel a swing in the opposite direction, a renewal of my wish to get rid of stuff. And, suddenly, everything around me looks like *stuff*. You contradict yourself so often, says Robin, the methodical scientist. In the *Sonnets to Orpheus*, Rilke writes:

Don't be afraid to suffer; return
that heaviness to earth's own weight;
heavy are the mountains, heavy the seas.

Even the small trees you planted as children
have long since become too heavy; you could not
carry them now. But the winds . . . But the spaces . . .

I long for the winds, the spaces.

Mark Doty wrote while his partner was dying of AIDS, "It's only animals now who make me believe in God." If I'd written that, I'd mean: only animals are full enough. We humans are full enough—in fact we are too full. I have so much extraneous junk that it's hard to see God clearly. Only animals are empty enough, then.

I am trying to get down to the simple animal. I am trying to get down to the moral weight of the heron who leaned her long neck on my shoulder a few weeks ago and died. To die that simply, one must practice by living that simply, with so single an eye.

I want to become the woman who disappears into the forest, raking away her footsteps with a broom of dry leaves. If I must leave, I want to leave no trace. I will be smoke in the air, resting, as the spirits of the newly dead hover in the valley, while the sun warms and disperses the particles of these dead, these waiting, these still-too-much-remembering spirits.

However, I do not ask for this path of waning and dissolution. Mostly it annoys me.

This winter I have been watching my mother progressively retreat from the world outside, refusing to leave the house. The more one's life becomes dominated by fear, the more the circle closes. My mother has confined herself first to the neighborhood, then to the house, then to the first floor, and finally to the sofa. In time, she will lose her physical mobility, the muscles will atrophy and literally cage her in her own refusal. One of Henry James' most terrifying short stories, "The Beast in the Jungle," tells of a man who retreats down the whole length of his life from the spring of a cat-like terror that haunts his imagination. At the end it comes to pass that the threat was simply and horribly this: that you can miss your whole life while hiding from it.

Robin and I spent the early hours of the New Year working our shift at the wildlife center. I had an unusual bat to nurture, a silver-haired bat with a puffy black fur-ball body that looks dusted in snow. He was not very hungry for grubs. We are also caring for a Baltimore oriole, a hermit thrush, and a Swainson's thrush that missed their planes south for some reason, along with the usual run of geese and mallards and coots. We have, inevitably, become fond of a long-term beaver with neurological damage, isolated now in the holding room because he has salmonella. He has become very doglike, sniffing at my feet as I tend the squirrel cages. He goes about slapping his tail on the cement and seems to like his warm bed of quilts.

Then, coming home, I went to sleep and had a dream that whip-stitched together the issues of my life and presented them to me in a tidy bundle. An old lover looked at me with big, brown, liquid, resentful eyes. He wanted me to go to a soccer game with him, of all unlikely things. I don't know what he was saying, exactly, but the feeling I got from the big, brown, liquid etcetera's was "You never give me what I want. You will never be enough for me." I felt a twisting guilt and also the rage I only feel (or only give in to) in dreams. The dream lover went on: "It's not that you do anything productive with your time. You just sit and stare."

I screamed at him, *"All the time I was with you I never created anything."*

The dream shifted to a tea shop, where we were attempting to continue the sort of decorous arguments we used to have in real life. However, I begin to throw dishes on the floor.

"I *must*"—I wake up yelling—"I *must* make the conditions in my life that allow me to create. It is *not negotiable.*" Smash. Smash.

In the morning, Robin and I had a disagreement about whether I would attend a holiday party, which would have been party number five in two weeks. For me, there was absolutely no question. I could not. I could not go shopping either, or talk on the phone, or do anything but sit still and knit. Robin did not complain much, but he didn't come back to my house after the party, nor call me the next morning, or pick me up for Quaker meeting on Sunday morning. In other words, those big, brown, liquid eyes were full of resentment. So what? Stephen and Ondrea Levine astutely call *resentment*, "a natural by-product of our wanting."

Of course I tore into Robin tooth and toenail. It must be so great for him to be the partner of a midlife wolverine. Yet he honored my need to sit still. I wish I were not so reclusive; am I turning into my mother? I missed, as usual, a good party. I examine my conscience for signs of *shutting things out*—but I think not; quiet time is where I *take things in*. It's such a delicate balance, each of us a tide pool from which the ocean withdraws and returns.

In the foreword to his new translation of Rainer Maria Rilke's *Letters to a Young Poet*, Stephen Mitchell says: "Whereas we find a thick, if translucent barrier between self and other, he [Rilke] was often without the thinnest differentiating barrier." Well, yes. Mitchell's metaphor speaks to my own long-time image of finding myself to be, as a party goes on, progressively *skinned*.

Perhaps Stephen Mitchell is describing the factory container of every artist, this too-permeable barrier. Women of my generation were raised with a lot of preconceptions about marriage—to site one locus of inner conflict—that made it hard for them to learn to deal with their own natures in the privacy the job requires. Despite having learned a lot about the conditions I need to thrive, I still fear for my ability to take care of myself when I'm with someone else. I give it all away. And when I can't give it away any more, I have a tantrum.

Surrendering to the needs of others is a peculiarly female way of avoiding responsibility for living out one's vocation and facing one's fear of the artistic edge.

Robin and I have made tremendous progress negotiating this issue, especially during our long vacations together, when I write and he paints. We keep silence and work in the morning, hike and tour in the midafternoons. It's a good rhythm.

What artistic men seem to need from women are cuddles and dinner and cowlike understanding. Do women cursed with poetry need something different? Perhaps not. But in addition they need recognition that they have a bridal engagement with solitude. The permission has to come first of all from themselves. *It is I, myself, who gives it all away.* Men need this tryst with solitude as well, but they have their deer stands and ice houses and seem to need no revolutionary energy, as women do, to claim those spaces.

And so I honor the contours of an introverted January, country of deep nights. This morning I lay in bed and watched, as the song goes, *the new Jerusalem come down, adorned with shining grace*: in winter, the skyscrapers of Minneapolis mirror the rising sun into my loft room. What a vision, all pink neon. The world is such a place of light, had we eyes. Then I lounged on the sofa for two hours with a pot of tea, finishing Gretel Ehrlich's *A Match to the Heart*.

Last night I took care of a flying squirrel in the mammal ward, probably a Southern flying squirrel *(Glaucomys volans)*. They are about the size of a chipmunk and chipmunklike in habit. (They survive well in captivity and, in England, are often kept as pets.) Flying squirrels are grayish white with huge black eyes, rather like the eyes of a meerkat. They do not of course fly, but glide with the help of loose folds of skin extending on each side of the body called the *patagium*, a physical adaptation that recalls every kid's dream of being able to glide off the garage roof. They are never seen by day, even in the mammal ward, where they hang out deep in a nest of boxes, burrowing like poets. They are extremely common in every Minnesota yard, but we rarely see them; they are another of those ambient ghosts who inhabit our world in a parallel frame without our knowledge.

This squirrel had some degree of damage to the cochlear-vestibular nerves, which made him careen and fall to the left when we examined him. "Look how vestibular he is," said Jim. I love to pick up jargon.

Also I had ten bats to feed, sometimes a tedious process, but I have gotten a better handle on tricking them into eating. They simply won't cooperate until they're good and warmed up. Each bat has a distinctly different personality, from gentle pickers to voracious snappers. Several were frostbitten on a wing tip or the penis, which did not improve their dispositions. Most had cases of "disturbed hibernation," brought on by the seasonal movement of householders to the attic to retrieve Christmas tree ornaments.

We finished up the evening looking at coccidia eggs suspended in a sugar solution under a microscope. The eggs belonged to an

Eastern cottontail who had, as one of the vets elegantly put it, "worms hanging out of his butt."

After being struck by lightning, Gretel Ehrlich tried to describe the contours of her psychophysical world. She compares it to wandering in the *bardo*, which in Tibetan Buddhism, is a gap between being alive and being dead. This displacement occurs, she says, "not only at the moment of death or the moment before death, but all during our lives; the bardo is the uncertainty and groundlessness we often feel." Like the Dark Night of Christian mysticism, it is a training ground for the work of detachment. It's a space of bewilderment, where we find ourselves without any logical transition, as though tripped off a cliff. In Ehrlich's case, the impetus was physiological shock, a lightning strike that disrupted the homeostasis between sympathetic and parasympathetic systems. After being hit, while she tried to make it home from the open range, the dangerous *bardo* manifested as a gray ocean. She would repeatedly pass out and waken to find her dogs pulling her away from the flood, as her blood pressure precipitately dropped.

In the year that follows, Ehrlich keeps finding images in the world that correlate with her inner state as she travels relentlessly north: "When the tides went out, all the seal-inhabited icebergs floated toward the bay, then back again with the swing of the tides. This was the inlet of devotion and transparency where illusion washed back and forth, a place that could teach me to see. Night came but it was not dark, only gray, and the face of the glacier turned bright, as if a huge slab of moon had been cut off and laid against the mountains."

Surviving lightning strike, she says, is a sentence to live. "The world falls out from under us and we fly, we float, we skim mountains, and every draught we breathe is new. Exposed and raw, we are free to be lost, to ask questions." If we don't have experiences like this, she continues, "we seize up and are paralyzed in self-righteousness, obsessed with our own perfection. If there is no death and regeneration, our virtues become empty shells. . . . A carapace had been smashed by lightning and all the events that followed—divorce, loneliness, exile, and unmasking—had exposed new skin."

Bardo is the name over the door of the prairie train station where I have been let off in the dead of winter. Another train may be coming, but when? *How long, O Lord?*—as the psalmist whined. Or has a decision been made, far down the line, to cut this station off the map? Here we stand, obedient, with our suitcases. But the train will never come again. Get used to it, traveler. What will you do now?

The Second Noble Truth of Buddhism is that "suffering is caused by attachment." This winter I have been struggling with a particularly lively set of attachments. I have seemed, over and over, on the verge of achieving some goal or another, and it's been snatched out of my hands. What a silly phrase. Nothing was in my hands at all.

This happens to me over and over, getting whacked by a dream on its way out the window. As a young married woman, I dreamed of living in the house of our friends Len and Sue MacEachron, who lived in an old farm on the edge of a wildlife preserve. In fact, I wanted to live the MacEachron *life*, which involved providing endless hospitality to all the musicians who passed through town and getting to sing the night away whenever we all wanted to. Out of the blue, one day, Len and Sue told me they were putting their house up for sale; they were moving to a simple condominium downtown. I was elated. But the very day they offered it to me was the day my husband, out of the blue, began to talk about divorce.

Quakers have a phrase about anticipating the future: *Way will open.* But Parker Palmer, the great Quaker writer, writes about how our path is more often defined by *ways that close.*

I have to stop and think about what would have happened if I'd bought the MacEachron house. Such a lovely space, so much room for animals, so close to town. But face it, the MacEachrons, God bless them, have already lived the MacEachron life. I'd have wound up with a funky old house and a marriage that, though I had been oblivious to the fact, wasn't serving either of our vectors of growth.

Desire causes pain, but I don't intend to stop having visions; they move us forward. I just need to stop digging my claws into them. It's easy to mistake our own desires for some providential plan: in fact, that's about the easiest mistake to make in spiritual discernment. But Buddhist detachment seems too passive for the seeker who is after real estate. We risk suffering when we love, when we have children, when we send them into the world after teaching them carefully about the Four Noble Truths.

I had three bats lined up on heating pads (medium) waiting for their ration of wiggling mealworms. It's no good trying to feed a bat until it's warm, because it will just twist its little Wookie face away like a cranky baby. But there comes a critical moment when the bat is both warm and hungry. It begins to bob up and down, echolocating, and its next move will be to launch itself off the heating pad and fly. Its instinct at that moment is to begin to hunt. We wildlife rehabilitators do not want our bats flying around the place. A small but significant number of bats are rabid, and we do not like them careening overhead while one person runs for a net, another has a panic attack, and all the intricate demons on their heating pads rise up and begin to echolocate in turn.

When you dance with bats, you have to be precisely on the beat. Don't get any more bats out of their aquariums than you can handle. Quickly clean the glass houses and change the diapers in the bottom of their nests. Put in fresh food and water, then run back and toss worms into the rims of sharp little teeth just getting ready to snap.

I was feeding water through a syringe into the mouth of a worm-satiated bat. Usually this means touching the plastic tip to its mouth, leaving a drop, and moving on. Suddenly this bat got hold of the syringe tip and started to suck. Some ragged memory of *Mommy Dearest!* woke in its brain. It relaxed blissfully and took 1 cc of water.

When an elephant mother sees her infant, the powerful hormone oxytocin floods her system and awakens a reflex that we can only call *love*. Humans, I'm told, feel the same powerful surge when they see a puppy, a sweetheart, or, of course, their own children. There's, literally, chemistry. Mistaken for a bat mom, I swell for a moment on the great tide of animal nature, its simple but fierce momentum to feed, care for, seek prey. For a chemically induced Zen moment, life seems of a piece, coherent.

animals
always waiting for us to wade among them: oceans of animals . . .

writes the poet Alvin Greenberg,

the same turgid oceans
we slithered out of once.

Robin and I came home late from a potluck at Quaker meeting and did a whole repertory of antierotic things: turned on TV, watched a video of *The Blackboard Jungle*, then segued into the Timberwolves' game. Robin was rubbing my neck in that hypnotic way he lulls me to sleep, curled against the spoon of his body, when suddenly we were ferociously and speedily and joyously loving each other, like teenagers in the back of the pickup without even taking our wool socks off—because—so ecstatic are these surrenders of the middle years—because we have no illusions about the body's frail capacity, because those cruel boys broke in and smashed the math teacher's precious Bix Biederbeck records, because we were caught in the great tide.

And so: on this morning, snug in our duvet, Robin is telling me about beavers in their winter lodges. Above the water, he says, they lie in semihibernation, all together. Now and then one wakes, uncouples, descends into the water, and swims off to the twig store . . . *Twig store?*—I question, imagining something like a Wal-Mart of beavers.

"Their store of twigs," he explains. "They eat twigs. In preparation, they store them."

Oh, yes. I think about the beaver I took care of recently at the wildlife center. He did not live sweetly in a flat above the water but lived more or less befuddled on the cement. We brought him red osier dogwood and he would slap his leather rudder on the cement; he had a head trauma; he was always, in his way, smiling.

The Owl Tree

OWLS EAT ALL KINDS OF STUFF they can't digest, but their systems are set up to regurgitate neatly wrapped sacks of garbage, called owl pellets, which pile up under their trees. That's how you can tell if an owl has been roosting in any given spruce: a trash heap of pellets containing fetal beaks, fur, half-feathered trinkets of predation. Little poems about the terror in the bones.

I carried a pair of latex gloves and my X-acto knife to the owl tree Robin has been casing out most of the winter, but our adventure was ambiguous in its results. We explored an interesting location in the middle of the city, a stand of evergreens and abandoned cars behind canyons of grain elevators, silent as the high desert. A woodchuck went trolling along past a wrecked house trailer. *The meek shall inherit the earth.* In our well-organized city, it's a pleasure to come upon this outpost of misrule and wilderness. Under a spruce tree lay a huge pile of saw-whet owl pellets, or so we had been told by a birder friend. We found what looked like a flatbed load of furry owl hair balls. But when, gloved and cautious, I opened one of the pellets, it yielded only seedpods. Vegetarian raptors? That's what city life will do to you. Living too close to the trendy Uptown neighborhood.

We sigh over the ornithological mystery, bag a few mysterious artifacts, and head out to the street. Lately we have been making a game of following people into restaurants and eating what they eat. In a multicultural city with lots of ethnic restaurants you can have a few edgy meals this way. Last week we followed some Somali people into a tiny room with two items on the menu, fava beans and goat. I brightly asked for the fava beans. The waiter rapped on the table impatiently, "You will have goat!" I shrugged. Later I heard two college girls whining, "But we're vegan!"

Emerging from the urban canyon, we followed a bunch of laughing Chinese students into a noodle shop. Robin has vowed to eat the weirdest thing on the menu and goes for skate and bean curd with sour melon.

The Chinese waiter grins, "It's too Chinese for you." With that provocation, Robin has to have it.

"It's not good for you," the waiter goes on. "You could have eggplant, maybe."

But Robin wants the dried skate. Did you see the movie *Babette's Feast*? Do you remember that scene where the Norwegian women were hanging salt fish to dry in the North Sea gales? I guess you can reconstitute such fish by soaking them in brackish oil: at least that was the look of what was placed in front of Robin. He tore into it manfully, and then pushed it aside with a rueful grin. As for my own food, the vegetables were bright and shiny, but I didn't feel hungry any more. I remembered that when I had gone into the restroom to wash my hands, there had been no hot water. Suddenly, I mistrusted a restaurant where there's no hot water for the benefit of those of us who've been dissecting dead things before dinner. I nibbled eggplant, and we both coveted the meal of a beautiful black woman with intricate braids sitting near us. She obviously knew how to say "fried chicken" in Mandarin.

And now *"The green fleas are all coming up,"* an elderly friend tells me, his articulation brillig with brain damage he suffered in a recent stroke. "The goldilocks are falling into the garden like suns. . . ." Which of us knows how to tell the real story of spring? What do words stand for, what relates the *word* to the *thing*? It delights me to contemplate the rain of goldilocks.

Bloodroot is three days into its show and the petals are falling already. *Eph-hemera.* In Greek it means "upon the day." Last week it snowed, today the spring comes quickly on. The garden I cleaned out ruthlessly last year looks waitful and ready to tell me something about green fleas. Last year, I wanted to cut it by half . . . this year, hmm, I see so many possibilities. I stop raking to imagine raised beds of container vegetables behind the fence . . . no, no, my goal is to *simplify. Lilies.* The possibilities come crowding in, meanwhile: *ephemera.* What we must love well and leave e'er long, whatever you think your timetable is.

When Dad went to the hospital that last time, I came up to his room. He was talking on the phone to my mother, who had refused to visit him—so excruciating was her fear of hospitals—and was threatening a series of melodramatic gestures to bring him home where he "belonged." I could hear her yelling as he drew the receiver away from his ear, pointed at it, shrugged, and rolled his eyes. My mother had come out of an unstable family situation, and he out of inflexible rectitude; the contract that underlay their marriage required him to be her rock. She saw his illness—anyone's illness, in fact—as an insult and a betrayal, no doubt because her own mother's decline had first manifested itself as a refusal to get out of bed for months at a time. Dad wanted to go home and take care of her. He had no thought for anything else. His marriage, its difficult spiritual practice, had carried him to the heart of compassion.

We went in the ambulance to the hospice, where the nun took his little plastic bag of hospital stuff, slippers, electric razor. "He won't be needing these," she said briskly. *Ephemera.*

The last time I saw my dad, he was wearing a yellow paper dress, and he looked as foolish as a dog dressed up by a little girl; worse, he didn't know how shabby he looked, or he had gotten past caring. He had been the nattiest dresser of all the dads. My mom even pressed his underwear. *The last time I saw him, he looked so frightened.* I had to call up the nuns at the Cancer Home after he died and demand to see his body. They wouldn't let me, there was some regulation. So then I called up the funeral director who had closed the casket and pleaded to know if he had still looked afraid or if he had calmed down at last. As if the undertaker would say, "Oh, he looked frightened."

Now, when my father comes to me in dreams, he is always calm. Sister Chris, my spiritual director, says the dead parent always brings a gift. Dad seems to have no idea of what to bring. He comes around and tells me the house is going to burn down when, for example, I've left the water running. When I left the iron on, he worried me about burglars. Spirits become aphasic about the emergencies of this world. It's all green fleas and goldilocks to them.

Robin scolds me, as we survey the garden, for "constantly reversing positions" about my planting scheme. It annoys his scientific mind. He doubles over laughing when I tell him that what I think at any given moment is a matter of *particles versus waves*. I am riding the wave of the body, the mind, the relationship, the garden. I want to pay attention to little internal shifts. I begin to discern a pattern but to name the pattern exerts an unseemly control over the process of what's coming into being. I say.

Robin keeps laughing.

Long Dance in the Sogn Valley

OUR TEAM WAS SCHEDULED TO GO into the woods near Kenyon, Minnesota, in the Sogn Valley at noon, precisely when the turkey hunters were required by law to quit shooting.

Had the hunters synchronized their watches?

We wore orange mesh vests, just in case.

About ten of us lined up an arm's length apart in the pouring rain and began an elaborate line dance through drifts of flowering isopyrum: the Swedes must have fiddle music for an exercise like this. Robin and I usually spend much of our weekends playing Scandinavian duets on our fiddles, which I would rather be doing, to tell the truth, than staring into the wet, green face of this cold woods. Robin has the look of a man who might be composing a piece called *"Langdans fran Sogn."*

Our task will be to count dwarf trout lilies for the Nature Conservancy. Trout lilies are about four inches high, the blossom rising on a solitary stem out of two mottled, elliptical leaves. It looks something like a violet, and, in fact, its common name is "dogtooth violet." But now think of a flower half that size, for it is the rare *dwarf* trout lily (*Erythronium propullans*) that we are looking for, also called the Minnesota Adder's Tongue. This ephemeral seems to be found only in Minnesota and Wisconsin, a ghost baby of its larger relative, a slip of thread. In early May, dwarf trout lilies are usually a full-quarter inch of flower; many specimens in this woods are in fact past prime, slipping into their almost invisible dissolve. Some have been nipped by a deer or flooded out—for this land we're walking was under the Zumbro River a week ago.

Our job is to spot each whisker of flora and mark it with a pink flag. Some old colonies are already marked with orange flags, mapped in a previous season. The number of plants in each colony—an average of six or as many as 125—is marked on its flag. We have to recount the old colonies and determine if populations are growing or declining, as well as search for new flowering outposts. We also note changes and aberrations—for example, instances of aborted flowering—that may signal something is going on in the ecosystem.

There's a baby stream to cross, running just above the anklebones. I was having more fun before I sank into that freezing current. Two hours into the task, two hours to go, it's zero at the bone, as Emily Dickinson would surely say. Then, too, all this davening among the sprouts has ground my hipbones; I'm afraid I will soon have to be airlifted out in a frozen squat. It rains harder and harder.

Nancy Sather, the biologist leading our party, knows how to keep our spirits up. She positions us newcomers in line with a mother colony, so we'll have some flamboyant success. For my part, I have come upon the body of a newborn fawn, drowned and teeming with maggots, which holds my interest. I peer into its mystery of bone and loops of innards until I almost lose my place in the human whip. Never let it cross your mind what a crazy task we are undertaking. What is the rest of America doing at this moment? Reading John Donne, watching the last episode of *Survivor?*—whoa! My fingers brush a leaf of bloodroot to the west and catch a spider's weft of trout lily thread in the middle of Sogn woods, latitude 44 degrees 39 minutes 19 seconds N, longitude 93 degrees 14 minutes 46 seconds W. In the next phase of this project, naturalists with global-positioning equipment will come in and situate these tiny lilies in the starry galaxy, accurate to a meter.

Later, Robin and I get out of our wet socks in the car and drink strong tea with our chocolate-chip pumpkin cake. Sometimes I think we spend exacting days like this just to experience the exhausted clarity of their finish, kind of like an exercise in Rinzai

Zen. In Rinzai meditation, monks race around at top speed, then halt abruptly in order to feel the grace of stillness. The tea of our present moment is delicious. In Nova Scotia, I've read, there are men who go out in trawlers to harvest the water off icebergs in order to make tea this good. Hot air blows on our feet, and Robin and I remind each other of all the places in the woods near Vasa church where we made love when the spring ephemerals were coming into bloom, how we ate those lemon-ginger cookies. We have been making this trip for fifteen years, since our dogs were young.

Robin says, pulling on his socks, "I wonder why we do this."

I am lost in the memory of lemon-ginger cookies, "Which?" I ask.

"Why we crazily save things." He doesn't mean "we" as individuals, but "we" as a collective of orange-vested hikers, or "we" as members of a subset within a species. He goes on to muse on his own question, "It reminds me of doing wildlife rehabilitation. We line up all those bats in their aquariums, feed them mealworms with tweezers, while all over the city people are hitting them with tennis rackets . . ."

I say, "My students will never do that, now that they know . . ."

"I suppose when you know, really know . . ." he responds.

We have begun one of our duets: ". . . how everything connects to everything else."

I hope that Robin will incorporate that theme into his *"Langdans fran Sogn."* But all music has that theme. The fear and flight and flooding, the doe giving birth in the rising water, they will run through our dreams and the dreams of our old dogs, who are waking up now in the backseat and wanting their share of pumpkin bread.

Robin looks into the trees, "Those orange and pink flags have plotted out the woods like galaxies."

The old religions have a phrase, "As above, so below."

A man named George Divoky—I read in the *New York Times*—spends every summer on a frozen barrier island in North Alaska charting the movements of guillemots, a husky bird in the alcid family. He lives in a tent, melts snow to drink, and eats Heinz products out of cans. His marriage broke up and he doesn't get to see his kids, who must be grown now—he has made this passage for more than twenty-five years. He keeps yellow journals of when the birds arrive, where they nest and with whom, the ratios of males to females. Most importantly, he notes the dates they return to roost and the conditions that seem to draw them, the delicate balance of freeze and thaw, the owl action in the vicinity, and so forth.

It seems that at first—for some twenty years, as naturalists keep time—he had no idea why he was giving up his chances in the world for the sake of guillemots. Until suddenly one day his life's inarticulate longings tied up with a vast current of global history—*what does anyone ask of life besides this one incandescent moment?* For George Divoky, that moment came when his data sets began to tell him a story about global warming, began to sound an alarm for the human species—as though he were meant to be there in that time and place, uncomfortable, lonely, often feeling (I imagine) half mad, obsessed and faithful, unable to explain to any woman or child why he was wasting his life this way.

The artist, Frederick Franck, now in old age, says, "When I start drawing I am scared. Drawing from life, which I do at least once a week, I have to prove I can still do it. I did a drawing yesterday on the beach. There are thirty figures in that drawing. I scribbled them down in a kind of ecstasy mixed with despair. I could never do that again. Drawing is a strange process, for even where it succeeds you never do justice to what you see. If you draw well today, you can't assume that tomorrow you can continue on that, you have to start all over again, from scratch. No guarantee of success, unless you are a hack who uses a routine."

"Are you able to live according to your own truth?" the interviewer asked.

"No," Franck replied. "But I am always aware of it when I fall short. I am awake to it—to the existence of my truth. Our own truth is our true selves. It can't be discovered, but perhaps it can be intuited. You can get in tune with its potentiality. And then you are out of tune again."

The old man's words seem to me so important. As the waters rush in to annihilate our civilization, I want to scratch them in the sand. His way is not a better way, or a worse way, than the way of people working late in night in skyscrapers, trading on the Tokyo stock exchange or scrubbing the floors of people who trade. But it's a hidden, mysterious way—who notices it?—that artists live, and kindergarten teachers, naturalists, and nuns in contemplative convents.

In a few months I will have made a new friend, the young painter Karl Pilato. One day we will be walking along the Salmon River estuary, near the Oregon coast, and he will draw in a breath. Karl is a quiet person, and this breath means, "Kingfisher!" Big tears will pop out of my eyes. Kingfishers are gone from my native lakeshore in Minnesota, though I used to see them every day. *"As kingfishers catch fire, dragonflies draw flame."* Gerard Manley Hopkins's poem comes to me, with its ferocious ornithological and artistic assertion: *What I do is me! For that I came.*

I think of grizzled, old ornithologists who would fall on their knees in their baggy shorts if they heard the tap of an ivory-billed woodpecker deep in the woods, that distinctive double rap.

It would be like finding the blue scrap of a letter floating over a burnt house.

For that I came.

Letting In and Letting Out

JUNE HAS PLOWED INTO TOWN, and I've been working three or four hours a day in the garden. Last year, when I resolved to cut everything back by three-quarters, a friend came and reamed out the Korean lilac, the dwarf euonymus, and the red osier dogwood—promising to relocate them on his own property—as well as all the junk shrubs and blackberry vines on the bank outside the fence.

This year I hired some women from a gardening firm to grub out more, but they rebelled and said that they were in the business of making gardens, not wrecking them. Instead we all got to work rearranging things so the management would be easier. Removing the bushes last year, which seemed so sad at the time, has opened my eye to the yard's beautiful terracing. Now, from the stone bench in my pergola, I can enjoy its variations in rock texture and foliage.

Pruning is the last thing we learn, and we only learn it when we have to.

I'm studying to pass the wildlife rehabilitation exam: *If your rabbit weighs 6 ounces and needs 125 k-cals p.d. calculated in grams, what is the rabbit's astrological sign?* The DNR has made the exam difficult to pass, because strange characters try to get into wildlife rehabilitation—people who suffer from an odd variety of obsessive-compulsive disorder that leads them to hoard animals, and people who want to operate illegal game parks, for example. Who knows whether such individuals will be put off by grade-school math? I certainly am.

There is a kind of superficial peace in my life, covering up an inner upheaval. I've learned to welcome such shifts in my psychic weather, though the attendant nightmares and anxiety are no fun. I welcome them because the alternative would be feeling stuck, failing the example of my garden: to grow. Such feelings of instability often come with summer, after the school term ends. Teachers traditionally get sick on the vacations; perhaps our immune systems relax and welcome invaders. Or it may be that the grinding pace of the last weeks of school knocks us out. We anticipate the "free time" of summer—this anticipation is one of the calming narratives that get us through our twelve-hour work days—but when June arrives, we discover, flummoxed every year, that our days are not going to be all that liberated. Pleasant as it is to be in the garden, I hear some murmuring under the leaves of *hurry, hurry*, before those blackberry vines take over, *hurry, hurry*, review your Greek, there is not really that much time before school starts again. We need to clean out our basements, shore up the fragments of our relationships, and take care of our aging parents.

That latter agenda item is claiming a lot of my attention this summer. A few nights ago, I woke up in a panic wondering *who is cutting her toenails?* My mother won't leave her house now, even to go to the podiatrist or the eye doctor. I'm trying to get her household help. In the last twenty-four hours I've interviewed (1) an expensive team of women from Uptown ("We're expensive because we don't have husbands and we do feng shui and read tarot . . ."), (2) two gentle artists who are asthmatic and can't deal with a smoker, (3) several snappish women without references, and (4) one born-again Christian eccentric. She may be the best bet. At least her references vouch for the fact that she won't steal.

Zen practice and Quaker stillness have given me a pretty good approach to the routine stresses of life; what contemplative practice allows, however, is a space for the underlying issues to rise. We make ourselves into vessels: the vessels fill with suffering, not only our own. This paradox is inevitably discovered on the spiritual path. Perhaps we begin to meditate to escape our problems, but we find that instead we have created a threshold over which the traumas of the inner world can emerge into the light. Worse yet (or better yet) we grow excruciatingly sensitive to the suffering of others. "Damn," says one of my young friends, "I'm discovering that the prayer for a compassionate heart is always answered."

"Firm as a rock my soul shall stand!" we boldly sing this Christian text in Prairie Harmony. Similarly, Thich Nhat Hanh taught us the *gatha*: "Breathing in, I feel myself become a mountain."

Stability of practice helps us to welcome (just a little) the emergence of the world's deep pain, and our own. My practice is none too stable, but I know that every time I survive my inner tumult, I move a little closer to what I think of as *integrity*. *Enlightenment* is way over my critical horizon. Father Thomas Keating, O.C.D., a priest-psychiatrist who promulgates "centering prayer," a form analogous to Buddhist meditation, speaks of the unconscious healing that goes on in this prayer of the heart. It is, he says, rather like psychoanalysis. Still, it sometimes feels like sandpaper. "As the deep peace flowing from contemplative prayer releases our emotional blocks, insights into the dark side of our personality emerge and multiply. We blissfully imagine that we do good to our families, friends and business or professional associates for the best of reasons, but when this dynamism begins to operate in us, our so-called good intentions look like a pile of dirty dishrags. . . . love by its very nature accuses us of our innate selfishness."

There is some quality of pain associated with caring for my mother that I can't get a handle on—so what? The handle would be the wrong handle, anyway. There is some residual emotion associated with the long-ago end of my marriage that still undermines other relationships of trust. Again, so what? My mind wants to work on these issues in its silly-mind way. That is the nature of mind. But under it all, in the storehouse of the unconscious, other work is being done, work we cannot imagine. Its results surface in dreams and poems and artistic forms, telling us the deeper story.

"Did your poem surprise you?" I always ask my writing students. This is my clue that they are working out of a more profound space, learning new things. They look at me in puzzlement, unwilling to be apprentices, like the student archeologists who spend long, hot summers learning how to dig and dust off old pots. Gently.

My dreams du jour are full of panic, but when I waken the fear often reveals its rational base. Last night, I heard a clatter on the roof. Raccoons, I surmised, and, indeed, the canny eyes shone back at me when I raised my skylight in the light of the full moon. Could they get in? I closed the skylight. I slept again and dreamt the raccoons were in the room. I wakened and closed the side window, as if they could shinny down a rope to invade my loft. Again I dreamt vividly of their filthy little feet all over me. The sensation of pressure on my face was intensely real. The power of the unreal— dream—to exert real physical effects on the body is so bizarre: *no, they are in here, they are pawing on my face with their garbage-sorting feet, their* Baylisacaris. I snapped awake to the familiar bedroom and rain gently began. The raccoons, I hoped, were routed back down the storm drain where they inhabit a vast Unreal City.

But this morning, guess what? Racoons *had* been on the porch; they had eaten through a board on the threshold and scratched so intently on the heavy pet-food containers stored there that they had cut sharp channels in the plastic and bloodied their paws, *getting in.*

Will I have to welcome them? Even them?

Pema Chodron writes

> Ego is like a room of your own, a room with a view, with the temperature and the smells and the music that you like. You want it your own way. You'd like to have a little peace; you'd like to have a little happiness . . .
>
> But the more you think that way, the more you try to get life to come out so that it will always suit you, the more your fear of other people and what's outside your room grows. Rather than

becoming more relaxed, you start pulling down the shades and locking the door. When you go out you find the experience more and more unsettling and disagreeable. You become touchier, more fearful, and more irritable then ever. The more you just try to get it your way, the less you feel at home.

To be fearless isn't really to overcome fear, it's to come to know its nature.

I meditate on this passage, trying to put my fears into separate rooms, so that I can have tea with each demon in private. Pema Chodron seems to be describing a kind of spiritual agoraphobia, from which I used to suffer on the physical plane. Once I cured myself of that, my problems just went to another plane. Do we finally run out of planes?

I feel that I'm shutting a lot of doors these days. Of course, you have to shut some doors to know which ones to leave open forever. The discernment is what's agonizing.

So, which doors to close, which doors to open, and how to sit with the fear that attends choice?

Choose, my financial adviser urged, *to put your money into the stock market!* I'm disinclined, however, to fund war machines and cigarette companies. Finally, I slotted my retirement into a Social Choice account, and then listened to the market news, which was all about downturns. I woke up frightened. *The raccoons are breaking into my house!* I spoke more gently to myself: You've put your money where your values are, now just let that part of your life rest. Stay organized, clean out your stuff. Be patient with a time in your life when all you can do is sweep clean and clarify, see who you are and what you need.

I'm sweeping out, getting down to the bones, so that I can see clearly.

Next, I go to Mom's and try to sweep out her house: overreaching. She fired the cleaning lady I hired for her, the fundamentalist Christian. I had thought they would make a good match, both being feisty and contentious. But they had a fight, in the midst of which Imelda said to Mother, "You need to have some respect for yourself and for me, not go around in your old clothes. You have to wash your face and put your teeth in when somebody comes to the door." Unbeknownst to us, Mom's mean little dog has chewed up her dental plate and she is too proud to tell us. We will find this out from her dentist months after her death.

Mom wanted to know how "a mere cleaning woman" dared to speak to her like that. "That woman said to me, 'What if Jesus came to the door?' I told her Jesus hasn't been seen around here lately."

Then Imelda called to bawl me out for ignoring Mom's "disrespect for herself and others." I've glanced away from it so long that I've failed to think about what it might look like from outside. What it might in fact be.

"Is your mother senile?" Imelda wanted to know.

"No, she's always been that way." Grandma Rose used to take after her for her housekeeping. Because Mom had no vanity, she paid little attention to what she wore; Dad always bought her clothes and made her groom. Since he died and her vision began to fail, she feels free to do as she pleases. That is, after all, one of the few pleasures of aged widowhood. She smokes and piles up ashtrays on every available surface, ignores her dog's hygiene. My sister and I sneak in and cart away her washing, bring her food and the cigarettes she demands. Some karmic knots are so tightly woven you can't get free in a single lifetime.

My cousin, the son of my mother's eccentric brother, whom I haven't seen for forty years, is visiting from California. He has been a police officer all his life. He told us several tales of corpses over breakfast, and we helped him to fill in the details of our scampy family. I suppose it is only writers and police officers who would smile at our genealogy of mayhem, rather than descent from some refined broodstock. My mother's bedtime stories began, "When we were rich . . . ," or "When we owned . . ." And there is a subtext of either "grandfather/mother dropped out of sight, leaving the riches behind" or "we were cheated out of our inheritance." My cousin, however, is a disciplined realist, which no doubt he learned in the cops. He told me that he had traced the family's history back to the nineteenth century, where they had starring roles on the police blotters of several western states.

Difficult as our parents, brother and sister, can be, they have done better than their forebears. They have not been institutionalized or committed a felony that we know about.

In fact, brother and sister will die, quite suddenly, within four days of each other. My cousin will call me to confide in his matter-of-fact police officer's voice, "My dad had the gift of seeing the dead, and no doubt she came for him. He couldn't stand anybody much, but he liked her the best."

"Be kind," wrote Philo of Alexandria, "for everyone you meet is fighting a great battle." I have been subjecting my mother to a lot of analysis this summer—as opposed to kindness—and it's no surprise she's rebelled, though I wish she wouldn't lash out at us when we try to help. I wish I could be more feeling-full, instead of ticking away appointments and solutions and cleaning women, "filling the house with strangers," as she puts it, "invading my space."

Hiking down by the river, the smell of the world washes over me, a mossy green drift. Rain I didn't hear in the night has turned up the spirit of leaf life, combed by the long toes of small beings who feel all the vibrations of this world.

I watch a huge turtle move out of her squat in the humus. The world has to stop for her slow rush to lay eggs. Now she delves in compost, digging down to the mud. A white rubbery egg, the size of a pullet's, falls and she scratches it into the ground.

Early this morning I wakened, agitated but kind of ecstatic, from a dream about my old friend and teacher, Joe Guerinot. It's such a blessing when the dead visit in dreams, looking hearty and young again. He told me he was living mostly in Milwaukee, trying to help a young woman get out of a relationship with a terrorist. I asked him about God. Joe said he hadn't seen him yet. He said the animals get to go first, especially the great hordes of the extinct and endangered. Then the dream opened into a vast blue space of animals swimming through the sea toward what looked like a great star sapphire. I woke up damp with tears, so happy.

Blue Grass

AM I MEANT TO LIVE ALONE, or with others of my kind? This is developing into the great question of my middle life. Robin and I are spending a few days at my mom's cabin, trying to see how amicably we can live together, which, in the many years we have been a couple, we have not learned to do at my house or at his house. We seek out neutral ground.

Robin spent the morning transcribing bluegrass fiddle music from a tape. There would be a few bars of whiny music, then Robin humming A *da deedle deedle deedle deedle deedle deedle dee*, then the *scree* of the tape machine reversing, then that virtuoso from Kentucky leaning into the downbeats—*a da deedle deedle*, and so on, then a few notes on the fiddle, *scree*.

I can't read or think or find my own rhythm. I take my pile of textbooks out to the car and sit. This is Minnesota, where we have delicately honed the tools of passive aggression.

Robin comes out to look for me. "Give me an hour of quiet," I say, making him the small, doling god of my time. How many hours at a certain age do I have to give?

My grandmother had a good way with summer's children. We'd get up early, eat soft eggs scrambled in the cast-iron pan. Then I did my round of cottage jobs, which, in retrospect, I realize did not represent jobs she needed done. They were the things I needed to learn how to do. Or, was it just that I needed to be able to do something, and finally, everything, in an orderly way? Sweep the front stoop, sweep the outhouse, and dust the lion feet under the table. But after the jobs were done, always by 10 a.m., the whole day would lie fallow and free. That's what I want! My time to lie fallow and free.

In those days we would do, eventually, wonderful things; perhaps take a trip to town in the pale green '48 Ford with its chrome-hooded eyes. But that would happen only once a week because we couldn't afford the gas. Or we would walk to the next farm for eggs and spend an hour playing with the new kittens. Most often we would go swimming, with Grandma sitting on her lawn chair drawn knee-deep into the water, her *Reader's Digest Condensed Book* on her lap. She would have on her twenty-year-old skirted swimsuit in which she would occasionally take a few strokes of the crawl, her expression as it rose and fell above the water, disapproving. There was nothing whatever to hear but the wren-calling-phoebe-impatient-cicada summer.

When did I lose control of my hours, give them up to lovers and committee chairs? Once a woman who wanted something of me snapped, "You're only reading!" I had a hard time explaining to her that this was my job—I was reviewing books in those days for the *Baltimore Sun* with a tight set of deadlines. "You're only staring into space," she said.

What I do is me. For that I came.

Perhaps I'm just whining for the aimless days of childhood. I don't want *play*, exactly, but I want aimlessness. It's aiming, aiming, and aiming again that makes me tired. As children we are rarely free of the leaning power of others, their gentle swishing chorus of *you are too small you are not enough you are not enough*. At my grandparents' house, this chorus died out. They didn't mind my staring into space. They had nothing better to do themselves, and I was at peace.

And now what do *they* want, the Saturday morning boys in their electric blue speedboats, cutting through the space of water where yesterday I saw two mergansers and a blue heron wading? What does he want, the pilot dipping his white wings over the lake where yesterday I saw eagles? A man and his child drift past in a pontoon boat, casting their red plugs over and over. On the back stoop—exiled now—another man plays the same bluegrass riff over and over on his fiddle.

The electrician from up the hill, who finally got our lights on, told me about how his neighbor wants to get a 180-horsepower Johnson motor. I know what I want: to step delicately over the rotting boards of the dock and sit in a lawn chair and hear nothing whatsoever. I do not think my wish for quiet is holier than the men's wish for sound and speed and the dip of wings, but I resent that I and my kind have to live in the chinks between their huge desires. By "my kind" I mean herons, mergansers, the little gray mammals who glide from tree to tree by night, the eagles commanding their empty space, space that—I tell the pilot—*only looks empty to you.* You, circling in your white boat with the stars and stripes astern, even you on the stoop whom I love—how dare you take what you don't value from those you don't notice?

I must acknowledge my own co-optation in this theft. I want light to read by at night and an indoor toilet, though, frankly, you might be surprised to know what I'd trade to possess again my stolen silence. "Power's on," says Merlin. Why do they call it *power?* (Why did they call him *Merlin?*)

Sister Anselm used to call me a "false mystic." But I've come to understand that the word "mystic" is simply a judgment placed by speedy people on the reality of the slow moving. The fast moving do not understand my reality any more than I understand the vision of the snapping turtle I watched last week as she made her way to high ground, clawed away with her sturdy nails the clay cover, and loosed her rubbery eggs. Two eyes peering over the parroty beak see places I visit only in dreams.

We go home and I settle into solitude again. It's turned hot. A little while ago, I leaned out the kitchen window to watch a juvenile squirrel, flayed out on my fence, uttering his perfectly timed *crack-crack-craack*, his fragile rib cage heaving in and out; I thought he was dying, but he was just stressed out by bearing the heat and humidity in his hairy coat. The animals are all going crazy in the weather. At sunrise, I watered the garden and filled dishes for the chipmunks and squirrels.

Before 7 a.m., the smell of baking chocolate cake drifted through the house. I've cleaned up the garden, located my sprinklers, organized my bills, written a note at the bottom of the cake recipe, "Try sixty to sixty-five minutes at 375 degrees." A load of wash bumps in the unbalanced spin cycle of the Maytag, harvest gold, older than the children I miss so much at the moment. To whom am I writing these notes in the cookbook? Why am I lonely today, among all other days, touched by the dark wing, when usually I rejoice in solitude and guard it against all comers? I'm out of balance, like my washing machine.

What are the components of this loneliness? Even dogs must feel it, because here comes Shep to lie at my feet. And when I rise to go and check the cake, she will pull herself up on her arthritic legs and follow me to some other space. Loneliness, then, is the particular face of solitude, unwelcome to any pack animal. The houses around me, other dens, are awakening to their summer business. I hear the whip of someone's sprinkler and the whine of humankind's devices for trimming and tearing and cutting through.

When my adult children are far away, we do keep up of course, but the daily knowledge is lost. They will not know how the dog grew old, or how the roses bent their canes this spring, or that the lilies were sparse in July. What, in turn, do I not know about my children's world? I grieve for this loss of daily connection.

And my loneliness has to do with not knowing what I am doing in this world, as if I have come here to gain so little ground and to feel my tether slip from God. I have a clear sense of what I should be doing, but the way does not open. I should be looking for a farm, I think, and going forward with my plan to establish a refuge for all beings, or as many as I can stand. Maybe not. Perhaps I should be sitting here.

I am yelling again at God, call it God, for a revelation and seeing instead the oriole tumble into the mulberry tree and the cardinal swell in the clematis climbing the rose. Green hearts of the garden long for things I also long for. A northern flicker spreads out her prom skirts and digs in the cracks of the stone path. Something is going on, I know, just out of my sight. This morning on the radio, I heard that a threatened leaf knows how to call up a scent that will draw a wasp to attack its preying caterpillar.

And I tell God I don't know what to do in this life.

A crow with a long tear in the wing goes over: how can he fly at all? He flies well, in fact, with a strong, flogged spirit.

This morning when I bent over to deadhead a rosebush, I heard a rush of wings and felt familiar claws brush my skin as they bit into the clothing of my back. It was a blue jay, aggressive by nature and no doubt addled by the heat.

I get out of bed early these days and try to answer the questions that rise in the deep sleep just before dawn, questions that fade as the light gains, that come to me at night like swimmers who greet the ship, trailing garlands of flowers and smiling with teeth whiter than human teeth. They take my pale hands in their brown hands and help me to dive into an element otherwise alien. Under this cool ocean, it is the things of earth I can't remember. If I think about my old black dog, she seems a familiar monster; the country where birds dip their beaks in spring water and feed on sweet fruit seems torn from a myth.

I have holes in my memory, like the holes my mother has in her vision, rubbed away (her doctors say) by years of smoking in small enclosed spaces, or perhaps by Texas dust storms, polluted air, or hereditary weakness in the organs of sight. My mother will turn her head and look where a garden used to be and see what? Something like a peeling green wall? A gauzy length of cloth? The spaces between molecules? I can't imagine the look of what's not seen. Bet on heredity. I will find out. The fabric of the world outside will tear, as already the world within has begun to do.

This is one of the holes in my memory: I can't recall how I got home one tumultuous day in 1982; it's a little mystery circling within the larger mystery of all that was going on between me and my husband at the time. But it's not because decades have passed that I can't remember. That very evening I couldn't remember just how I got home.

It began simply enough when I jumped out my husband's moving car. I have to tell you—if you haven't gone through a divorce or horrendous breakup—that most women jump out of cars now and then. Not that I recommend it. It's a wonder the roads aren't littered with us, as with dried-up squirrel carcasses. The day after I jumped out of the car, I tore around looking for help, therapy, girlfriends. It seemed to me that things were getting crazy, and maybe I should be put in restraints or something. But my friends—even my physician—just said, "Oh, I did that once." My doctor, in her gray-blue, practical tweed coat: "Oh, I did that once. At least it stops the argument."

So that's how I formulated my theory. Girls, raise your hands: how many of you have jumped out of cars?

Although I can't remember how I got home, I can tell you what I was wearing when I jumped out of the car, as though I had it on video. Shades of opal: a gray gabardine suit, pearlescent earrings, a pink silk blouse. Pale nylons and black patent-leather, sling-back pumps. My hair was shoulder-length, then, and I had gotten a perm, strategically straightened every day with hot curlers so it looked natural. A soft lipstick called Cranberry Veil. When we were preadolescent, my girlfriend, Carmen, and I used to play with our mothers' lipsticks, enjoying their fanciful names more than their greasy reality: Candy Apple, Cherries-in-the-Snow. The names were little haikus that defined how desirable we would be some day, to a man with an eye for cold fruit.

I remember what I wore because that whole year I had been looking in the mirror compulsively, searching for the mystery of why I had become unlovable. And I had bought new clothes, clothes for a different person, clothes for a delicate and fragile doll whom I loved very much and looked at constantly in the mirrors and in the eye of my mind. I could run a movie for you, so keen is my recollection, of a night I went to the chamber orchestra alone, row three, center. I knew that everyone in the auditorium was looking at me, groomed and mysterious and dressed up to the gills. If I could have gotten more love, I would have stood up on the stage and taken a bow.

Back then, mid-divorce, I would have split my skin for affection, like the Little Mermaid. See, "dressed to the gills," I wrote, and it was literally true. And gasping, not able to breathe the human air of O'Shaughnessy Auditorium, running out between the first and second movements of the Mozart concerto, *excuse me, excuse me, thank you.*

The night of the concert, I had my own car. Several weeks later, when I bailed out on the street, my husband and I were coming home from a wedding. We started to argue, not surprisingly, about some particulars of our own marriage, and the next thing I knew I had jumped out the car door. I found myself in an inner-city neighborhood of boarded-up crack houses. Not the place where a lady in sling-back pumps can knock on a stranger's door and say, "Excuse me, I've just jumped out of my husband's car, and I wonder if I might use your phone?" It was beginning to sleet a little, and that's all I have of this memory, which had begun in a shaft of light from a church window. The opening scene was bright enough: wedding-cake figures lit by a clerestory window, far away as though in the wrong end of a telescope. All those pearly grays shot with light, of rock wall, of bridal veil, of my gabardine suit, of winter street, sleet. How did I ever get home?

And *where am I?* Why am I pondering this *today?* Sometimes I waken with a childish concern on my lips, the questions of a little girl spirited away in the night who wakes in a strange bed. Perhaps

I have dreamed again that I am still married although it has been over twenty years since I jumped from that car. And what is it, exactly, that I think I'm doing in my life?

Spirituality was introduced to me on an ideal plane, and in the years after I left the novitiate I tried to be good. Very good. Perfect. When women—especially—learn to be sacrificial lambs, it serves the establishment, both religious and secular, very well. In graduate school, I tried to write perfect papers, and, as a young teacher, I tried to get perfect course evaluations. When I married, I pored over trendy manuals that advised wives to be attired in Saran Wrap when their husbands came home from work. When we had babies, I tried for high scores at natural childbirth and breast-feeding.

Why would anybody divorce a perfect person? A Quaker elder once spoke darkly about religious people "trying to be better than they are." I didn't get it. As a young person, I was engaged in the willfulness model of spiritual progress—which most education encourages, of course. I thought if I tried very hard I could change myself into something more presentable. Will and self-discipline can be our worst enemies in the spiritual life. If we are very disciplined, we can truly deform ourselves in trying to create an ideal image. Rebecca Parker writes: "Sometimes we live for a long time with a certain belief, like the belief that it is best never to speak about pain and abuse in our lives. We hold fast to our belief and live by it. But then something challenges this belief. We see it may not be the best way to live. We defend our old belief, fearing that if we let go of it our life will fall apart. But then we find we can't hold on. Life has asked us to let go. So we let go. We relinquish the way we have held our life together, the ideas that have guided us. It feels like falling, or dying."

If we can speak of a spirituality of divorce—and we had better begin to try—it must start with this sense of radical displacement. I talk to many women, and a few men, who feel the pain of a broken marriage as a kind of dissolution of personality. They think they will never be happy again. They will never be happy in the way they were, but this is the important point: *they will not be the person they were.* Divorce is a radical makeover. Rebecca Parker is not talking about divorce, but about the larger spiritual patterns of life, when she says, "We discover that by letting go we have opened ourselves to something better. Grace comes to us, and we discover a life that is richer, freer, more joyful."

Many of the people I work with in spiritual guidance are ministers and therapists: people who are supposed to have their lives together, people who are supposed to be models of "wholeness," "integrity." For those of us with high standards, breaking a relationship can be particularly shaming; most of us have internalized the Calvinist notion that runs so deeply in American culture: if you do the right thing, you will be rewarded. We in ministry or the helping professions may be able to give up the perks of consumer culture, but we expect to be granted a happy family life. Divorce lets us know how screwed up we really are: how deeply damaged by our upbringing, our choices, and our malevolent, septic culture. *Dispossession* is a more radical course than Calvinism. But it is a spiritual path, a way; in the end you can get somewhere. We have to live the truth of our condition before we can hope to change our own lives or the course of our planetary folly. Divorce can be a deeply holy process: it replicates the most ancient patterns of death and rebirth that define our life in this world.

It lets you start over from the green ground.

The moon is full, and because of wildfires in the west, it rises in a red veil. My relationship with Robin has progressed into full catastrophe. But tonight, or rather early this morning, I woke in my loft bedroom and looked at the red moon through the skylight. "I will call Robin," I thought. "He would like to see this."

Well, if I want to look at the moon with him, I must care about him. Part of the summer's leaden feeling has come from our loss of communion. Robin is struggling with the koan of his mother's illness and decline, far away in Princeton, New Jersey. He seems to be cocooning himself against his history: Cynthia Fox, his mother, was a challenging woman. He seems to be shutting me out as well. Excuse me, *I am not your mother.* But, inescapably, I am.

Why doesn't he go to her? This is my koan. No, it is *his.* Not knowing which koans have your name on them is one of the mistakes that subvert our peace.

Many of my men friends are struggling, in midlife, with becoming more sensitive to caregiving. Many of my women friends are negotiating the midlife role of *wolverine slashing mate.* Our oxytocin has leveled off.

Much later, after my own mother's death, Robin and I will finally verbalize our struggle with these riddles and karmic knots. "Why didn't you go to her?" I will at last demand. Now, while his mother is dying, I know this question is too tender to ask, perhaps for both of us. I am pulled in two generational directions. I have chosen to stay near my own feeble parent, yet I withhold my personality, my story, from her. I am merely dutiful. And full of suppressed rage.

When I finally ask the dangerous question, Robin, with his relentless honesty, will reply, "Because I *couldn't* go to her. Because there is a place in me that's dark and cold, and I don't deal with it very well."

I have that place, too. It takes Robin's blunt honesty, as ever, to point us to the truth of both our lives.

My Grandma Rose was often baffled by the stories on TV in its early, serious days. The dramas on *Playhouse 90* and *The Twilight Zone* did not always come out as they did in her beloved *Reader's Digest Condensed Books.* What did those books condense? Anything troubling or out of synch with the cultural script of the fifties, which preached that virtue will be rewarded, hard work will amass riches, people will forgive each other in the end, suffering will make us grow. But in the early days of TV—nothing like the pap we get now—serious playwrights used to present the occasional open-ended, postmodernist story with a dark conclusion or some sort of churning at the end to leave my grandmother querulous: "What are we supposed to make of that?" She wanted all the strings tied up and a happy restoration of order at the end, or at least piety. Angels should come down from the sky and carry off Little Nell.

But neither Robin nor I will manage a deathbed resolution with our difficult mothers. Real life is different from fiction, and mine is not predicated on the white male quest myth. We will both have treated our mothers carefully and justly, but without the open channel of affection that I cherish in my relations with my own children. Our failure will damage us. But if we are brave and honest, will it not lead to deeper understanding and reconciliation?

I lift up my arms like Little Nell.

Great Lake

HONEYBEES FEEDING ON THE GOLDENROD are active and agitated as if they had a clock to punch, longing to sate what one of their poets might call *thoughts too deep for tears*. There seem to be large honeybees and young apprentices. The older ones do more crawling than sipping, epicures of the deepest throats. The young ones pull at every yellow trumpet.

We are in a cabin on Lake Superior for our annual holiday. The relentless pounding of the lake puts me into a semistupor, broken by full stupor. I want to sleep, and then again I want to read the books I've brought, or do schoolwork. This is a conflict that stupor ought to win.

Because of a broken water heater in the cabin we usually rent, we've been placed, at least until today, in a larger house with a second story overlooking the mighty wave action. With storms in progress as they are, it's like being in the echo chamber of the gods. I find it hypnotizing, healing, and stirring, though I can also imagine that it could make a person crazy. Robin can't sleep. Myself, I can barely pull out of the sea caves of night to drag myself down to the kitchen for a cup of tea. Then I go back up under the eiderdown, deliciously safe and warm on the edge of chaos.

Yesterday I nearly drowned. I went down to swim in the freezing surf and quickly got disoriented. Huge waves began to break over my head, and I started to get water in my lungs. I began to dog-paddle furiously and felt my energy drop into the danger zone. To Robin, on shore, I humbly called "help" but he couldn't hear me. Then—thank God I'm an English teacher—I remembered what Joseph

Conrad recommended in *Lord Jim*: "to the destructive element submit yourself." I wonder how many people have saved their lives by reading Joseph Conrad? Within seconds I got my legs under me and was able to fling myself toward shore, a depleted creature. Then I went right back in the freezing water, which I love.

Far away in Princeton, Robin's mother is enduring her long protracted death, and I am courting danger in the deepest lake I can get to. Gulls walk disconsolately on the beach, their bumper stickers read, "I'd rather be flying."

Robin continues to distance himself, but that is not what is making me sad. I'm upset because the center of *nothing* holds. I hold onto marriages, family property, old phone numbers, less out of faithfulness than through a kind of preserving and caretaking and burrowing instinct common to woodland mammals: what will people come home to? I have not noticed sufficiently that no one wants to come home, really, anymore.

Where does my feeling of isolation come from?

Bill Moyers had a special on PBS about death. The subtext I saw was the abandonment of women by men. In contrast, men were being taken care of by their hovering wives (four stories), mothers by their daughters (one), a sister by sisters (one)—even a renter by her landlady.

I have decided to lose track of dates this week, one of them being my birthday, days like stones found on the beach, distinct but anonymous and lost. Distinct only if looked at. Why single out any day for special notice, old-time Quakers would ask. But I know when Sunday rolls around because it tells us our vacation is almost over.

This is what Robin's Quaker ancestors would have simply called "First Day." We took our First Day business to a little evangelical protestant church near the center of a nearby town. Not much was going on; one woman talked about real things. She told about nursing a sick calf through the night and how the vigil tired her out so much she missed her Sunday school responsibilities. When I go to church I like to come away with something concrete, like the weight and coloring of a calf, its sire and dam, and a circle of barn light in my mind's eye. The pastor, by contrast, seemed to have a kind of pastor-film over his body, which the day—Sunday of a particular month and year and weather—could not penetrate. His mind was in the past, dressed in a white toga, or, alternately, in the famous future where death shall have no dominion, and Robin and I will have to deal with each other's mothers for all eternity, though they will presumably be better behaved.

I *hope* we go on forever, slipped back through the interstices of this world, caddis flies into the air. I like it here. *Love calls us to the things of this world.* I would like to be a bright wing dropping at the edge of someone's peripheral vision.

Shades of basalt, chalky green and gold lichens, ledges still flashed with Queen Anne's lace and campanula, a granite altar waiting above the surf for the descent of some minor deity. I suppose people make art because they are surprised to find themselves alive in this world of artfulness, feel drawn into participation. Left to itself, the natural world composes and recomposes the beautiful. I could sit for eons and watch the erosion and rebirth of Hollow Rock, with the surf whipped, breaking, upon it. So much to notice of color and design, but I am unable to inscribe the revelation, that white flash when it comes.

Far away at the end or the beginning of the inland ocean, the seals under the boreal ice keep smiling. We are born, like them, for the deep cold swim and pearly twilight, the crescent moon lighting. I read, as evening comes in, the words of one Richard Hibberthorne, an eighteenth-century Quaker minister: "Do not seek to hold me, for it is too strait for me; and out of this straitness I must go, for I am wound into largeness."

Opal light wanes into indigo, setting off the moon. I mourn for everything that changes: gray on the dog's muzzle, love in its seasons, babies outgrowing their newborn clothing. I grieve for my grandmothers' recipes, children who do not stay, colors, and finally fabric and lastly thread. I grieve for wallpaper pulling back from the damp kitchen corner, becoming, anyhow, outdated, and for the habit of gathering there I grieve. Grieve room to room for the carpet torn by the cat, and for the cat, and thus on and on, wind pulling grief through the chimney of every house in the world . . .

Abandoning Control

LUCE IRIGARAY WROTE, "If anything divine is still to come our way it will be won by abandoning all control . . . it is through risk, only risk, leading no one knows where."

Hollow Rock Creek runs high this morning with the detritus of inland forest. There was fierce rain and thunder in the night, and today waves crash and tunnel on the beach, as though the bowl of the world had tipped. I can't stop roaming up and down the shore on some excuse or another and swimming a little and even just sitting in the 50-degree water when it's too wild for me to swim. In this surf, the big boulders roll around and come crashing through the waves; even I wouldn't want to paddle in that.

What does Irigaray mean by "abandoning all control . . ."? I am thinking about Margaret Atwood, the Canadian writer, whose novels and poems often deal with women going feral in the wilderness. Like me, Atwood was raised in casual contact with the northern wilderness, a place where one might entertain those kinds of fantasies yet know that, if one were to surrender to this territory, a lot of control would be necessary. Every move would have to be orchestrated just to ensure survival. No getting wet feet or losing the matches. (Maybe Virginia Woolf was only rock hunting?) Perhaps Irigaray means abandoning habitual ways of thinking, patterns of behavior? Narratives of culture become so habitual that one doesn't even know one is imposing them as a standard.

For example, the marriage narrative. Robin and I vacation in the country of marriage, or perhaps retreat into it as a quasi-religious exercise that we undertake in the same spirit as the desert abbas walling themselves up in celibacy. Relationship—the surrender of precious solitude—is a primary challenge to the habits and patterns that ego loves so well. It is salutary to live with another person, who lives differently. Last night I told Robin he was grumpy and hard to live with, which he took with good grace and no diminution of grumpiness. ("I don't even *see it*.") As I don't see *myself*, except slantwise, like an elf sister in my peripheral vision. Or when Robin gently calls some transgression to my attention—which in fact, he rarely does, having the most accommodating of natures, unlike me—I see my gorilla face.

"If anything divine is still to come our way . . ." Every manifestation of the god signals a break with the known world and not necessarily a happy one. Sitting on this shore I think of the Ojibwa people who lived here two hundred years ago, watching the laden canoes of the French explorers ride out of the mist. Unfortunately, it was the native people who submitted to the disruption of their categories, simply by force majeure. Power, for the bearers of the white god, lay in holding tight to preconceived notions, although in the process they missed out on anything divine coming *their* way.

Nothing worthwhile ever comes to me except slantwise, when I'm not attentive.

Robin goes out, leaving the door open, and the roar of the surf comes in, making me want nothing so much as sleep. It seems not a desire for rest but for unconsciousness, access, and descent into the shafts of the mind.

"Disavowed murderousness is the ground from which little murders crop up. The grudge itself is a kind of endless little murder. Born in hurt, it is often nurtured by relentless self-righteousness and a refusal to see oneself and one's own complicity, to budge from a psychologically self-protective place," writes Robert Karen in *The Forgiving Self*.

It's no wonder, I now see, that my divorce caught a thread that unraveled the whole sock of my religious system: this may, of course, have been a gift, but how many socks can one knit between age forty and death?

Before that happened, I thought I was a good person, striving to get better. I more or less held with the Judeo-Christian outlines of God, modified by what I thought were sensible embellishments of my own. I worked hard at being good. What I see now is that I white-knuckled my way through life on nerves and will, trying to conform myself to some plaster image left in the wreckage of my religious upbringing. Thus it became necessary to my self-concept never to admit such inadequate human feelings as jealousy, abandonment, and loneliness. For a long time I resisted the lessons of the divorce, trying to blame the failure of our marriage on my husband; how could I be culpable? I couldn't admit that idea into my self-concept. The evasion cost me precious knowledge, delayed, for example, my discovery of Mary's Third Law of Marital Thermodynamics: *you always marry somebody as crazy as you are*.

I didn't marry for love—although it may be that I thought at the time I was doing so. I married because it was time. Time, above all, to have children. I married, that is, according to the terms of another family narrative, which, before TV, was what we had for good or ill to guide our perceptions. Grandma Rose often told me she had no love for my grandfather and simply wanted to have children with a good man "with good blood." My grandparents were completely unsuited to each other, it always seemed to me, loving them both— he, mystical, brilliant, and reclusive, and she, extroverted and practical. But, in truth, I watched them fall for each other in old age, when both of them had gentled down a bit.

I didn't marry for love but, like a Hindu bride—like my grandmother—I learned to love the man I married. It was in that marriage, I suppose, that I came to understand relationship as a spiritual discipline, a path in which the rough edges of the soul are buffed by daily contact with another.

In the last few years of our journey together—Robin will attest to this—I have become both more difficult and more relaxed. At Plum Village monastery I learned to sit in meditation and simply look at feelings: "Breathing in, I know that I am feeling [insert your feeling here]." I learned, as Thich Nhat Hanh taught, to let "older sister,"—the wiser self—take care of "younger sister," the one with the passionate feelings. I started to know myself, for the first time, in my forties. Yet in the presence of another person, I regress. That is why I think of relationship as monastery, as testing ground.

This may seem unromantic to those who have a softer karma.

When we contemplate how strange our lives are—Why did I marry that man or woman? How did I come out of that family? Why am I so anxious? Why is my living room full of lawn furniture?—it leads us to the edge of the abyss, where all radical understanding of life is forced on us. That is why I can't write "spiritual autobiography" in the traditional sense: counting none but the sunny moments, as the old sundials advise. If I did, I would understand nothing, manifest nothing. Most spiritual writers turn away from the things that make our human journey human. I think of Dorothy Day renouncing, once she became a Catholic, her love for her common-law husband. I find her description of him unbearably poignant, perhaps because he reminds me so much of Robin: "I loved him for all he knew . . . I loved him for the odds and ends I had to fish out of his sweater pockets and for the sand and shells he brought in with his fishing. I loved his lean, cold body as he got into bed smelling of the sea, and I loved his integrity and stubborn pride."

To leave such a man behind seems to me—to use old-fashioned language—a *sin*, but Dorothy Day considered it a necessary sacrifice.

Role and vocation inevitably imprison, but there is probably nothing we can do about that, or should do. It is part of the creature's inexorable spiral toward death and whatever we know of resurrection. Our famous stem cells can become a Taoist Ten Thousand Things, but they cannot become *anything*. We can perhaps regenerate bone marrow and perhaps, someday, spinal neurons, but we cannot become a ferret or an angel or a Scotch pine. What's remarkable about the human condition is that we can imagine or play with the idea of becoming a ferret. To the best of my knowledge, becoming human is not a speculation that troubles ferrets.

This week's rhythm of work and rest and companionship feels, at the moment, right to me. We are relaxed and lazy, yet keeping to a reasonable schedule of activity. Robin works on his music and drawing, I write; we stroll in and out of the natural world. We keep silence together from breakfast till noon. Every year that we come here to this borderland I feel we are living precisely the way we are supposed to live, simply: staring down the eye of the merganser now and then, his little flighty topknot too damp to show off, noting how the loon calls just as he breaks above the water. Nothing much, but looking at these things should be in *somebody's* job description.

Some patterns in nature are orderly, some—the arrangement of purple campanula, a spiderweb, the crunchy gnats caught in it, grass, white lichen, gold lichen, bumblebee, little yellow flower growing out of the boulder I'm on—are random. And on the black rock fundament, there are tunnels of quartz rimmed in rhyolite or porphyry, rods tunneling downward like thresholds into the black rock. All of these streams of molten jewelry were most important to themselves at one time; later, they found themselves caught, cooled, entrapped, and castled *till God shall bid them fly.* Fish scales made of gemstone, desire of lava.

Anne Carson, in *Eros, the Bittersweet*, makes the ancient case that *desire demands absence*, longing requires distance and rejection, does not require the red stream, porphyry, to be trapped, cooled, and held. *Stay forever:* what a fate, to make a cradle for this lake's turn at insistent desire, its ever-changing devices of seduction. Today sucking and sliding over the impervious granite body; yesterday turning its huge waves inside out with attack, blowing east, blowing west, blowing both ways together.

Robin did his undergraduate degree in geology, so I am always begging him for the names and habits of rocks. "You'll just make up metaphors with them," he mildly scolds.

The people in the cabin next door are taking pictures of their beautiful, healthy children—two rosy girls of fourteen or so (twins?) and a fat, sweet-faced boy perhaps a year younger. All of them are dressed roughly alike in baseball caps and black pants and shirts with white stripes emblazoned "Tartans." Now they are in the canoe traversing Hollow Rock and the dad scrambles along the rocky shore, photographing. Then they all come ashore. Are they canoeing or being photographed canoeing? In thirty years they will look at the photo: *We did that. We were happy and strong.* Or, we were sad and a little soft, or soft and bitter and happy and loved, whatever people find they have given back to the little eye of the camera. It's an odd preoccupation, photography. At night the family sits on the beach. Flashbulbs pop, then they go inside and TV lights up the picture window, through which Robin and I nonchalantly watch them from the beach.

Photography is a way of "dealing with things everybody knows about but isn't attending to" Emit Gowin wrote about Susan Sontag, an idea similar to Karl Pilato's notion that snapshots cross easily into the realm of image.

My dad's photos were fashion shots. He liked to take pictures of us all dressed up in clothes he had bought for us, being in that respect not much different from the burghers of Amsterdam who hired Vermeer. No need for Vermeer in 1958. I remember the hot smell of the melting flashbulb, how sometimes I could not resist snatching it up and getting burned. I see my sister in a gauzy dress and straw Easter hat with pink ribbons, posed in the conservatory at Como Park, her color high and her eyes happy. Fathers laid down trails of photographic proof that their children were carefree. In my world, it was mostly dads who did the photographing, especially the complicated shots where the guy set up the tripod and timing mechanism and jumped in at the last minute, a bravura performance of how they behaved in real life. Then they jumped out.

After my husband left, photography declined in our house, though I indulged a brief, weird vogue for having studio portraits taken at cheesy malls. As if to say, *we are complete, we fill the silver gaze*.

Robin is sitting, looking at the lake in his black baseball cap and flip-up sunglasses, and I am here on the sofa, swatting every fly that comes in. The window is thick with a lech of gnats driven to grate themselves on the pane. Calm today, the gulls bark to each other, circling down the air. There must be pleasure in it, *extend aileron far to the left, spread spotted tail feathers and glide, slop of dead herring draped on the bill*. Is this what we aspire to, a condition of pure intent? Is the gull, then, enlightened? Or do we just long for the end of longing, each minute eaten by each successive hungering minute, bloody against the bill? I think not.

Soon Robin and I will love each other a little bit carefully, then we will drive into town and have a fried walleye sandwich. Last night we sat on the beach, creating the possibility for these acts and others, while the gulls merely circled mindful or mindless and still do.

Rhyolite runs ribbons through the substrates of basalt and diabase or gabbro with insouciant willfulness, as though back in the molten times it shook its little red fist at Creator and cried, *"Non serviam!"* Refusing its turn to melt into the common fundament, it appears in calligraphic traces across the black and gray cliffs and in perfect Zen circles or lines on round, lake-tossed stones. It's hard to believe the designs aren't laid down with a good Japanese brush. They are geometrical and controlled, giving calligraphers a quick lesson, or maybe a slow lesson.

The soul flies in circles, the Sufis say.

Love Story

WHILE WE WERE SLEEPING, I dimly felt Robin's hand tighten around my hand, clench and free, as though we kept up an old and cordial argument in our dreams. I think about all the lovers waking up under all the chimneys of all the houses around us, making holy the Sunday beds and reading the *New York Times* in the first bright autumn cold.

Today is the day of our friend James's memorial service.

This is a love story: when James went to prison the second time, he was so alone that when the warden gave him a book to sign the names of any visitors he expected, he wrote, "Jesus." But after a year had passed, a Quaker prison-visitor named Mary Beth came along. She and James fell in love the first time they saw each other, and they made it work, too. "She is my light," he would say again and again. He would be on parole until a month before his death. I will miss James forever, how he could stand up in Meeting and call a bunch of middle-class people to attention with his deep black voice.

Italian Catholics say, "Every baby comes with a loaf of bread under its arm." I believe that is true of relationships as well. You have to discern the gift. There is one for sure, but what is its nature? What is the face of God in it?

I don't think James and Mary Beth asked so many questions. They had a knack for accepting grace when it came their way.

For much of this summer, Robin and I worked in the mammal nursery of the wildlife center feeding baby rabbits, animals who confidently slouch in a web of connections. How hard it was for us to find the mouth in that tiny pucker, how easy to nourish the nose instead. Sometimes a speck of blood flows to warn us we are moving too fast. The mouth of a newborn cottontail is not an easy door, and sometimes you have to wait at it for the pink point of tongue to determine its own fate—*lick lick*—*at this rate I'll be here till 1 a.m.* When we lift a rabbit out of the nest to feed, it struggles; sometimes it utters a piercing scream out of proportion to the baby-sock size. *Mister, do I look like a hawk?* Rabbits miss the furry pile of brothers and sisters; they have no idea they aren't each other until the horrible moment of separation: *they do not know they are not each other.*

Going through my dad's color slides—a task of historical preservation I took on after our mother died—I retrieve a slide of Peggy and me, bonneted and overdressed, squinty in the sun, standing next to an arborvitae that would grow taller and taller along with us through years of Easter photos. Here, this moment, fourth grade, I am wearing a yellow satin dress overlaid with white lace. It's the most beautiful dress I have ever owned. Not only did I get to wear it at Easter— white patent-leather sandals, too—but, also, that year I would be Queen of the May: just in my own classroom, mind you, not for the all-school extravaganza.

Still.

My teacher that year was an old nun called Sister Euphemia, who did nothing wrong, nothing right. We did not look to her for ecstasies of love or terror, as we looked to Sister Mary Adrian, who flashed into temper and threw things, or Sister Michaeline, sentimental, needy friend of small girls. Then one day, out of the vast cape of her innocuous bland nature, Sister Euphemia pulled the announcement that I would be Queen of the May.

I had long ago given up hope of being Queen of Anything. I, formerly the boldest girl in school, the child who expected to be queen of the world, had learned some terrible mutability by fourth grade. Sandy Schultz had begun the process of my erosion, her skin so milky, her eyes so black, her red coat so trimmed with fur.

"Daddy"—it was autumn—"may I have a coat with a hood?"

"Coats don't come with *hoods* anymore. Who do you think you are, Snow White?" This latter comment had no edge to it beyond a practical transfer of information. It was important for kids to learn what role they were cast for in the drama of Roseville and not to have uppity notions. He hung a practical, thick, gray garment on me with a plastic buckle that cinched the grommeted belt, "This is a storm coat." Around the neck, a plushy fake-fur collar could be turned up around my face. "This will keep you good and warm when you walk home from school." Wool, plaid headscarves were the big fashion item of the day; the fast girls knotted theirs at the very point of the chin. When I tried that, my scarf slid up and the knot lodged under my lower lip, where it would soon be damp with winter drool.

The ugliness of my storm coat was beyond expression. Sandy Schultz's red hood—somebody certainly did think she was Snow White—dipped before me into her elderly parents' heated car. Sandy's mother wore a storm coat; Flora LeTourneau wore a storm coat. She was chubby and overgrown and looked, in her own storm coat, like a girl made of sausage. Flora, a new girl that year, had fallen in girlish love with me, and I gratefully loved her back. She followed me around and told me obliquely about such things as "periods."

"Something's gonna happen to you," she warned. "I can't tell you now. When you're older." I regarded Flora with the tenderness such girls, heavy and kind, always roused in me. We were the same age, but she was a head taller and a little developmentally delayed. Our friendship drove my parents crazy. They were afraid I'd pick up Flora's bad grammar or table manners. It would have been a good thing if I had picked up some of her weighty kindness. She was another kind of angel in my life. I didn't tell her I knew all there was to know about periods, since she took such pleasure in enlightening me.

When I was Queen of the May in fourth grade, I chose Flora to carry the flowers and Sam Ippoliti, beefy and tripping over his feet, to carry the incense and be King. Geeks on parade. Why did Sister Euphemia give us this moment? I can't imagine what prescience moved her. Flora was one of those girls pregnant by sophomore year in high school, and Sam would crash his Thunderbird and die in a strip-mall parking lot.

After I crowned the smiling statue of Mary with her sticky little wreath of artificial flowers, Flora poked Sam and pushed him forward, "Now you can kiss the bride," she said, a little weak on liturgical distinctions. But he wouldn't. He was a good Catholic boy.

I am feeling the surge of energy I get when daylight saving time ends. We get that hour back—actually I got it over and over because I set some of my clocks ahead instead of behind and set others not at all, in my dither. So I entered into *central cuckoo time*. These governmental manipulations of time are such a metaphysical buzz. I get up at 6 a.m. now, which is really seven, and the morning stretches before me like a smorgasbord of things I passionately want to eat.

"There is no such objective thing as time," my physicist friend, Andy Pico, used to tell me, with all the authority of his discipline. This morning I was lying on the couch reading Plato and thinking, "If I prepare my class conscientiously, I won't get to work out in the gym." Then I remembered that there are not really twenty-four hours in the day—thanks Andy. Time is merely a convenient fiction—and what's not done today will be done soon, or it was done already done in some time warp tied up in string theory: why worry?

The Soul Flies in Circles

"THE SOUL FLIES IN CIRCLES—" Sufis say, always coming round to a few stable points, returning, not always wisely, but certainly on purpose.

One day, some twenty years ago, my soul was flying around to the idea of reconnecting with what is so oddly called "organized religion"—a phrase that begs many questions about the nature of our spiritual business—and so I decided to find a spiritual director. As noted earlier, spiritual direction is a traditional Catholic practice; when I was a young person pondering a religious vocation I began to make monthly visits to a priest who I thought would give me prayers to say and guidance in discerning my call. I soon found myself in the care of a gentle and canny counselor, who awakened me to the nature of poet-mind and prepared me as well as he could for all hell to break loose once I set foot in the novitiate. He gave me great spiritual guidance, like, "try to grow some rhinoceros hide." He offered mysterious advice about animals: "If you have a backyard full of junkyard dogs, you'd better learn how to feed them and then they will work for you very well. Otherwise, look out."

I've been fortunate in my spiritual directors.

There is a certain kind of student who takes classes from mean professors, thinking that kind teachers are lying to her. For similar reasons, I look for rigorous mentors in the spiritual life, but instead my soul flies around to people like Sister Chris—whom I chose because she was elderly, and a nun. Maybe she would hit me with a ruler. Contrariwise, she was full of warm hugs and wacky new-age ideas.

Sister Chris died in her sleep, suddenly, a few months ago, on the first leg of the trip to England she had been planning for years. When last we met, she spoke as though presciently: "I can't wait to die! I can't wait to see what happens!" Yet no one was more full of life than she. At seventy, she thought, given her good heredity, that she might have thirty years to wait. As I go about my days, now and again it comes to me, "I must speak to Chris about this—" I hope I can go on speaking to her. Her last, most astonishing advice to me was, "Why don't you goof-off and try getting something for nothing?"

What kind of a koan is that for a disciplined person? I had been complaining about a colleague who was vexing me by behaving irresponsibly, when Chris came through with this piece of Lutheran counsel. It's often the case with spiritual wisdom that the teacher ascends or transcends or simply dies gently between dark and dawn before she can add all the footnotes and warning labels. So I remain to ponder her question, conjoining it in my mind with the last lunch I had at my Uncle Boo's house as a five- or six-year-old. Boo used to make us a meal of white bread covered in syrup. This was his idea of lunch. After we finished this delicious repast, we would pick up the plates and lick them. I think that this may be God's idea of lunch: *goof-off and get something for nothing.*

My affectionate cat, Fluffy, died this summer as well, and Robin's old dog, Rosie. There has been a great passing over lately of the good and innocent, as though, between worlds, a strong team is being lined up for duties I can't imagine.

It is windy today in the crest of the cottonwoods, shaking light. Two women go by pushing the huge prams in fashion for the one or two precious babies people allow themselves. My own babies, after brief visits, are back in their real lives. Jude and his fiancée, Leslee, were here for the weekend, seeming relaxed despite a hectic schedule. Their wedding is planned for spring.

Unlike my wise son, I used to have a pattern of turning to the wrong people for love; my soul circled to that place as if tuned to country music. My monthly visits to Chris for spiritual direction were the beginning of breaking that pattern. My soul is almost steady now. Perhaps we come to earth just to acquire that steadiness. I have been slow to gain it; it doesn't take much soil to get something decent to sprout, though maybe not what you want, not a cottonwood.

I hope that Chris and Fluffy will come to meet me when I die, along with my friend Joe Guerinot and a procession of dogs and swans and Eastern cottontails. We complain about our families-of-origin while God is laughing: "You didn't know who your real protectors were, they were Chris and Fluffy, Joe and Shep!"

We would do well, defining family, to look to the souls who are really guiding us, even though that doesn't seem to be their official job description. We think we have a right to find that guidance in our parents, but universal love is not bound to genetics, nor does it operate in an orderly way through space and time. When I think about my own children, for example, Galway Kinnell's phrase comes to mind: "a backward spreading brightness." They are true spiritual teachers of mine, comforters and exemplars. An old Roman named Marcus Aurelius spoke up off the library shelf and saved my bacon when I was a teenager; a black cocker spaniel, who lived only a few weeks, got my childhood off to a very good start.

One reason we see ghosts, I suppose, is that the dead are slow to give up their reality, or, more likely, we are unwilling to give them up: thus the recurrent thought, "I must tell Chris—," or the emergence of Fluffy in his customary light at the top of the stairs.

On a thick bed of petunias, sphinx moths dart from flower to flower, their orange-red double wings a blur of energy around the compact, bomber-shaped bodies that look too heavy to fly, and indeed require this intensity of expression to get lift. The proboscis of the sphinx moth is a straw as long as the body, designed to pierce to the heart of its longing. So wide the bed of temptation here, so short the season, that these insects don't even bother to retract the instrument. It's all plunge, plunge into the full throats of their only desire.

In *Death Comes for the Archbishop,* Willa Cather wrote that "Miracles . . . seem to me to rest not so much upon faces or voices or healing powers coming suddenly near to us from afar off, but upon our perceptions being made finer, so that for a moment our eyes can see and our ears can hear what is there about us always."

This is more than an injunction to stop and smell the roses, which don't smell all that much anymore—they've been hybridized right out of their pheromones—or a plea for us to regard the sunset as something more than a blinding distraction on the freeway. It's a statement about the nature of consciousness, and perhaps a comment on developmental psychology. As our perceptions become refined by age or grace or spiritual practice, we literally see more going on around us, which we may as well call *miraculous.* It's as though the eyes of our mind acquire a kind of built-in telescope, which we can switch on at will, or in moments of will-lessness.

Did you ever know someone who took up serious birding? My son told me about a popular ornithology course at Swarthmore, which attracted students in droves. In my motherly way I suggested he take it. But he didn't want to.

"Those students," he told me thoughtfully, "are hard to hold a conversation with. Their eyes are always on the trees."

I respect his position. The eyes of an ornithologist, which might be locked to yours, instead *flit.* It can be annoying, especially if you are not a birder yourself. Anyone who studies nature, however amateurishly, is awakened to amazement by all the flashes of yellow and blue and spotted feathers newly available to the eye. *Mira!*

Surely those birds cannot have been there all along and I failed to see them? If your friend learns birdcalls, on top of it, he will not *listen* to you either.

Ornithology is one example of the alternate universes we can productively or unproductively get lost in. Dislocations like this are essential to the contemplative vision, though they may cause us to afflict others both skillfully and unskillfully. If one spends a lot of time in silence, as we do in Quaker meeting, we become a bit like those young ornithologists, suddenly seeing things that others do not see or care about, distracted from social contact, demanding that others look at things they do not want to see. In the process, we may become perhaps lonely, perhaps ecstatic, perhaps prophetic, perhaps revolutionary, perhaps "a peculiar people," as Quakers used to call themselves. In Plato's *Allegory of the Cave*, a teacher returns to his origins in darkness to lead other people to the light, but the cave dwellers hate him because he has become odd-looking, like certain university professors who seem to have lost their pocket combs, and he refuses to follow the fashions of the cave.

If you are in the right mental time zone, miracles happen. Humans operate in two time zones at once, like parts of Indiana: *clock time* and *high time*. This is an idea that obsessed St. Augustine and later philosophers such as Henri Bergson, as well as any first grader who is trying to get to school before the bell rings while *also* paying attention to the single once-in-a-moment descent of the tiger swallowtail onto a tea rose, devoid of smell.

We are always torn like this between the school bell and the butterfly. The conflict seems to be wired into us. I shake my fist at the creator every now and then about it. It's like trying to get from Earlham College to make a plane in Cincinnati: you have to drive through Indiana central time and through eastern standard to central daylight, and the airline doesn't care about your problems.

Miracles happen, in my experience, on the edges of time zones, on the border of the woods, in the void between perch and free fall. The beautiful, fancy word for this space is *liminal*, the Latin word for "threshold." Maybe there are even bigger miracles over the border. I suspect there are, but I have not been there.

Rather, I tred carefully down my garden paths, which are as likely as not to be decorated with dog poop. My eyes are no longer sharp enough to pick it out amongst the woodchips on the path or in the dirt, so I am instead attentive to the buzz and lift of flies. As I get older, I begin to understand what a blind friend once told me: "I have a way of seeing. It's not just that my ears have become more sensitive—in fact, I'm deaf in one ear—but rather that my senses have scrambled themselves around in my brain and triangulate on an object in a way that I can only call *seeing,* though of course it is different from the vision I used to have." Unable to pick out the dog poop visually, I am attentive to other data. This reorganization has gone on without any particular training or discipline. The brain wants to see, or needs to, to survive and keep its renter's shoes clean.

It's a breezy blue autumn day, chickadees scolding for their hand-out as I check the wash. An old purple heirloom variety of morning glory called "Grandpa Otts" is opening now on the pergola. It's not effusive. It never gets enough sun. Nor do my sheets and underwear. Tossing my frilly lingerie into the basket, I think My *husband had the worst of me;* he got cotton briefs and wifeliness. Perhaps I was made to be a lover, not a wife, of God or man . . .

"Not that God's love is much like human love," my friend Peter's phone call, tempting me away from work, announces this thesis. "If we think it is," he continues, "the Trinity must seem quite a dysfunctional family."

One of the recurring patterns in ministry is that women come to me—rarely men—and say they feel called to leave their family because God is in some way leading them. A few years ago, I spoke to a woman whose husband was a pastor, both of them active in church and community, with four young children. She told me she felt called to be a hermit.

I thought this idea of "call" might be illusory, but I did not tell her so directly. In spiritual-director school we are taught not to tell people what to do, but to sit with them in discernment of how God might be leading them. Nevertheless, we have our opinions. I thought that this woman—call her Clara—should probably stay with her husband and children. There is an old guideline in Christian spirituality that God's will is best found in "the here and the duty." Four young children and an active ministry can lead anyone to daydream about a hermitage on some picturesque spot of ground. She sensed my negative assessment, of course, and did not return.

Later I heard she had gotten a divorce. I don't know what became of her—good things, I hope—or who took care of the children, though I know that both the minister and his wife would have put their care uppermost . . . and I hesitate as I write "uppermost" because Clara was, of course, putting her sense of call or her inner voices uppermost.

"Beyond ideas of right and wrong," Rumi wrote, "there is a field. I'll meet you there."

I don't know where, out beyond ideas of right and wrong, Clara bravely makes her way. It so happens, however, that I've kept in touch with her husband. The scandal of the divorce ruined his standing in his small-town religious community. He couldn't get a job. What ending would you write for this story? He spiraled into despair? Wound up on the streets? Became CEO of a munitions factory? No, he went back to university as a music major. He became a church organist and composer. He plays in a rock band on weekends. The worried creases that used to cross his face as he ascended the pulpit have softened in the strobe lights. That loss was the channel through which he entered his life.

"*See,*" says Peter. "What do we know?" From his parsonage in Massachusetts, Peter functions as my "supervision group." Spiritual directors, like psychologists, are supposed to report to people older and wiser to make sure they don't go off the rails. In my life, however, Peter's role is to kick the rails away.

The Christian tradition does not give a lot of comfort room for scenarios like "There is a field. I'll meet you there." One can find examples of virtuous men and women who have gotten their confessor's permission to retreat from marriage into religious communities; there have been couples like Jacques and Raissa Maritain, who vowed themselves to celibacy out of religious devotion. But Christianity has no models for the kind of insouciant, careless love that one finds in the Hindu or Sufi traditions. I think of the fourteenth-century renunciate, Lalla, who left her marriage to take up life as a wandering poet. She wrote

My teacher told me one thing,
Live in the soul
When that was so
I began to go naked
and dance.

The great Mirabai, a thirteenth-century Rajasthani woman, flung herself, in her jingling ankle bells, onto the path of *bhakti* (devotional) yoga with a similar (as we might say in Minnesota) excess of emotion. In the Western tradition, women, at worst, defy their parents. When Peter really wants to get my goat about how conservatively I'm managing some situation that rises in spiritual direction, he'll say, "You're pouring holy water on the status quo." He hates religion invoked to support bourgeois social arrangements. He'll say, "Don't put chocolate over that shit."

The *here* and the *duty* tether us to the world as it is, a consecrated landscape. That's good.

But Peter pushes me to sense, beyond truism, another field of possibility. There is a riff in Sacred Harp music that I steal from the bass section whenever I get the chance to bawl it out: "Could we but stand where Moses stood and view the landscape o'er / Not Jordan's stream nor death's cold flood could fright us from the shore." Cross over. Get soaking wet and cold. Christianity and Buddhism both make this demand—which I so far have managed to ignore, like a border collie who would rather bark than jump in.

Out beyond *ideas*, there is a geography of prophetic witness, and timorously as I stand here barking, I know it's not only for the bass section.

Live in the soul. My teachers—Chris, Peter—taught me that, too. Then why am I stepping so timorously around this garden?

PART THREE

Fire Keeps the Memory of Form

Walking Point

WALKING MEDITATION, AS IT'S CALLED in the Mahayana Buddhist tradition, has become a vital practice for me since I returned from studying with Thich Nhat Hanh at Plum Village several years ago. As the euphoria of the millennium—does anybody recall that media event?—dissolved into an epoch defined by terrorist violence and incoherent counterattack, I began to frame it with new urgency as what soldiers call "walking point": taking my turn, that is, to hike along the perimeter of a dangerous situation in order to keep a circle of safety around those I feel called to protect. All the great Buddhist traditions, knowing the nature of our world, draw analogies between the training of the monk and the training of the warrior.

My dog, Shep, smiles at me. This is no big deal to her.

I'm told we come to resemble our dogs, or perhaps we get involved in the first place with animals who share our temperament. I have two border collies living at my house now, both of whom, as spiritual teachers, offer me plenty of negative and positive examples. Border collies think they are responsible for everything that goes on. Star, the young one, needs to be taught to rest now and then: no barking. Take a nap. But she is a border collie, not a golden retriever and not a poodle, and we have to yield to our natures and do the job we think we are assigned, to go from window to window if we need to, and yelp. I'm teaching her to meditate, or, as *Dog Training for Dummies* would have it, I'm getting her accustomed to a half-hour down-stay. She loves it. Creatures as anxious as this one appreciate being completely relieved of their sense of obligation. Every morning, as soon as I come downstairs, she goes to the meditation corner and flops beside the *zafu*. She herds me over there if I think I have something better to do. The rest of the day, she paces relentlessly, wearing out the carpet with her sense of responsibility.

By contrast, my old dog, Shep, is arthritic and conserves her resources. She doesn't get to her feet unless there is a serious food issue. She knows I will carry her downstairs if the need arises. She has always been, temperamentally, a Lutheran dog. In youth she would "sin boldly," as Martin Luther recommended. Once she stole and ate five loaves of unrisen bread. They fermented in her gut, and we awakened in the night to find Shep leaping around the kitchen, hiccupping drunkenly. In old age, she relies on grace, like a good Minnesota church lady, and my neighborhood fish merchant rewards her from his store of salmon scraps.

Both of these dogs are great examples to me, and to the young ministers who come to my house for what their churches call spiritual direction. I mistrust the language of authority implied in this job description, but any dog, even restless young Star, can redefine it as "being with," nose between paws on the rug. She senses when someone just needs *presence*, which is, really, what most of us need all the time. Young ministers see as much of the raw side of life as do young cops, and they often think that people in difficulty need a high level of theological analysis. The dogs refute this idea.

One thing ministers have to deal with that cops do not is banality. A young pastor may go from comforting the victim of a tragic accident to meeting with the committee to hang the advent wreath. This is why I teach walking meditation, and why it seems so important to me. When you do walking meditation, you try not to make judgments about the relative importance of the stops on your journey: you just put your feet down and go calmly from one thing to another. No yelping, no dashing from window to window.

On the morning of September 11, 2001, I was stumbling around the kitchen, inattentive as usual, when the phone rang. It was someone calling from the middle of the country to cancel some business we had scheduled, ". . . because of all this terrible stuff."

"Huh? Did you lose your job?"

"You don't know what I'm talking about, do you?"

"I guess not."

"Some terrorists have crashed an airplane into the World Trade Center, another into the Pentagon. There are thousands of people dead. Don't you ever watch TV?"

The World Trade Center. I'm kind of ignorant about the international world of power and prestige, so I wasn't even sure where this building was. It amazes me, in retrospect, how insouciant this conversation was, how my friend and I changed the subject and caught up on our kids and gardens. We didn't quite get it. It was all so hard to grasp.

Outside under the bird feeder, gray squirrels were retrieving seeds. *In all creation*, says the Ojibwa prayer, *only we have left the sacred path.* I thought of Alyosha, the cottontail, and how he would stir in my lap and spread his delicate toes when a plane flew over. I'm not sure it was fear he felt, exactly, but certainly a vibration of threat to his environment. Thousands of people dead, and I'm worrying about rabbits.

Finally, I start to take it in: it's near the end of September, and I'm trying to sit and look at the birds feeding and the garden drooping in the rain without forming an opinion. Here a chickadee, there a house finch, flash of the last roses—time rushes against us. At rest under the canopy of Virginia creeper, the birds fluff out their feathers just a little. Water beads at the end of each twist of vine, each bead a world, each world flung prodigal into the dangerous path of consciousness. Four or five chickadees fly into this place of stasis, red leaves of oxalis bob a little under a droplet or draft. All of us longing for safety, shelter, and dark seeds. Fly in, fly out, afraid more than anything to rest.

After a few hours of work in the garden, I go inside to read. The elongated shape of a snail bends down from my hair onto my glasses. He falls down onto a page of some significant Western philosopher and begins to telescope himself into a gray viscous jelly. Antennae in, antennae out. Then he drags himself across my desk. Shall I let him go on his way, which will lead to no great good for him? It is not his fault that he migrated into my hair, but neither do I feel like trucking him downstairs and into the garden, the better to eat my hostas. I will, however. There are many dead ends in the universe, and grace abounding to the chief of sinners. Over my pencil he goes. What a job.

Yesterday, while I was quietly kneading bread, my mind reproduced a snapshot of the gray morning garden and the bird feeder, as they looked on September 11. Perhaps what we call "memories" are merely moments of presence, comfortable or uncomfortable, to which something has opened us: my son's newborn, cross-eyed look, the way my daughter could regard her long baby fingers by the hour, memories of being married that come to me in dreams, spliced with falling towers.

Now the snail crosses my page. *Tap. Tap. Tap.* He startles and pulls out his tender-looking horns. *Tap. Tap. Tap. Tap.* He stops and telescopes into a hump. *Tap.* I will take him back to the garden. Perhaps Creator has intended him to inherit the earth.

Thomas Merton wrote: "We do not detach ourselves from things in order to attach ourselves to God, but rather we become detached from ourselves . . ." It is not the created world that is the problem, but rather any use we make of it to "increase our attachment to our illusory self." I'm told the Jihaddists hate us because of our riches and our depraved TV and our thong underwear. I wonder why the Amish don't bomb us? What's the difference? The present crop of terrorists identify evil as *something outside the self.* So do most Americans. That certainly makes us brothers in spirit. I look at the photos of the 9/11 terrorists in the paper and see the boys of Derry or Columbine. What have we done to our children? Woven out of sacred connections a shirt of flame.

❦

The elm is full of goldfinches today on the fall migration, not as bright as the spring passage; they are outdone by the yellow-turning leaves. Yet each bowl of a body is formed to contain its desire. I feed them black seeds and white grain. They gather on skeins of air. They fly as the soul flies out of the body's knotwork, as the soul takes off from a knob on the spine.

Pacing

ALL BORDER COLLIES NEED TO LEARN the difference between walking meditation and *pacing and yelping.*

At a recent arts celebration, I became obsessed with the need to talk to everybody in the room about working for peace. I forgot to eat. Ten minutes before I was supposed to go on stage to give a speech, I realized that (1) I was freezing cold and shaking, and (2) the room was spinning. Clearly this would not be a good condition from which to address an audience.

Priority: get warm. I backed with Robin into the nearest bathroom—which happened to say Men—and begged him to find me a cup, a glass, anything to hold hot water. He went off on this errand while I ran hot water on my face and hands. Robin came back and held me against his big warm heart till I stopped shivering, at which point someone gave one of those peremptory knocks on the door, then came right in. A very surprised man. There goes my reputation in this town.

Without a lot of conscious practice and mindfulness, I waste my substance. Learning how not to do this has been one of my great struggles in the world. When I entered the novitiate in my late teens, I felt a conflict between what was then called the *active* vocation versus the *contemplative* one—intuitively, as I now see it, I was trying to work out a compromise between over-working and *overdreaming.* My first sense of call was to one of the contemplative orders, the Carmelites or the Poor Clares, who spend their lives behind literal walls, praying and trying to be present to God.

166

My dad felt this would be a colossal waste of time and talent. The very idea of my entering an enclosed order broke his heart. He opposed it with every fiber of his being. He could get his mind around losing me—as he saw it—to an active community of nuns, where I would be doing useful work like teaching or nursing, and where I could get a leave of absence to come home now and again. A contemplative nun, in his eyes, might as well be dead.

I didn't have the stamina or the self-understanding to oppose my parents when I was eighteen, so I entered a teaching order instead of following my first instinct. It was not the best fit, but it was the snug fit I required in order to make spiritual progress. I needed to struggle and understand the difference between the two calls I felt. It's too bad the old spiritual traditions didn't create a third category for people like me: active, contemplative, and *hermaphrodite*. I left the novitiate, still feeling these opposing tugs as sources of pain and friction, and tumbled into the social-justice struggles of the 1960s.

That was fine. The world needed me, and I was young and strong, though always teetering on the edge of burnout. Just in time, I became a Quaker and discovered a way of being an activist rooted in the contemplative silence of weekly Meeting. So. There was a place for hermaphrodites like me. Buddhism, especially my study in Thich Nhat Hanh's monastery, gave more structure and coherence to this mixed vocation, as well as a deep commitment to the idea that all beings are interconnected. Things inevitably come full circle. As a young Catholic, I had been taught concepts like "the mystical body"—which is a Catholic way of saying all beings are connected—and that the prayers of contemplative nuns and brothers nourish the whole body of the faithful. If all beings are connected, then the vocation of any one person, however hidden or humble, nourishes the good of all. Thich Nhat Hanh taught, "You sit for the world." Paradoxical as it may seem, he told us, our prayer, call it prayer, supports the work of those called to active work in the world. *Médecins sans frontières*—Doctors Without Borders—was his favorite example. We would be down on the floor once a month or so with our noses on the cold monastery tiles doing protestations in support of some medical team working by candlelight.

All mystical insights seem to have in common the perception of human connection and, even more strongly, the uniqueness of every human soul. The poet William Butler Yeats, for example, wrote of awakening at night "lying on my back and hearing a voice speaking above me and saying, 'No human soul is like any other human soul, and therefore the love of God for any human soul is infinite, for no other soul can satisfy the same need in God.'" Similarly, on a street in Louisville, Kentucky, Thomas Merton was suddenly lifted out of time into a transcendent vision of the people he walked among: "Then it was as if I suddenly saw the secret beauty of their hearts, the depths of their hearts where neither sin nor desire nor self-knowledge can reach, the core of their reality, the person that each one is in God's eyes. If only they could see themselves as they really are. If only we could see each other that way all the time, there would be no more war, no more hatred, no more cruelty, no more greed." Because we are connected in something like a body, all religious traditions seem to discover the idea that people on the front lines are supported by those who pray—whatever we may mean by that word—in solitude and silence. In fact, the great contemplative writers suggest that the stakes are high: Reshad Feild quotes his irascible Sufi master as telling him—in 1976—"If real change is not brought about, if people do not become *saliks*, then there is a very real danger that the earth will revert to a state of primordial chaos. It could be, if enough work is not done at the highest level soon, that we will see the end of civilization in our lifetime." Thomas Merton believed this as well, writing in his auto-biography in the 1950s that "the prayer of contemplative monks keeps the world from spinning off its axis."

I used to feel that these ideas might be grandiose, at least as they impinged on my meek existence. Now I feel an urgent responsibility to live more contemplatively. Every once in a while, even Thich Nhat Hanh would get just a little impatient on this subject: *get on with it. How much time do you think you have?* Considering that I have been dithering since my teens, it has taken me quite a while to get the point. Yet as I look back over my shoulder at my life, I'm aware that my feeling of struggle between the active and contemplative vocations has fallen away. Or walked itself away, into this world we are given, where I am walking point.

The Teabowl of the Heart

THE WORLD IS IN ITS CUSTOMARY MESS; my son is on the West Coast, making visits to a local Muslim community; my daughter is in Philadelphia, training young activists in social-justice work; I am mostly in the basement, trying to center clay on a potter's wheel. This is either a meditative exercise, or it is an occupation along the lines of what Henry David Thoreau called "weaving toilet cushions against the last day." Perhaps it is both; this year is a sabbatical for me, and at least I am able to spend my days in what is for me a perfect rhythm of writing and manual work. "What have you written today?" asks my old friend the sculptor, Peter Lupori, with whom I have studied since high school. We are hanging around the studio, kibitzing and playing with clay.

"One sentence: *Fire keeps the memory of form.*"

"Like in the kiln!" says Peter, delightedly.

I am grateful that these words make sense to one person, which is all any writer can hope for.

"And what are you making in the studio?" Peter goes on.

"Bowls."

"Teabowls?" he wants to know.

"Oh, I wouldn't dare."

"Me neither," says Peter Lupori, now in his eighties. The Japanese pottery tradition has a saying, "Only the master may make the teabowl."

As an apprentice potter, I'm fascinated by the form of the yunomi, or teabowl, which I do not dare to make. Here is a question that must trouble the apprentice potter: *is it a bowl or is it a cylinder?* All

170

traditional vessels begin in one of these shapes. Most of us learn, in Ceramics 101, rules like this: a bowl must be a bowl from the moment it appears in the mind. You should center a bowl differently from the way you center a cylinder. You begin with a lump of clay shaped rather like a doorknob, you scoop out a belly-shaped interior, always thinking *bowl, bowl, granola, soup, beef stew, haggis*, whatever. A cylinder, if we contrast it to the loving open heart of the bowl, is a martial form. You flatten the bottom and pull up the side at a 90-degree angle. While you are doing so, you think entirely different thoughts from the thoughts of the bowl maker. You think *efficiency, time management, must clean out my sock drawer.*

But now try to imagine the yunomi, a bowl within a cylinder. It boggles the apprentice potter's mind. Forming it requires, perhaps, both action and contemplation, *strong practice*, as Buddhists use that phrase. That is why only the master may undertake its form.

Caught in the heart of paradox, the potter must, in the same breath, obey the rules and transcend them. Obeying the rules is deeply engrained in most of us. It's funny, we spend so much time in school rebelling against our teachers, sticking out our tongues behind the algebra book, and making fun of Sister Mary Paperweight. But the rest of our lives, we try to do exactly what Sister Mary Paperweight told us to do, no matter how stupid, and we try to make everyone we know conform.

I know a man who had learned in school that it was not polite to eat a piece of pie that was pointed toward you. He swore this was an important piece of etiquette, and he judged everybody who came to dinner in terms of pie-attack. Sister Mary Paperweight had taught him this and, though nobody else in the world had ever heard of this rule about pointing the pie toward you, he was hanging on like grim death.

As a college teacher, I confront this phenomenon—the persistence of high-school discipline—with every batch of freshmen. One of two things has typically happened. Either they cling to every word their high school honors English teachers taught them and they will never under any circumstance begin a sentence with a conjunction. That's one possibility. The other is that—high school being the haze of confusion it is—the student has heard the rule exactly backward: "Always begin a sentence with a conjunction," or "When faced with a piece of cherry pie, back up to it." This student will also cling to the rule.

My Grandma Rose had a story about rules. She was a girl of about seven years old, back in the old neighborhood, studying for the sacrament of Holy Eucharist. The nuns had worked very hard preparing the children for any interrogation the priest might offer on the Baltimore Catechism. They could all recite the Seven Gifts of the Holy Ghost and the Twelve Fruits; they could rattle off the commandments and they could enumerate the sins against each.

One day a new priest came to the parish to visit. He was from Ireland, which gave him a particular cachet, and the nuns were very excited about having him meet the children in an assembly and run them through their catechism. Unfortunately, as my grandmother told me, the new priest was either completely insane or else he had "a wee bit taken." That was my grandmother's opinion, but I'll leave you to judge. He lined up the children and said to one boy, "Well now, Jimmy, if you take a nickel from your mother's purse, tell me is that a sin?"

Jimmy dutifully responded, "Oh, yes, Father."

"'Tis not," said the priest. "Now Molly, tell me, if you corner Jimmy here in the cloakroom and give him a kiss, is that a sin?"

"Oh, yes, Father!"

"'Tis not!" the priest responded happily. He went on like that for an hour, demolishing the edifice of catechism and sin and guilt the nuns had so carefully constructed.

For my grandmother, I think this was a story about the craziness of men or the dangers of taking a nip of the creature before catechism class, but I took away a different moral. "Imagine how confused those children were," she always wound up, but I, her ardent listener, was not confused at all. I was set free, I was on the path to becoming a Quaker. From then on, whenever a teacher told me in what direction to point my pie, or what to believe about Socialism, I heard a small voice in my mind saying, "Tis not!"

It is hard to figure out what is right and wrong in the world, what is the best course of action for a society. It is hard to figure out, in each individual case, what we are called to, especially if our call seems a bit different from those around us: the Quaker in a militant society, or the warrior spirit in the midst of Quaker meeting, or the artist or poet in the commercial world, or the scientist in a popular culture of unreasoning mush. In order to figure out what's right and wrong, we have help from orthodox religion, Miss Manners, Martha Stewart, and the fashion police.

Rules, however, are not central to the Quaker path. I spent nine months at Pendle Hill, a Quaker community for study and contemplation near Philadelphia, some fourteen years ago. A refugee from Catholic higher education, I was delighted by a word I came upon over and over, tacked onto the refrigerator, headlining the protocols for scrubbing floors, and so on. The word was "guidelines." Since I came home from that sabbatical and went back to teaching, I have always headed my course syllabus with the word "guidelines." This word and the set of concepts it protects are not always congenial to my students.

There is a part in most of us that wants to know exactly what to do. We are afraid of freedom—but that is understandable. To ask a student to find his or her true path, true voice, true character in the world is to ask that individual to surrender a set of behaviors that have worked well and brought success. Teachers who teach this way are asking a good dancer to lay aside a practiced routine and be clumsy again, in front of an audience and for a grade. Very little in the average student's previous experience of family life, school, and situation comedy have formed a personality that can respond to "guidelines."

But in the Society of Friends, this, if anything, is what we are good at: trying out the terrors of freedom *within* a circle of support, *within* a loose series of agreements and testimonies that keep us, with luck, from anarchy and narcissism. We are, to return to my central metaphor, always trying to spin that teabowl of the heart, the circle within the square, to protect an area of religious experience that honors both prophecy and order.

When I talk about *prophecy*, I always have to screech to a halt and explain what I mean, because people get it mixed up with fortune-telling. I have in mind a more theological application. In the Hebrew Scriptures, for example, there are books of law, like Deuteronomy, which gives rules geared to the daily survival of the human community: "Thou shalt not kill," or "Don't simmer the kid in its mother's milk." The prophetic books, by contrast, call the community to higher ground, to better behavior, to things so difficult that they can't exactly be mandated. They require inner change and discipline and grace. We might contrast, for example, the dietary laws in Deuteronomy with the diet recommended in Isaiah 59: "Is not this the fast that I have chosen? To loose the bands of wickedness, to undo the heavy burdens, and let the oppressed go free, and that ye break every yoke? Is it not to deal thy bread to the hungry, and that thou bring the poor that are cast out to thy house? (6-7)"

So, when I encourage individuals and institutions to nurture the prophetic—rather than simply keeping the rules—I'm encouraging them to seek new and original and daring solutions. Breaking the law is not a step I would take lightly; anarchy is a condition I eschew, because I like to find my drawer full of matching socks. Order is important to the survival of a community, but the prophetic spirit must also be nurtured if we are to get anywhere, as a world, these days.

Prophecy is, in my mind, allied with the creative, the poetic, and the contemplative, which is why I'm so eager to water those seeds. I used to teach a humanities course, which, in about the third week of February every year, required me to lecture on René Descartes. As soon as I would start to explain his famous dictum, *Cogito ergo sum,* my words would be cut off by a relentless cawing of crows outside my classroom window. There was something about the third week of February and the migration of owls or the pattern of freeze and thaw in Minnesota that attracted those raucous birds. Surely it could not have been that all nature convened in horror to block transmission of the *cogito* . . . Later, however, I read Thomas Merton's indictment; he calls the famous Cartesian statement, "the declaration of an alienated being, in exile from his own spiritual depths, compelled to seek some comfort in a *proof for his own existence (!)* based on the observation that he 'thinks.' If his thought is necessary as a medium through which he arrives at the concept of his existence, then he is in fact only moving farther away from his true being. He is reducing himself to a concept. He is making it impossible for himself to experience, directly and immediately, the mystery of his own being." Those crows were on to something.

Thinking is fine—I sign on to the bumper sticker that advises, "Commit random acts of rationality." But in Zen sitting, or contemplative practice, or poet-mind, we *caw* at it; something in nature, something at the root of being, encourages us to make rude noises.

I am not equipped to write a book about contemplation, or Zen practice, except as it filters through my own experience. But I would be unfaithful to my deepest knowledge if I did not remind the world at every opportunity that—as the poet William Stafford wrote—"the darkness around us is deep," and, if we have a call to this contemplative way of being, we can be of some use in the world.

Buddhism talks about the importance of "first thoughts" rather than "thoughts about thoughts." *Thoughts about thoughts* include clichés, cultural assumptions, slogans, commercial messages, sitcoms, inherited prejudices, and propaganda. Contemplation, by contrast, calls everything into question. That's why it's a painful and difficult path. Merton observes that contemplation, by its very nature, "mercifully examines and questions the spurious 'faith' of everyday life, the human faith which is nothing but the passive acceptance of conventional opinion. This false 'faith' which is what we often live by and which we even come to confuse with our 'religion' is subjected to inexorable questioning." He calls the suffering of the contemplative vocation a kind of "holocaust"; the "worst of it is that even apparently holy conceptions are consumed along with all the rest."

I've read Merton over and over since a kindly adult friend gave me a copy of New Seeds of Contemplation when I was fifteen years old, and I don't know when I put that exclamation point in the margin, but I'll hang another one out there now beside this section: "In the end the contemplative suffers the anguish of realizing that he no longer knows what God is. He may or may not mercifully realize that, after all, this is a great gain. . . ."

In my work as a spiritual director, I visit mostly with young protestant ministers, for whom this conflagration, this process of becoming a contemplative, can feel like loss of faith, feel like having a breakdown. But it's really a process of maturing—becoming more than a thinker—and it's good to open yourself to it. I'm convinced that all human institutions—a marriage, a scientific paradigm, a job—are subject to a similar trial by fire (which keeps the memory of form). Because poetry, dream, and a call to stillness are not much respected in our culture, it's easy to evade this trial. Much is lost in this evasion; in fact, it's possible for all to be lost.

I wish that in times of crisis the president would institute a national day of silence and discernment, a news fast, a darkening of the nation's TVs. What might come of that? What new voices might be heard?

Hugh Prather says about silence: "There is no problem that a quiet mind will not answer, because all problems arise from intense mental activity. Stillness permits a gentle correction of perception to occur. . . . How can stillness allow this change of perception? Because what is real is also obvious. If the mind is busy, it is attempting to overlook the obvious. . . . Stillness allows you to see what is, which you cannot do when you are mentally striving, searching, confronting, taking warning."

I take refuge in food and beauty, arranging my dinner of fresh corn and peas on a hand-thrown plate. In the clay studio, I'm trying to master a new form, after seeing a recent retrospective of the potter Warren MacKenzie's work. Once the wars started, I couldn't go to the woods for solace, so I go to my wheel. Other wildlife rehabilitators and naturalists reported a similar tendency to stick close to home, near the stove, in the world of human artifice. In the wilderness, all eyes are upon us.

People are learning—and they learn rather easily, if at some cost—to live with fear. I was scared to begin with, avoiding the rush, so I feel more detached.

At the heart of all spiritual consciousness is a struggle between fear and love, which I began to feel definitively when I was about five. Every religion has some version of Jesus's droll comment, "Perfect love casts out fear." Perhaps it's important to remember that, in the Greek texts, the word "perfect" *(telaios)* doesn't mean "flawless." Rather it recapitulates an agricultural metaphor from the Nichomachean Ethics. "Perfect" is said of bulbs, like the hyacinth bulb, that's capable of going through a healthy cycle of lying in the ground, then flowering into the goal *(telos)* for which the organism was created. So, if the bulb of one's life is endowed with good genetics, well nourished, and placed in the right soil, it's going to repel fear like any other workaday threat to its growth and development. My own roots were rather shallow, and I have come to understand that most people's are. Perhaps this is a young planet, perhaps our soil is blowing away in its first strong wind. Perhaps there is some other intention governing the process, which we cannot fathom any more than ants can comprehend a picnic.

Over and over throughout religious history, huge numbers of people manage to get the point about love, and, in the same historical space, huge numbers mill around unable to escape their fear. So

Rumi got it, Kabir got it, Jesus got it. What a radical thinker was the seventeenth-century Quaker William Penn to contrive the bold and tentative experiment, "Let us try what love can do." "To try," in Penn's sense, meant "to put on trial, to test." This is *hard love*, not romantic-ballad love. And the outcome of the experiment is still not clear. The trial may fail. But right now there is an urgent need to *try*. I would like to try to banish hatred and judgment from my mind, be it judgment of terrorists or of political parties or colleagues at work. And this is so hard for me that my little piggy eyes screw up with tears of effort.

Throughout late September 2001, I sat in front of the TV and knitted a shawl. The stitches were so tight I could have used it for chain mail. Finally I unpicked this armor of wool, gave away the TV to my niece, and went out among humans again. Somebody wrote of Christian community that we are like climbers tied together on a mountain.

Why are we tied together?

So that the strong ones don't go home.

I am bound to my mother, who calls me up demanding cigarettes, to colleagues lost in intellection, and to all my ex-boyfriends. American individualism has taught me that I am in it alone, my job is to get myself safely off the mountain. But that is wrong. The job for each of us is to get the team home.

I'm tethered to a few people who desperately need my help and, fortunately, to many others who are strong on the ropes.

Passages

> Yet no matter how deeply I go down into myself
> my God is dark, and like a webbing made
> of a hundred roots that drink in silence.
>
> —Rainer Maria Rilke

I THINK OF A WOODCUT by Hiroshige, *Sudden Shower over Shin-Ohashi Bridge and Atake*, which represents a village scene, its indigo space bisected by a delicate orange bridge, people covering their heads against the black slant of rain, people who will never in this world get home. Things happen, time shrugs its shoulders, and we complete our passage not in Osaka or St. Paul, but where? And what do we do now? We shake our heads like old dogs coming out of the water. The world is changed. We fling ourselves down on the strange shore and fall asleep, unable to face the gravity of it.

That, at least, is the response of most people, including myself, to dislocation and crisis. It's not a bad course of action, or inaction, compared to the political imperative to do something, anything, immediately.

I awakened this morning from a dream about jagged shapes of broken glass, images of the world's fragmentation, I suppose. I had been dreaming about the summer I spent in Guatemala City on a student exchange when I was fourteen years old. That was the year I discovered that the stories I had been told about the nature of reality were mostly false.

In Guatemala City, wealthy landowners—mostly employees of United Fruit—would embed broken glass in concrete walls around their houses. Cristina, my Guatemalan host sister, and I would pass the houses of the rich every evening, on our rambles around town. One night, we found the streets crowded with men in suits and women plainly dressed, with sensible shoes, mostly teachers from the local schools. They were singing and making speeches in a relentless and unimpassioned way.

"Who are they, Cristina?"

"Communists!" The women's low heels offended her Latin sensibility more than the political issue.

For my part, I had been taught that communists were ferret-faced rapists, sadists, and torturers. But here were teachers and journalists agitating for the poor against—*us*—Americans, United Fruit, and the Chiquita Banana with her saucy cha-cha-cha. My mind reeled back to a summer evening when I was seven or eight years old, packed into pajamas to go to the drive-in theater for yet another movie about planes, war, sadness, and heroism. Something with June Allyson in tears at the end of the runway. Dad would always become very grim in the course of these movies and when we got home he would lecture us about patriotism, as did the nuns and priests, endlessly, because in those days the Catholic church was eager to transcend its immigrant roots.

"*Listen, America's Princess,*" Luis Echeverria is hissing in my ear, "*what you believe is shit.* You have been lied to since you were two weeks old." Luis is an intense boy of Mayan descent who has just gotten back from a year in Cincinnati perfecting his English and learning the ways of the oppressor. He is so fierce that most of my fun-loving Guatemalan friends avoid him and his house with the dirt floor and the blind grandmother in the corner singing to herself in some ancient language only Oscar understands.

I was so frantic with political confusion that summer that I started to get up at 5 a.m. and attend daily mass. The streets would be washed clean, the town smelling of new bread. I would hear goat bells, the light would be pale and clear. Mario, a cousin of Cristina's, came to pick me up every morning, and we would walk to church together through the white-washed clarity of the city as it was at dawn. Mario was an unmarried intellectual in his thirties: there was a mystery about him. Perhaps he was holy. Like Luis, Mario was respected and avoided in the family. The shabby colonial cathedral would present other mysteries to us, the only young people in church. Old ladies would gather around the altar singing in a high-pitched whine, "O Maria, Madre Mia . . ." Walking back down to our street, we would inevitably pass Luis speeding by on his black bicycle with a load of bottles on his back to sell. He would wave and sneer. That summer I had an angel on my right shoulder, Mario, and an angel on my left, Luis. *O madre mia!*

When I came home from Guatemala in the fall, my friends found me *changed*. They thought I had fallen in love or something girlish. Of course it was impossible to tell anyone in Roseville about the oppression of indigenous people in a remote Central American country—their mental image of that place was something from *Road to Rio,* starring Bob Hope. I could not tell them how the big American companies supported the wealthy landowners, how the Catholic church had allied itself with the wealthy against the poor—except for the Maryknoll priests and nuns and the little bands of base Christian communities, who were practicing a new kind of guerilla religion I found powerfully attractive. There are stories you can't tell when your listeners have no imaginative space in which to hear them, unless you have greater powers as an artist than I had at fifteen. My trust in America had been shaken; I had entered an inverted world where capitalism was manifestly doing evil and communism seemed to be doing good. From grade school on, I had been filled with rabid tales about the torture of priests under any available communist. We were always being schooled in the immi-nent possibility of having to "defend the faith" against atheists, who would torture us into denying the church: a strange mix of sadism and surrender passed for religious education in my youth.

Coming home for my junior year in high school, I acquired a downward-looking posture to hide my soul, which was full of foment and cynicism. Almost all the girls at my Catholic high school were supporting the handsome young John F. Kennedy, with his photogenic wife and children, in the upcoming presidential election. Something was happening in Vietnam that everybody explained to me as an assault against godless atheism. I sat stonily through the standing ovation that greeted Kennedy's election—not that I liked the other guy!—suffering the incommunicability of what I knew. I wandered out and joined radical student organizations full of boys and Jews. I always got to be secretary. I read Simone Weil and took to wearing a black trench coat. These days, they'd have me in counseling, pronto.

I never told anyone my stories about Guatemala until I was a young professor, eating sandwiches with some colleagues in the faculty lunchroom, in the days when everybody was trying to figure out what was going on with the Sandinistas in Nicaragua. Well, let me tell you. My startled colleagues put down their forks and listened, as with rising heat in my cheeks I told and told and told. There was a silence. One of the old profs patted my hand and looked around the table. "Our own little *La Pasionaria,*" he said, clearly signaling his colleagues that it didn't mean anything and they should give me tenure anyway.

Some nights, Luis and our gang would go around the city taunting the army gunners on every corner, singing ditties to the tune of "Let Me Call You Sweetheart." Since we sang them in English, they did not shoot us dead: "Come and join the party, be a Communist! Come and join the party, brother, clench your fist!"

I had come to believe my dad was wrong in his unquestioning patriotism, but I didn't trust Luis, either. I had no intention of becoming a communist nor, as it turns out, did Luis, who wound up as an accountant in Sacramento. But given a slight shift in the tectonic plates of destiny, so unstable there in the highlands, what might have happened? I have always understood the fate of Patty Hearst.

Boundaries

THE LOMBARDY POPLARS GO ON lightly moving to the inner music of the world, poplars my neighbor planted to demarcate a tense boundary between himself and the slovenly occupant of the house next door, as we humans are always trying to do: knowing ourselves so narrowly that we have to keep drawing lines and marking edges of our ego-domains.

I am stifling just now in an America that, it seems to me, will be at war forever. Even without TV, I walk around trying to shield myself from electromagnetic fields. I hate the daily debasement of images and words, the thoughts about thoughts about thoughts. I soothe my spirit over and over by looking at art. Just as some people start to go to church, anticipating the Rapture, I go to galleries. I keep breathing in the craft of MacKenzie's teabowls and plates: *this is the best of us*. I carry this plenty before God's face to argue against our destruction.

Suzuki Roshi writes, "Suppose you recite the *Prajna Paramita Sutra* only once. It might be a very good recitation. But what would happen to you if you recited it twice, three times, four times or more? You might easily lose your original attitude toward it." In sitting mediation and walking meditation, we are trying to be with *mind* as it rises and reveals, with the flash of wind in the poplars, the play of sun. By contrast, TV and its pundit culture smother us in endless permutations of recycled ideas: the nobility of the fire fighters and police officers at the World Trade Center, how like Pearl Harbor, the mantra of supporting the troops.

With all this repetition of thoughts about thoughts, at a certain point no one will dare to say *it was not anything like Pearl Harbor, at all.* Creative response—response to the present moment, not some other moment—becomes almost impossible. If the mouths moving on TV can convince us that whatever war we are running is just like some other noble conflict, they can convince us to retaliate, be brave, cut our hair short, and stop complaining about the degradation of the environment.

I have no intention of waving from the end of that particular runway.

Saved too long, the pomegranate on my kitchen counter has convoluted inward on its own decay, giving up chamber by chamber to soft rot. I am thinking about the bounty of the world, a ripe seed webbed by its neighbor, death; sun streaking the gold and surrendered hive, full moon sinking at dawn upon its stars, how another neighbor stood a moment too long on the porch yesterday as though he would have said—what was it he would have said? He was afraid to say. People look at each other with suspicion. The politicians keep reassuring us about safety.

This country has puzzled me since 1960, when I belatedly began to think. Where did we get the idea that we are entitled to be pain free and worry free, that accidents must always be someone's fault, that all cancers should be gotten in time, that babies should be born flawless, and that death could be relegated to the back burner? What is the implicit idea about being human here? Confronted with international terrorism, we cannot be safe, even marginally safe, without an expenditure of money and curtailment of freedom that no one, not the wealthiest and most fearful, would sign on to. Yet fear is irrational, as I know from carrying a lot of it for a long time. Under the rock of every fear is the refusal to accept the contractual conditions of being human. I don't know why I came into the world or where I will go when I boil over on the back burner, but I know that I was born into a condition of radical instability: at any moment the car may drop its muffler, my heart valve may clog, or somebody who thinks too much may discover a novel way to surprise me with a dirty bomb. The only way to overcome fear is to accept without equivocation the worst it can propose, belay your ropes, and step across the next crevasse. We have no choice, anyway, about stepping. So why are my ex-cop cousins making money in "the security business," while I'm in the insecurity business and not making much at all?

The farmhouse that Robin and I go to look at is desperate, its log shell is crashing by inches into the cellar; yet, in the neighboring field, blonde autumn corn makes a sound like the rubbing together of thousands and thousands of dry wings. I want to sleep next to the corn, as if it were the ocean. I sense that if we could lie one night next to that field in a warm sleeping bag, something amazing would happen. An animal with red eyes would arrive on slow paws to tell; or just at dawn, a raven would fly down to say something about the moon. Or out of the smoky basement, a burned edge of old scrip would lift on the breeze. An ear of corn will rap another, the barn finally fall, grain dust, ashes fly up . . . there will be a run among the mice and one thing after another will implode until I am used to it. I will fear nothing ever again, whatever falls, whatever skitters over the bluff. *I will know I will know I will know.*

Instead we go home and sleep in our own bed, and I dream about a dark opening, like a keyhole between two cliffs, and beyond the keyhole a space of water, and beyond the water an island running with young black horses and horses, too, swimming. The cleft in the rocks begins to narrow and darkness grows at the edges. A voice in the dream says, "Earth demands a few million of you in order to preserve herself." I waken sobbing and gasping for breath.

Robin says, "What's the matter? Did you dream again about the children dying?"

"No. The horses."

One afternoon, I got in the car and went to visit Warren MacKenzie. He is a world-famous potter, who trained with Hamada in the Japanese Mingei tradition, yet he lives simply up a country road. Word gets around when he is doing a firing and buyers come from all over the world. He puts his own vessels out with the work of his friends and apprentices—wonderful potters like Randy Johnson, Jan McKeachie, and Will Gibben—so it's hard to tell what is and is not Warren's work. He doesn't sign things any more, preferring the anonymous tradition of the village potter. You just put your money in the can, honor system.

When I got there, there was a bad feeling in the shop. Collectors were arguing among themselves about what was and was not "authentic." One lady reared up and said, "Well, I'm just going to go and *ask* him if this is his. I've come a long way." So off she went to his studio, and Warren came in, all covered in clay dust, but affable and friendly.

I was so embarrassed to be in the room by then that I just introduced myself and said a quick hello. Warren had written me a kind note inviting the visit. We had not met before, but I had written to him after the show at the neighborhood gallery telling him how important his work had been to me in the days after September 11. Why? I couldn't say, then. To do the work you are called to do with a perfectly simple intention seems the most radical action of the moment—to look at work accomplished in that spirit is infinitely calming, restoring to the balance of the world's soul. But it was both impossible and unnecessary for me to say any of these things to Warren MacKenzie, so I just stood there tongue-tied, playing with my hair.

It didn't matter. I stared at pottery for an hour while the collectors came and went.

When all was quiet, the door opened and MacKenzie came back in. "Mary," he said, "come visit my studio and we'll chat." He remained working at his wheel—what more could an apprentice potter ask of a master—putting that elegant little finish of his on the foot of a bowl, patiently showing me how, while we talked clay gossip.

Then, after I had gone back to contemplating every piece in the salesroom, he came in and presented me with my own beautiful bowl, saying, "I hope this will give you as much pleasure as your writing has given me."

I was so touched that, in leaving, I dropped my car keys and had to search for them almost an hour in rising panic. Finally, I went back to the salesroom and saw, sitting on a shelf near the money jar, the pot Warren had given me as a gift. "Well, that's providential," I thought. "He would certainly have thought I didn't value it much, if I left it sitting here." So I wrapped it carefully and put it in the car. Then I discovered my keys in the grass and off I went.

When I got home, I discovered that I had two identical Warren MacKenzie bowls, one of which I had *stolen.* I sent him a check for the looted item, feeling like a complete fool. I think at some level I had wanted to impress this man I admired so much, whose work had communicated such transcendent spirit to me. Perhaps I coveted his spiritual condition or the graceful foot on his pots. Instead I managed to convey what a flighty idiot I am. And, fortunately, I conveyed it to myself as well.

This panicky afternoon in the country mirrors the larger patterns of spiritual greed and pushiness in my life; the insight makes me laugh. I am always tripping off the paths of art or spirit where others tred so gracefully. Yet I meet kind friends along the way who tolerate my skids.

Warren lives not far from a Fleet Farm store, so I was able to stop in and buy a pair of rubber work boots I've been needing, another well-made item, and similarly soothing to the soul.

The other day Robin began teasing me about spending so much of this sabbatical year obsessively throwing pots. I felt affronted, and retreated to baffled silence: *why am I doing this?* The response that tempted me was to defend the *difficulty* of the apprentice potter's task: "I'm exhausted! I throw ten-pound intractable lumps of buff stoneware. My back is killing me. My arms hurt. I work all afternoon like a field hand." I'm enmeshed in the American habit of evaluating the worth of a job by its difficulty rather than by its mystery.

Yet, *why* am I spending all this time wrestling ten-pound wedges of earth?

Mary, I tell myself in my kindest voice, as if I were speaking to a very dense animal, it's okay to throw pots all year. You don't have to write a book, you don't have to dig out the buckthorn, you don't have to look at property around Lanesboro or put an end to war. You don't have to learn Spanish, walk the dogs, or clean your office, sort your drawers, play well with others, learn a new musical instrument, take your wildlife exams, buy a computer, knit mittens, decorate for Christmas, make a quilt, call Sally, call Ann, write poems, visit your mother, clean the house, arrange Thanksgiving, get the leaves out of the gutters, read more postmodernist criticism, keep up with music, art, literature, your children, your friends, your dogs . . .

When I deliver that list to myself, I know why I feel so embattled; I feel the texture of a cloud of obligations pushing back from inside that ten-pound wedge of clay: *should could would need might ought to.* But some indisputable inner wisdom has whispered back, "Mary, just throw pots." Well, I do have to visit my mother, and dig buckthorn.

The soul is here for the lessons it needs to learn. It's having a junior year abroad in this skin. Some it will never get right. My soul will never clean the garden tools, oil them and put them away for a winter rest. My soul will leave the best terra-cotta planters outside to crack. It will be looking for the lawn mower under the snow in December. My soul will not put on winter tires until it foresees an engagement in Northfield, across a field of black ice.

But this soul vacationing in my skin has learned some lessons well. She likes the flesh enough to stay until they drag her home, the way some kids fall in love with Paris or Atitlán. She wants to stay at least through the major festivals: toleration, forgiveness, and the deep loosening of snow.

I know where my soul needs to go by a kind of leaning I feel within. Usually I get up in the morning and climb down the ladder from my loft through a room full of obligations that leap on me like dogs. My soul has learned to have a cup of tea and sit on my zafu for half an hour. When I get to my feet, I inevitably feel clarity about the day. For six months, I have inclined toward the clay studio. I assume my soul is learning what it needs there, but I cannot say how or why. I cannot justify it.

Mary Caroline Richards wrote persuasively about the relationship between centering clay on the wheel and centering the self in time and space, as though one act bore critically on the other, but from my own experience with pottery, I think the two are unrelated. Centering on the wheel is physics and craft. Centering the self is infinitely more difficult. A scattered person can center clay; Pablo Neruda could create poems edible with the yeast and grain of lived experience, while being, in his personal life, quite the shit.

Being able to center clay is unrelated to the state of the soul. Being able to write a poem fine and true is unrelated to the state of the soul. To evolve a good form at the wheel, you must, however, manage almost imperceptible imbalances. I work with a lot of cheap recycled clay, and its imperfections are a source of joy to me, except for the pieces of ground glass which occasionally spin out to slash fingers. Clay, a living substance, is always eating and digesting its environment, coughing up now and then slivers of wooden tools or, last week, two inches of chamois leather. I suppose in that respect at least, we can compare it to centering a relationship. Love also eats the house and car, problems at work, and memories of childhood, how you would not help with the dishes or say please. Nothing that won't go through the pug mill, nothing you'd even mention till suddenly under your fingers it slashes or pulls down the wall.

So, "centering" does not demand an undivided pure spirit, but rather a kind of animal attention to multiple imps of destruction.

Okay, I take back what I said before, or at least I modify it. Centering clay and writing poems are related to the state of the soul.

But the relationship is more complex than what I, in my dim-wittedness, took away from Mary Caroline Richards. Perhaps an artist's only gift is a peculiar quality of attention. While she minds the trivial details of balance and form, the soul can slip free, have a clear run toward its truth, the truth for which it came into this world.

Christmas is wheeling round again. When I think about God's birth, my mind fills with something like the night rush of luna moths in their iridescent dark. Such mysteries belong to some such world as that, not this.

I have received an invitation to go to Oregon for four months after Christmas, to be the writer-in-residence at a place called Sitka Center for Art and Ecology. This has put me into a panic. How will my mother and sister and Robin cope without me? How will I live all alone in a house in the woods—as I'm told is what I will have to do. Are the animals speaking to us again? Shall I rent a car? Surely my old Volvo will not make this trip across the mountains in winter. Whenever I have to deal with the jackals of the world, suited up in car dealerships, I just go to pieces. Am I doing the right thing? Feeling quite the coward, I inquire of the center's director whether living in the woods will be safe for a woman alone? He assures me that "those incidents have stopped."

PART FOUR

Learning the Coast

Echolocating

IMAGINE A ONE-ROOM GLASS BOX surrounded by woods. The top half, anyway, of my house at Sitka Center, has windows on three sides. Nobody gets to see my knees, if there were anyone to see, and, indeed, there are a few. The house I had imagined completely surrounded by moody spruce turns out to be attached to a deck, which attaches to an empty room, which attaches by a series of wooden bridges to eyries inhabited by the other artists-in residence, the young painter Karl Pilato and Brad Mattson, the latter a man about my age, who writes about ocean ecology and other adventurous topics. Still, my house is just isolated enough at the end of the Sitka complex to let me feel both alone and safe, a rare combination for women of my generation. The illusion, at least, of secure privacy allows one to feel like a solitary hermit in a grove of old-growth spruce. This illusion, I will discover, is much cultivated by West Coast architects.

Last night, sitting at the kitchen window, I felt the forest watching. Isn't there an old *Twilight Zone* episode in which the husband and wife discover at the end of their domestic evening that they are exhibits in some extraterrestrial zoo? I could imagine bear and deer and elk meandering down the Nature Conservancy trail for popcorn and an evening of watching *homo sapiens*.

Nothing Robin and I worried about happened on our journey from Minnesota—I, at least, worried—though other things happened that we could not possibly have anticipated. The old car did not break down passing over the winter mountains, but we did find ourselves the only guests in a ramshackle hotel near Coeur d'Alene run by a tattooed woman who slept all night in the parlor with a gun in her lap. That evening had begun with a young Canadian trekker also in residence, but he cleared out when the woman accidentally bolted into his bedroom to check out traffic on the street.

"Darn. I forgot he was there," she told us later, regretfully.

She mentioned we might also expect some old whores and young loggers, as well as people brought in by the police in the aftermath of road accidents. When we are on a trip, Robin and I like to stay in old hotels in small towns rather than in chain motels without any character. Unfortunately, these charming—or merely dilapidated— hostels often lend themselves to multiple use these days, of which the most benevolent may be "homeless shelter."

Robin is going to spend the first week at Sitka Center with me, then take the train back to St. Paul, leaving me to my solitary time. I'll drive him to the train station in town, then come back to my glass house and—be very lonely? Work hard? Have a breakdown? Meet the dark animal who wants to tell me something?

But let us continue to tour my one-room house, which is about 25 feet by 25 feet. As the visitor enters, he or she will walk between a sofa bed set under the north window to the left and a woodstove to the right. As you cross the room, continue past the desk, set between windows on the east wall and enter—if your goals are any- thing like mine—into the food preparation area. Overhanging the south end, next to the tiny stove-sink-and-refrigerator unit, is a sleeping loft, which I climb by means of a daunting ladder. The western half, without windows, is taken up by closets and a bathroom.

My little house connects on the west, windowless, side to an overflow-sleeping area called the bunkhouse, and, beyond that, the other artists' sleeping quarters and studios are connected along a series of decks. My space, called "The Tree House" is the most isolated. Brad and Karl have neighbors in each other, while I have Sitka spruce and Douglas fir. They are also closer to the office where, at least during the week, three people work, Randall, Amy, and Dee. Beyond these few acres, other neighbors live, though they are mostly in residence only on weekends.

I'm coming to understand Sitka as a kind of conscientious private development, not a gated community, exactly, but not a place where trespassers are welcome, either. Years ago, the surrounding acreage was set aside as an investment opportunity and then entailed in covenants, most of them oriented to environmental protection. A great deal of the glorious headland on which we sit, Cascade Head, has been ceded to the Nature Conservancy. On the other side it abuts the Salmon River and its fecund estuary; beyond lies the wild winter ocean. Most of the rest of the land is closed to development, and houses built on the open sites have to pass administrative scrutiny; each one must be judged eco-friendly. The founders incorporated in their plans the idea of an art center, inviting artists and writers with an environmental bent for four-month residencies, and in the summer a variety of classes are taught, ranging from sea kayaking and tide-pool ecosystems to every kind of art and poetry.

We pulled in on a Saturday night and decided to look for a church to go to the next day. Robin and I go to a lot of different churches, often evangelical protestant, out of a kind of instinct, when we are on the road. I don't know why we do this. We don't even talk about it, except, afterward, inevitably, to say, "Nothing much happening there." I think we are looking for a level of passion and intensity that would be the objective correlative, the adequate metaphor, for what we might timorously call our religious feelings. Mainstream churches have domesticated Jesus, exiled him forever among the lambs. I don't know much about Jesus, but I know that if half of what the Bible says is true, Christian churches would have signs in front saying, "Danger, proceed at your own risk." Looking for this energy, perhaps fearing to find it, we're drawn to scampy little independent churches. Snake handling might work for us.

We didn't think there were any Quaker communities around, so we looked up "Mennonite" in the phone book and reached a pastor somewhere inland, an hour's drive he told us. Then he began to pray, "O Lord Jesus, thank you for these seekers coming to look for you and bless them on their way, amen." Since both of us come from either silent or highly liturgical traditions—it comes to the same thing—we are always touched and puzzled when people take the trouble to pray over us. So we left seconds on the pancakes behind and got in the car. I put a scarf in my pocket in case they were head-covering Mennonites. We took a beautiful drive along the ocean, then inland along the Sesskit River through small towns that got poorer looking and poorer looking. It was my first sight of the economic devastation and poverty sprawl that coexist beside the environmentally fastidious architecture of coastal Oregon. Ten percent of the adult male population of the state is unemployed.

We followed an old pickup into the churchyard. The truck had a bumper sticker reading, "Hug a logger, you'll never go back to trees." The church was a simple white stucco building with a plain wooden cross in the front of the sanctuary. Lots of people were standing up to make announcements and offering public messages of one kind or another: how my dad made me get on the Sunday school bus and how glad I am because I still walk with the Lord.

The congregation sang strongly and stayed on the beat, as Mennonites know how to do, helped out by a lady at the piano and another in a honky-tonk pose with a guitar. A couple of giggly kids had the job of putting pages of hymn verses upside down and sideways into a projection device that shot them onto a screen, stage left.

The minister wore a brown knit shirt and black Sansabelt pants. After the kids were dismissed for Sunday school, only about twenty adults remained to hear a lengthy sermon on how Jesus could be both king and priest, leaded out with baseball metaphors. The minister seemed kind and sincere and, as we went out, he shook hands and remembered who we were from our phone conversation.

"You came such a long way," he said, "but it's a beautiful drive. I love where those alder trees branch over the road like a chapel." He formed his hands into a little steeple-house. Robin likes alders too much to have them stand for anything, but he smiled kindly as he shook the hands of the minister and the old men who had raised their arms in the air like bandits when they sang, "I surrender, Lord." What could they be feeling, waving their arms like that? I really want to know.

Robin, back in the car, was puzzling over why anybody cared how Jesus could be both king and priest. Having come from six generations of Quakerism, Robin has no space in his mind for theological hairsplitting, something Friends (me excluded) have little time for.

"I suppose that in the nineteenth century it helped people to keep their minds alive out in the country, debating stuff like that." All that catechism I memorized as a child gave me, at least, an inkling of taxonomy, even if applied to strange objectives like the ranks and rights-of-way of angel choirs.

We passed a shanty, the entire yard crowded with what could be the contents of three small houses. "Somebody saves things," I said.

"Somebody *male*," said Robin. "When I go to church, I would like to hear a sermon about how not to end up like that. What was the deal with those guys raising their arms in the air?"

"That was new to me."

"It's kind of moving and kind of creepy all at once."

"As if they were making themselves into lightning rods for something . . ."

". . . that isn't coming down."

"That isn't coming down."

I wonder how many people have had a religious experience sitting in a dusty classroom in Johns Hopkins University—Fort Hopkins, as we used to call it when I was studying Greek there. Few, I'll bet. I was translating the Gospel of John painstakingly out of Greek with my friend Stephen, a Jew. When you come to Jesus through a couple of foreign languages, it's possible to meet him with something like Beginner's Mind.

"If any of this is true," Stephen said suddenly, "it puts the whole world up for grabs."

We looked at each other for a suspended moment in which anything could have happened and nothing did. Then we went back to
figuring out the grammar.

So how can I blame the minister in his elastic waistband for not
helping us to get a handle on the thing? It surely took more gump-
tion than I possess for him to get up and preach to twenty people on
a Sunday morning.

The next day we took an old road along the ocean, winding up
in a coastal dairy capital, pea green in the rain and vaguely sulpher-
ous with what someone later told us was manure being sprayed into
the air—perhaps they meant chemical fertilizer, using the word
"manure" in a generic sense. To the Midwestern eye, Oregon's dairy
industry seems disconsolate; the cows look sad, the barns need a
government grant.

We stopped at a coffee shop in town and were served by an
aggressive man in suspenders. Neither he nor the woman who was
helping him could find the tea I asked for, though we all rifled
companionably among their piles and turned up something without
a label that smelled like tea. I taught her how to make it—to be fair,
it was a *coffee* shop. She had a kind of late-sixties, druggy air.
While we were chatting, other odd folk wandered in and rooted
around. We stopped later at a fish store and talked to three other
fairly demented people behind the counter. Another slice of the
seaside demographic.

Robin introduced me to the man behind the coffee counter as
"an environmental writer," which caused the man's suspenders
to swell over some internal combustion. He began to tell angry
stories about lies told by Oregon environmentalists in senate com-
mittees, stories in which the spotted owl was featured as a canny
opportunist building its nests in the buckets of logging rigs. Some
people near Sitka told me that when the Elks Hall burned down
in a nearby coastal town the fire fighters found a closet full of Ku
Klux Klan regalia.

Where *are* we? What is this place?

We have been, like bats, echolocating, trying to get a sense of the coast we have landed on. Without knowing it, by the end of that first week, we had laid out the geography, both physical and psychic, of my investigation into Oregon.

That particular day, we finished with a stop at the Oregon Coast Aquarium. Here, we discover live sea jellies encased in elaborate tubes of light; beside them are crafted sea jellies the artist Dale Chihuly has breathed into a shimmering glass display. It would be hard to choose, here, between art and nature, if both were for sale and one had a possessive spirit. Chihuly's, to their advantage, have the potential to exist forever. The pulsating, bottled sea creatures will, however, die; already they are translucent as ghosts, never more hardy than spirit on a good day. How many worlds like this are happening in our veins? Creations bodying forth forever this pulsing light?

Outside it rains.

Seahorses, curling their tails on each other, seem to be family, humorous; they swing in sargasso grass. Robin and I struggle across a deck in the pouring rain to visit other ocean creatures in their glass-fronted caves. The hundreds of discs of a pink octopus command her window. No one could make her in glass without losing her playfulness. But she is mortal, too, as are the drenched onlookers. Old fishermen down to the brown grandkids—all of us grinning at things we never imagined under the keel. The neon anemones pulse in their tank; beside them, glass anemones are for sale. Which is more real?—both doomed to be lost in the volcanic litter of this world, spun out, like me, in crystals finer than nerves, all things, because so unstable, beyond price.

What Are You Doing Here?

Inside you
there's an artist you don't know about.
He's not interested in how things look different in moonlight.
If you are here unfaithfully with us,
You're causing terrible damage.
If you've opened your loving to God's love,
You're helping people you don't know
And have never seen.
—Rumi, "Say Yes Quickly"

ROBIN HAS GONE HOME, and for a few days I looked into the eyes of the great solitude; no sooner have I begun to make my peace with it than visitors start to arrive—by a series of historical accidents, I have as many friends on the West Coast as I have in Minnesota, and a son in Seattle as well. Then there are my fellow "hermits," Brad and Karl. We have been told that artists-in-residence at Sitka Center sometimes become grouchy and reclusive, so we three have resolved to have dinner together once a week. It will turn out to be a good decision, for we are compatible buddies, gregarious over lasagna but respectful of each other's work time. And I, for my part, will learn a tremendous amount from these two.

People keep asking me what I'm doing here.

Just now, I'm sitting at the window with the heat turned up too high. Outside, globes of precipitation left over from morning fog shiver at the tips of the spruce candles as though awaiting a signal to change form. That's all that's going on in the world today. Millions of beads sparkle as the sun gets up; nothing more. Should I count it a productive morning, having learned to watch drops of water stand at attention, or do I have to write a double sestina to earn my keep? One by one the beads gather and fall into the grass. By evening they will all have made their passage or lost the chance: or a breeze will have whipped up and tossed them, or a hotter sun dried them to the boughs. That's what they do in the world, as the great spruces keep the hill in place and hold onto *sky holes*—as my painter friend, Karl, calls them—and only I in this patient, ancient action am new and restless. Wind stirs up a little circus of refraction. Everything we humans can make or imagine—chandeliers, bead curtains veiling mysterious doors—already exists here in the woods and our kind only comes along and copies it.

Usually when I go to the woods it takes me only a few days to slow down, but my rhythm has been interrupted by those welcome visitors, my relentless *going out* (complains the tide). I can't seem to still myself.

Someone—the artist who lived here last?—has left a pile of stones and shells on the table outside my house. They've gotten muddy and rucked with fallen leaves and spruce needles; finally, I rinsed the table and laid the beach combings out on the deck rail. I could not quite dispose of them, they were important to somebody for a day; somebody found them neither significant enough to take along nor insignificant enough to toss. How long will history pile up such shoals of stuff and how long will we keep it for each other as if they were coming back? Perhaps because we would want our own shoals preserved for our return, to ensure that we will return, although we won't. Mussel shell, trilobite, sea-sanded quartz.

Ashamed of my candy-ass boots from L. L. Bean, I walk into the margins of the Salmon River estuary at low tide. Wrack, riot, and sea will; a white heron fishing—what if I could learn to stand so

still? I smell silt and process, layer upon layer. I feel a claw of loneliness under my rib cage.

That's what I'm doing here, feeling that. If I open myself to
silence and solitude, I make it possible to see this much of what
Heron sees: the ripple of what's going on *underneath* the water. The
shadow of my prey.

Not that this makes me what passes for happy in the world, feeling loneliness, for example. Not that I am ready to accept what the
tide and weather toss my way. Often I don't care what's going on—
why are these stars flung like a net over my skylight? I want, at the
moment, baubles instead.

Today, wind has taken even the crystals out of the trees. Wind
came up in the night with a rioting sound, setting off lots of things
in the woods, bumps and scampers and the motion detector beside
the house. The motion detector, which ensures my safety in the
woods (as if we could be safe), flung bands of light in front of the
stars and woke me. I had had a good dinner of prawns cooked with
garlic, olive oil, kalamata olives, lemon juice, and thyme over angel-
hair pasta; yet I woke up at 3 a.m., hungry and listening to the wind.

That's another thing I'm doing here, feeling hungry.

"The care of rivers is not a question of rivers, but of the human heart,"
writes Tanaka Shozo in the frontispiece to a book I'm reading on the
ecology of rivers and estuaries.

It is tempting to close myself to the strangeness of this world,
simply shut down. I know oak savannahs. I know boreal forest. But
this country confounds me with its tidal river, its pulsing estuary and
the demented ocean beyond, crying for human sacrifice. Like a
student who has taken one class too many, I want to quit school.

Today they came and taught me to pray a new way, at the null
point where salt and riverine waters oppose each other, neither side
winning, and there is a lot to win: sharp glance of the spruce in these

parts, standing up to its wind. Today they came and taught me to name the claw in my heart *no one*, how the tide withdraws yielding plastic and jellied wrack, *nothing*. It is so painful to absorb these lessons that I flee to the library for consoling facts: "*An estuary is the wide lower course of a river where its current is met and influenced by the ocean tides. It can also be thought of as an arm of sea extended inland to meet the mouth of a river.*"

The catechism defines *prayer* as a lifting up of the mind and heart to God. Prayer is a word that has become so vexed in our modern consciousness that I cannot hear it without a crash of gears. How can one have "first thoughts" about prayer? Gulls are good at *lifting up*, the deer that browsed by my window this morning never travel without their hearts. What funny animals we humans are. How did we get this way? We seem to have evolved *away* from a state of simple blessing—toward what? The pleasures of the freeway.

If I cannot lift up my heart—it is too heavy—and if I cannot decide if God is up or down—I can unleash my heart. Let it run.

This whole shitty business of going off to the woods and trying to be solitary is about what? Limitation. Simplification. *So that one can see.* During my time of echolocating, I drove up and down the ocean road, trying to get a sense of the larger placement: on such and such a coast, not far from such and such a small town, under this head-land with its history and lies and half-buried dead. Over the skylight above my bed is flung Indra's net of stars—or, to be accurate, only a few feet of net—tails of constellations I can't get a fuller sense of. Is that line of stars Orion's belt or someone else's belt, trying to mark for me where I've been or where I'm going?

In sixth grade the nuns gave up on me and my friend Gregory Kinney, and we just sat on the floor in the back of the room reading protestant science books about Cowboy Hal's nature trips with his L'il Podner, Timmy. Gregory and I would quiz each other, mispro-nouncing the Pleiades, full of wonder that there could be a dog in the sky. We thought it was all better than Jesus and his dubious resurrection. In the Cowboy Hal science books, dotted lines connected star to star. When I went outside, however, it was all dis-appointing star soup. Where were those helpful lines? I could not, still can't—by the light of poetry or science or calligraphy—connect the dots.

Instead, I make another trip down to the Salmon River estuary at low tide, determined to get a grip. This time I can't actually wade in the water. My boots sink sludgily up to the ankle bones and remind me of all the stories I've heard about quicksand. Heron, her aerodynamics apparently so unsound, takes to the air a few yards ahead of me. For the first time I notice that there are little houses set into the oceanside everywhere. People around here make simple shelters of unpainted wood and gray shingle—for all I know there's a rule, a good rule, about fitting yourself anonymously into the wilderness. Houses pop out of the bushes like little nests of winter wren in blackberry. No one is home, though. These people seem to inhabit their spaces only in summer, maybe on weekends, maybe never. My own home is far from here and I'm hermit-crabbing in somebody else's shell.

Do any of us belong here at all?

My library book is willing to reply, but perhaps it has not grasped the extent of the question: "In just 142 years, from the start of Lewis and Clark's epic travels in 1803 to the end of World War II in 1945, we in the United States have achieved the technological capability of disarranging and disarticulating the basic biological functioning of the world."

Winter Coast

Let whoever brought me here take me back.
—Rumi

ON THIS COAST, IN WINTER, the sea does not come and go, it stands forever and roars. It doesn't rise and fall and tickle the gravel, it lies there yelling. The sea gets up in its cradle like a child with a tantrum and never stops crying out. I used to sleep next to freeway noise and pretend it was the ocean. Now I sleep by the ocean and dream of relentless cars.

Breakdown. I don't know how to look at a new coast. In the center of some wheel a rattle begins and a wobble starts. But the mind will not stop demanding order, looking up words in the dictionary, getting a library card. Mind struggles against the new coast as though something were trying to drown it in a burlap bag.

My sense of oppressive loneliness is getting sharper. It comes on in the morning like a kind of jaded flu and it feels in the stomach for all the world like fear. I feel as though I can't see myself in the mirror; I feel like I've lost my shadow. The natural world of the West Coast is vast and overpowering. I have no chance against it. There are warning signs everywhere about *tsunamis* and *subduction zones*. And the people around here are, as we say in Minnesota, *different*. I keep looking for my own kind. I had to go grocery and household-trinket shopping today, out among the coastal tribes: on the one hand, you find the wealthy and well groomed; on the other, morbidly obese women and unshaven men pushing their carts in the (so-called) Safeway. Here, the social classes seem sharply divided in a way you don't find in the middle of the country.

Over our weekly potlucks, Brad Mattson helps me with the sociology. He calls the Northwest an "extraction culture"; big, brawny men have been imported for the sole purpose of taking things out of the land without putting things back and, now that everything extractable is gone, the men are standing around angry, disheveled, and looking for trouble. Perhaps this history, what Thich Nhat Hanh used to call "environmental karma," is what makes me feel, in the midst of so much beauty, unsettled. If Karl Marx were correct about the roots of class warfare, which he seems not to have been, this coast would be fomenting revolution. Instead, I think the displaced loggers and fishermen turn on themselves and each other and their wives. "They're all on dope or Jesus," Brad tells me.

The farming culture I come from—though it has its bloody-minded aspect—cannot be based on extraction, but rather on the careful return of what's taken out, so that morning comes and evening, the pace of work is consistent, and the rest deep for man and animal. I think farming is closer to a natural rhythm of life, what was intended for this creature by the creator. I say this with a xenophobic sniff.

But Brad, who is so full of ideas new to me, says we mustn't try to turn the whole world into a farm. For example, he inveighs against farmed salmon, because he says that only men who fish in the wild take care of the wild. He espouses, I guess, Gary Snyder's land ethic as opposed to Wendell Berry's. These are two distinct ways of being in the world, not quite opposed, but yielding, certainly, different environmental perspectives.

There was a beautiful sunset, though I saw only its reflection in my little west window. Four small, brown mule deer came to browse near my house. I report finding bear scat just up the hill.

"Oh, no," Brad hoots. "That was me."

❀

I do not share Henry David Thoreau's contempt for news. I call my friends and loved ones, though I have little to say: I saw four mule deer; I saw two herons or the same heron twice. This is not social currency. I fall silent on the phone, watching the waves turn over.

Might this trip to the west have been a terrible mistake? I could be in England or in Costa Rica learning Spanish or visiting my kids in their far-flung habitats. Instead I am lost in the Safeway, my stomach a bowl of hunger for what I cannot name. God, on his usual trajectory across the heavens, does not pick up his cell. Robin, who does, says that talking to me is like talking to a child at camp: "In a few weeks you won't even remember being homesick, and then you won't want to come back."

Here comes a young deer out of the wood. What drives them out among men? The grass cannot be so much greener. Is this God's answer?

Every day, like patient evangelicals, the animals come out of the forest, out of the ocean, down from the headland, to instruct their whiny, recalcitrant pupils.

"Why do you keep warning each other about *subduction zones* and *tsunamis?* The real tsunami is in the unfocused brain. I wouldn't have your wits for the world," says Herring Gull, "your pity and sanitation. You have no wings to speak of, you worry about death and whether the work will be any good. I have no idea why I face north for hours when the wind blows. I just sit on the grass in a wedge of my kind looking down the throat of it all without any strong opinions. When the winds die, I might chase the brown yearlings a little, show the wing; otherwise it's just fish shadows and maybe the pleasure of hovering."

Heron speaks: "You stand there on the shore in the dress of your life, tattery strings loose in the wind, waiting to be something as elemental as that log, waiting to disappear, waiting to get a window again on that opal sky just as the sun slides off the ocean's face. The tide keeps giving and taking, you alone think about it."

When I get back to Minnesota, Robin will ask, "How did you know when it was time to leave the woods?"

"When I began to think I could understand what the animals were saying, I figured it was time to drive to Seattle."

He will smile enigmatically. "Maybe you missed your big chance."

The Productive Animals

BUT I STAY. BUDDHIST PRACTICE HAS TRAINED ME that the edge that feels like breakdown is the edge you have to lean gently against. I have fallen back from it a thousand times, refused to grow. What we might call a mature practice gives one little more than the ability to hang a minute longer on the verge of annihilation. I think of myself as a bat on the curtains, resolving to hang. The curtains are on fire.

But gratefully I realize that this life at Sitka is giving me exactly the conditions I need to work and make progress, the rhythm I love best: I get up with the sun, have a cup of tea, sit meditation, and get down to writing till noon. Mostly I write poetry, a discipline I have followed all my adult life, more precious in that it comes to what the world would call "nothing." I seldom send my poems out, I don't exert myself to publish them. But I know that whatever else I do in the world I do because at birth I was poured into a poet's skin. If I don't practice this craft I am being unfaithful to the core of my identity, like a musician who refuses to practice scales.

Spiritual practice—as distinct from religious belief or intellectual assent—has to be daily and regular. It's more important that the exercise be regular than that it be difficult. If we skip the practice, it's as dumb as going on stage at Carnegie Hall without that daily foundation of scales. When you are stretched or frightened or shocked, when grief has just crashed through the picture window, you have to fall back on a practice that has become second nature. When the curtains are on fire is not the ideal time to start spiritual practice—although it can be a moment of awakening.

There are exceptions to this rule, which is why Luther spent such a long time in the outhouse pondering *grace*. I know musicians who practice little and play well. Every symphony orchestra is full of such stories. Perhaps these musicians are carried along on some ancestral gifts or gilded DNA. There are people gifted like that in the spiritual realm. Some children are born into families irradiated with spiritual presence; such children seem to go out into the world with the right wardrobe, as it were, and all the moves in place.

For the rest of us, there's practice.

After these morning scales and calisthenics, I like to spend the afternoon in some physically strenuous activity. I had hoped my afternoons would include work in the ceramic studio or volunteering at a wildlife rehabilitation center, but both of these alternatives have been blocked. The potter's wheel at Sitka has been set counterclockwise by the Japanese potter who preceded me, and I am too inexperienced to reverse it. The wildlife center in town has been closed by local ordinance, and the next alternative is several hours' drive over the mountains. None of these setbacks surprises me. When you set yourself up a spiritual program, a pilgrimage, or a retreat, it's inevitable that your plans fall into ruins from the get-go. If you miss your train or break an ankle in whatever Kathmandu of the soul you are visiting, it's a sure sign you are on the path. It's another version of the first law of spiritual dynamics: breakdown is the path to breakthrough.

So instead, I throw myself into hiking and coastal exploration, or I swim laps at the pool in town when the rain is sheeting down.

I love the two-hour hike up Cascade Head, some 3,000 feet above the ocean. All the flora and fauna are new to me, and I carry a backpack full of field guides. If something runs past you at mouse-height, it's a winter wren, skidding along the top of the underbrush, lying about the location of its nest. Salmonberry (*Rubus spectabilis*): magenta blossoms, leaves alternate, deciduous; three sharp-toothed leaflets. The ripening of salmonberry is associated in many native cultures with the call of Swainson's thrush. I love learning about these cosmic connections, the things animals take in, nose to the ground, without ever thinking about it: call of thrush, scent of magenta blossom, time to fly. Patiently I apologize to the animals as I sketch pistil, stamen, feather: this is how my kind orders its world. *Spring Beauty* of the portulacas, purslane family. *Claytonia sibirica* ("Miner's Lettuce").

Sitting above the ocean, I consider the possibility that, paging through my field guides, I am trying to get the effects of grace without working too hard. I'm a lot like my dog, Shep, who hates to retrieve sticks from the water, but will steal them from a more compliant, wet dog and lay them at my feet. I spent yesterday trying to live in the present moment and doing walking meditation much of the day, but now I realize it was mostly to have the effects of walking meditation, the lifting of loneliness and homesickness, or to gain the beginning of some insight. Did Thoreau go to the woods hoping to come out with an analysis?

Well, probably. We can't seem to help it. We are the *productive animals*. (Now I generalize my personal problem across the whole species.) I sit here looking into a beautiful woods, but it's no good unless the deer emerge. Which makes me, too, a member of the extraction culture.

I lack faith. I'm not sure that stillness opens onto anything but dread and panic. Dread sends me back to listening to my Spanish tapes or studying forest ecology. Which journey of the mind should I follow—to be still and open, or get something the hell done? How can I be both faithful and practical? How hard would it be to justify to my grandmother or to my mistress of novices that I sit all morning writing poetry? I don't want to change my program just because things are difficult and unrewarding; but neither do I want to waste my life.

Having thought this, I open the volume of Rumi I'm packing and find

"Is this stuff poetry? It's what birds sing in cages.
Where are the words spoken by the birds of Solomon?
. . . .

Suppose your leg is gimpy and you have to hop, what's
the difference?

I'm gimpy and it makes no difference. This is the life I am.

Later, I hiked a mile or so along a forest trail at the top of the
Salmon River estuary, where I find alder and western red cedar, at
one point three big trees growing out of the fallen body of a huge
nurse log. I miss my dear Robin for many reasons, not the least of
which is his handiness as a walking, talking guidebook. I see more
than I used to see in the woods, perhaps more than the average
English major, but nothing compared to what he sees and hears and
does not tell unless asked. I love how he traces our past in the world
by guideposts like "that hollow where we heard the white-throated
sparrow." As other men might say, "Seventh and Wabasha."

Around 5:30 p.m., I go down to the river to catch sunset where
the Salmon River flows into the ocean. Who ever named her
Pacific? I would have named her *Dementia,* throwing herself at the
cliffs there in front of me. The winter ocean, here, I'm told, is as wild
as anything on earth except the Bering Sea. No ebb and flow, no
melancholy long withdrawing roar for her, just Roar. If one were a
painter, this would be a place to paint, or a place to stop painting
forever in humble surrender. I watched an otter surface in the river
and roll over, showing a good broad back like a husband turning in
bed. The otter did not rise again, but swam out toward the reefs.

By morning, the Northwest coast will have given itself over to
the chill incessant rain that makes it fecund. Rain on the skylight
three feet above my head, and the ocean at ear level, keep trying to
charm me back to winter hibernation.

That first bitter loneliness has given way to a more tranquil solitude. I wonder what emptiness I can create inside myself to meet
this relentless woods outside my window, that just implacably *is?*
Would it even be safe to try? If I found it, would I have words to tell?

I'm not a great vessel, anyway, to be filled. There's a common
fungus in these woods that I find on my daily penetrations, a

gastromycete called a "Bird's Nest." It presents itself as tiny cups, no more than half an inch at the mouth, laid out along a branch. The job of each tiny cup is to catch a raindrop, which will scatter its spores; then its work is done. Everything in the woods has its mouth open somehow, like me, but not very wide.

Rapture of the Height

QUITE SUDDENLY IN FEBRUARY, wind and bright weather break through and everything speeds up, except, of course, me. As I drive into town, I see a high field full of brown horses, ponies on a background of brown grass, easy to miss, laid out in an orderly pattern, each animal giving the others a precise measure of distance. They look like horses sewn onto a medieval tapestry. "Funny," I think, "I've never seen horses pastured around here before." One animal, who seems to have positioned himself in a superior hierarchical position, raises an antlered head. Elk.

I couldn't get close enough to see the composition of the herd. At this season, I'm told elk travel in separate male-female herds and only get together for Yearly Meeting. Some young males may hang with the females, tolerated by the matriarch, rather as young bull elephants do.

On the beach by D River a man is flying a motorized kite, half engine of wind, half will. He aims it at children, who scream and run. A dog goes crazy trying to get a snap. Old women with curly white dogs they apparently wash every day give him a wide berth. In their windbreakers, pink, acid green, lavender, they try to make it a few feet into the gale. They carry their lives in big plastic purses containing all the reasons they got to this beach in winter, loving yappy dogs more than anything, sad-looking or triumphant, seeming to call the day a good deal.

There's so much going on around here. The San Juan de Fuca plate, for example, is pushing inexorably against the North American plate, creating that infamous subduction zone, a space

214

where anything can happen. Coastal people are supposed to know how to handle earthquakes and tsunamis, the way we in Minnesota handle blizzards and tornadoes. It's dramatic and sublime. My son says that when he rides his mountain bike into the rain forest, he wouldn't be surprised to come upon a brontosaurus with a stalk of Douglas fir in his mouth, like a piece of broccoli. Then there is the San Andreas Fault to think about. When I tell her about this on the phone, my sister, Peggy, says it doesn't seem fair that all this innocent country could fall into the sea, brontosaurus and all. San Francisco and Los Angeles might be, in her view, fair game.

There is so much happening. My head was being turned and turned again, as I drove down Three Rocks Road toward the estuary, by the emergence of skunk cabbage, its yellow cobra-headed bracts shining lantern-like at the damp margin. The Northwest coast tribes used skunk cabbage leaves as wrapping paper for food, shelf lining, and so on. It was the all-purpose plant. They ate it, too, when no other food was available. According to a Kathamet story, its central spike is a war club given to the plant by Creator, as a reward for feeding people during the famine time.

Last night, exploring the mouth of the Siletz River where it pours into the ocean, I looked across to a bank of whitish rocks, uniform in size, that looked like an array of flour sacks. Then I saw that they were seals, laying up, about a hundred of them. I spent the next hour informing every child I met on the beach about the seals. It was fun to watch them run and tell the grown-ups. Soon I was seeing seals, playing or working as the case may be, all through the surf as I walked along the ocean. I wanted to get in and swim with them, sure they would welcome me with cold nudges and svelte kicks.

At low tide I put on my stupid boots and went back to the river to see how close I could get to the seal bank, but it had moved into the ocean, where I could see a couple of hundred heads and flippers flipping. There was a strong northeast wind; a big black standard poodle, daintily clipped, ran along the beach. Seldom have I seen a dog looking so out of his element, which was, maybe, Manhattan. A bunch of boys in Bob Marley shirts were building shelters of drift-wood and hauling crab pots down to the water. They'd built a huge fire, and were dragging sleeping gear and coolers down into their structure. Those boys were getting ready to have the best fun of their lifetimes, and I wish I could have tucked myself away in a corner of their fine shack.

I'm keeping in my heart today the anniversary of my student, Juan, who committed suicide last year. *Poor foolish boy, he might have lived to see this.* Or maybe he is this. If I were a benevolent god I would send the souls of those who kill themselves back as seals on the Northwest coast—playing a lot, it appears. Or working very little.

The sun sets in the Pacific Ocean below Cascade Head; over my southern shoulder the full moon rises. I have to take my walks by the clock, so as to be off the headland and into the woods by 5:30 or risk being caught after dark. Something like "rapture of the deep" affects one, rapture of the height. I always want to walk ten minutes longer than I should. Douglas fir outlined against topaz, amber, the color of the bottom of a beer bottle, as I hurry home. A crash to the left of the trail—it's the female elk, big uncouth beige animals who seem composed of equal parts llama, camel, and deer. Around their necks are tatty collars of darker brown fur. I catch a scent reminiscent of—rabbits. Well, they are herbivores, after all. I hope they can smell herbivore on me and will stand still for a photo, but they will not. Deer and elk will stare at you just till your hand goes into your pocket, at which moment they exhibit the instincts of my cousins in the police. I like to get out of the woods before Cougar Dating Time. Cougars stalk people out of curiosity, for practice.

I jog back to my glass house, read in bed, and listen to the wind rise. Twice in my lifetime, trees have fallen on houses I've been living in, narrowly missing the inhabitants. Surely a third will arrive. It's only a matter of time. Therefore, whenever it storms, I lie wakeful under the wind and expect to be pinned to the mattress.

Tonight the ocean is on her toes, and into the full moon a cougar screams. I'm at that age when dreams are more real than e-mail. I wake with a mandate, but what is it I am called to do? I can't remember what the dream told me. Maybe get out of my dangerous bed and climb by moonlight up Cascade Head, traverse swollen streams in the dark, and look straight into that firing golden stare I caught in the headlight coming home. *Cougar* crouched in the dogwood, waiting for me. Maybe the wind will keep her at home tonight.

I yawn and drag on my boots and jeans, head out for the trail. Sometime before morning the tree falls, an old-growth spruce that made this appointment a long time ago. When I get back from the woods, I find the tree asleep in my bed. Or is it the cougar asleep in my bed? No, I am asleep in my bed, dreaming the cougar's dream as maybe she is dreaming mine. *Where am I? What time is it?*

The beginning of March slipped past me, many days spent entertaining visitors. It's such an effort to swim through the layers and layers of white, green, silver, and ice to the space where humans breathe. Today it's raining. I'll go to the beach at Pacific City and sit between the SUVs; I'll listen to the relentless whining of motors and teenagers. Perhaps I will put on my seal costume and walk on the beach, leaving humans behind.

The Danger of Something Happening

ANOTHER RAGING STORM HAS LULLED ME to sleep late, past 8 a.m. Something big as a mother comes to sit with me through these nights. I waken calm and pacified, washed clean.

But my eyes flutter open and I have to pound out of bed and into the car. It will take me at least an hour and a half to drive north up the coast road to the Friends church. My son found this church for me on his drive back to Seattle. These are not "our kind" of Quakers, but rather an evangelical community that established itself on the edge of the known world a hundred years or so ago. Rather than sitting silently in a circle, as we do at home, waiting for an individual to speak or "minister," these Friends have something like a regular church service, with a pastor and a choir leader. The only thing that's familiar to me is the twenty minutes or so of silence in the middle of the service during which members of the community can respond to—what we would call—*spirit*.

As I reach the distant coastal village, the ocean suddenly rears its gray self to my left. I pull up at the church. Tears begin to crash down my face, one after the other. I'm not exactly *crying;* I'm just responding. To what, exactly, I don't know. The little church seems to sit on some eruption of holiness, like a natural spring. When I quit being religious, as a graduate student, it was a quit of the mind; my mind went to work on the religious stories of my childhood, judged them, and found them illogical. But my heart has been wandering along for many years complaining: *What am I supposed to do with my love and my longing? What am I supposed to do with all I know about surrender and connection?* Nowadays, I've made some degree of

218

peace between my mind and heart. The more a church tries to make logical sense of Christianity—as do the Episcopalians or Unitarians—the less I can stand it. The pastor at Friends church is intelligent; he quotes C. S. Lewis; he does not fret about how Christ can be both priest and king. Yet, without being sentimental or manipulative, he leads from the heart. When he talks about his longing for "revival"—a vexed word—I feel hunger for some big takeover.

But I'm impatient with religious words. I want to go into the woods, like the porcupine I met on the road as I was driving to church, without a conceptual frame. It was a kick to encounter that quilly perception boring into the blackberry vines, his joy in stripping the green shoots. As I parked on the narrow road to watch him, he looked without envy at my car, flashing its warning lights to the weather. The new candles of Sitka spruce stretched white against the sky. The wind just whacks off the dead stuff. Spruce doesn't have to try. Spruce has no knees to fall on.

The Quaker meeting I belong to in Minnesota—"unprogrammed," as we say—is eclectic in its alliances. There is a study group on "Quakers Without God," for example, and another called "Friends of Jesus"; many people caucus with both. We are pretty serene in the midst of such mental gymnastics. But most people in our meeting have never encountered the kind of evangelical Quakers I met on the West Coast.

Nor have evangelical Quakers necessarily dealt with our kind. In this small, rural Oregon community of loggers and fishermen, I could never describe myself in a way that made sense to people. I would say I was, hmmm, a Philadelphia Quaker. This was by way of explaining why I got red in the face when they talked about Satan. One woman there mentioned that she had once fetched up at an unprogrammed inland Quaker meeting where everybody sat in a circle and kept silence. "Somebody must have had a clock running," she said, "because at a certain moment they all leapt up, shook hands, and started to talk about politics." I got the feeling that the time had been *interminable* for her. She said, "That was one of the strangest experiences of my life." She looked at me suspiciously.

Many things about this rural church were uncongenial to me, the Tabasco dash of Satan, the *music*: lurid and sentimental Christian soft-rock love songs, full of feeling and big brown eyes. I think of it as music trying to get Jesus into the back seat of the Chevy. But surprising as it may seem, given the levels of suspicion between our two synods or schisms, I fell in love with the Friends church.

I loved this church and these people and this pastor, despite Satan and the music. If I could have gotten saved to please them, I would have. Because something was happening in that church. Something was afoot, as Sherlock Holmes would say. The prophetic spirit was wildly loose in this Friends church. I felt as much as home there as I felt in the woods. And as much in danger.

Half-Assed

THE MULE DEER, WHICH OFTEN COME to my window in the morning, have a peculiar high-stepping gait adapted to rocky terrain and getting the hell out of vertical spaces. They come to the windows of my house as if I were mule-deer TV, and they look into my eyes like nervous sweethearts. Wait—are they mule deer or are they black-tailed deer? I look them up in my natural history books. The distinction between these two subspecies is almost irrelevant. *Columbianus*, blacktail, has no white at all on his tail, while *hemionus*, ("half-ass") i.e., mule deer, has only a black tip. They are smaller than the whitetails at home and have big (mulish) ears.

Like geese, deer tolerate humankind quite well. They applaud our deforestation because meadows and second-growth forest provide them with succulent browse. We have chased back the cougars and wolves that once reduced their numbers. Our dogs trouble them, but perhaps provide a tempting model of domestication. High stepping closer and closer to my window, the doe comes on, as though coveting the tea things.

Like every animal I've seen around here, deer love to strip blackberry canes. Cud chewers need little bits of this and that nutrient to feed not only themselves but the bacteria that handle digestion in their first stomachs. These bacteria are what permit them to survive on a high-roughage diet, but the bacteria in turn must be supplied with their protein requirement. So the deer instinctively eat for two orders of being—or probably for many more—as do we. These dietary choices often make little sense to the observer: the old-man's beard lichen the does strip off trees has no more nutritional content than a Popsicle. Yet they must have it. The naturalist Daniel Mathews believes it "enhances the deer's utilization of plant nutrients in the winter diet of twigs, evergreen needles and leaves." Huh? I'm staring out the window, too warm and sleepy again. It's been stormy for two weeks and I haven't gotten out as much as usual. The forest trails, precipitous and muddy, aren't a safe bet for the solitary hiker. So I go into town and swim or walk the forty-five-minute circle route along the road by the river and up the hill. Last night, I met a woman running alongside a white pony.

Yesterday, Sunday, I drove across the mountains to Salem for the unprogrammed Friends meeting, the "Philadelphia Quakers." I felt I needed to regain perspective on my own tradition. In comparison to the coastal Friends church, this inland community had the air of a depressed little circle sitting in the rain. But appearances are deceptive. A silent meeting sometimes feels strange to the interloper, and, unaccountably, I felt like an interloper. But the minute the circle was released from silence there came a great spring into action—rally in this corner, good deeds in another, children pouring in, full of energy.

I wish these two traditions could better tolerate each other, the head and the heart. To many unprogrammed Friends, Jesus is a great embarrassment. Just to see a picture in the vestibule of those great turned-up brown eyes would make them hightail it, like mule deer. To the evangelical Friends, conversely, Jesus is the *sine qua non:* once you have felt this reality, you are obligated to declare what you have felt.

"Do your children know the Lord?" one of the doughty coastal women asked me recently.

I actually started to stutter. "I don't know." Maybe I should ask them. Both of my children seem to be religious as casually and calmly as they are Midwesterners. Without making any big deal of it, or suffering through the kind of crises that characterized my own religious upbringing, they could fill in a couple of blanks on any questionnaire about religious beliefs. But I don't think anyone in my family can fathom this idea of having a personal relationship with Jesus. It makes me think of the teenaged girl I hitchhiked with in England, back in the sixties, who fantasized a personal relationship with Ringo Starr. It makes me think of people who believe Elvis rose from the dead.

The fact that I have thoughts like this is what keeps me an unprogrammed Friend or crypto-Buddhist, or maybe it just keeps me sitting in the religious baby chair. When I make an act of faith, it is in the possibility of human connection, the potential of each individual to burn through to a bedrock of integrity, and the responsibility of us all to try to do, for purely rational reasons, the corporal and spiritual works of mercy. I profess *religion without belief*.

The churchwoman went on to ask, "If you don't know the Lord, what's the point?" I think I can answer that. Give me a moment.

Despite all my intellectual reservations, if that's what they are, I feel a dark room in my house-of-being fill with light at the Friends church. This room is only rarely illuminated at an unprogrammed meeting. Robin says simply, "There is not enough passion."

We feel, we humans, a longing that pushes beyond the boundaries of species, like that of the mule deer that wants to sit at my kitchen table. *Maybe*—see, I don't know—some people put this feeling in the Jesus category. Jesus, the Concept, is as good a place as any to put it.

Does this mean I *believe*? That I am *saved*? That I have taken Christ for my Lord and Savior? Well, I don't think so.

The Hermit's Candle

The candle the hermit lights goes out in the worldly church.
—Hafez

I'M LISTENING TO NEWS OF ENDLESS WAR on public radio, while looking at a Christmas cactus somebody else nourished in my glass house and left to bloom, with careful instructions for a faceless new tenant, me, whom she imagined would be provident enough to water it. Some of our visions do come true. The plant's transparent red flowers, flecked with orange, surge out of each green base, bird-like. How different would the world be if men sat around in kitchens thinking about the flamingo forms of Christmas cactus, dreamed of the dresses they might sew, red-orange flounces feathering off green hips, instead of dreaming about rocket grenades? Why do we laugh at drag queens but, for generals, cut our hair and try to look noble, as if we could reclaim the purity of our grandfathers with a buzz cut and a bombing run?

I look up. *There is always a face at the window*, always interrogation from landscape: sometimes a mule deer or that rollicky porcupine perfectly aware that he is God's mistake. He is glad to be excused from the rocket science and petting, not hunted, and with only a small gullet to fill at the blackberry table. Sometimes I'm aware of the heavy root of the sky that holds itself to the headland out of fellowship; I suffer the bruising inquiry of rough-needled stars; of small critters needing a leg up to look in the window. There is some form of ranuncula climbing up the moss on a Sitka spruce nearby; there are alders crying alder tears so different from ours that we

224

never know they are desolate. I have had so many wild visitors this week, licking, tapping the glass they could break if they wanted to, asking the answer to all the things that I know. Whilst, for their part, *refusing to tell*.

To call this "landscape" begs an epistemology. I am their house-scape, their polymechanical horror, an asteroid crawling with virus crashed on their hill. Listening to the radio news, I want the animals to run from me, never grow tame to my kind. This house is the ark of a terrible covenant spilled in their woods. *Flee, be silent, pray, while you have the will*, St. Procopius counseled the Desert Fathers.

Nose to nose at the glass, the alder tears they have taught me run down my leaves.

Yes, I'm sitting here crying over the woods. Repudiating my white, furless skin.

Yesterday I went down to the Sitka office to beg a copy of the *Sunday Oregonian* to get the latest scoop on a man "nicked," "wounded," or "attacked"—reporters' opinions vary about what might be the appropriate verb—by an owl he was feeding. This man and his wife founded the raptor center in Bend, Oregon. They had a long-resident pet owl that flew to the man's glove every day for a frozen chick. That pet attracted another owl who also got into the snack line. A talon of the wild owl "nicked"—let us choose that verb—the man through a hole in his gauntlet.

A few days later he came down with a devastating set of neuro-logical symptoms. He almost died—had I been he, I would rather have died—but he survived, both mute and quadriplegic. After many attempts at diagnosis, the doctors settled on viral hepatitis. The owl disappeared, so they thought she had gone off to die. The man, however, remains alive and in possession of his faculties. What is more surprising, he continues brave and engaged in the work of wildlife rehabilitation, despite his new limitations.

When I asked in the office after this article, which I had glimpsed at the library in town, heads went up. Everyone immediately swung in with spirit, against the reporters and on the side of the owl.

"They made it seem like the owl cold-bloodedly went for him," said Amy.

"Nobody knows how you get viral hepatitis," said Dee, whose husband is a physician.

I saw this same partisanship with the wilderness years ago when a friend's daughter was attacked by a bear in Yellowstone. My friend complained how the rangers seemed more worried about the reputation of the bears than about his daughter. Fortunately, she made a good recovery. So did my friend, Laura, a naturalist park ranger, who was pulled out of her sleeping bag and slashed by a grizzly. For Laura, the attack was a metaphysical challenge. She loves the wilderness, but her injuries were soul searing. She quickly turned her anger on tourists. She ranted about humans who feed bears and harass and semitame them, so that they have the gall to see a solitary tent as a kind of wilderness refrigerator, with Laura on the shelf.

The religion of my youth counseled me always to take the difficult path, to be suspicious of the easy victory, the full stomach, the good sleep, in favor of rigor and sacrifice—*but why?* the black-tailed deer inquires. Follow my path up to the mountain meadow and notice how in every respect I head for blowsy pasture. Your chosen path would go straight up into the brambles. My trails crisscross, traversing the mountainside so that it seems to my brain that my hooves are always on level ground. While easily moving up the slope, I crop continually my heart's desire and give thanks after the manner of my kind. All of our paths on this mountain are so hard, finally, that when the path is easy, take it and make a memory of plenty to console you through grim days. When no one has an arrow trimmed on you, give thanks and forage for the greenest shoots you can find.

Sea Lions

ON THE WEEKEND, I DROVE EARLY to Newport and spent the day with my old friends, Eileen and Jim Flory. We went to Corvallis, an hour's drive over the coastal range, to a "Philadelphia" Quaker meeting, where Jim is clerk. We did a little touring on the way back of the sea lion colony in Newport, old dads fighting with each other for a place to nap while their harems raise the pups down south. Here (Eileen told me) is the difference between seals and sea lions:

Sea lions: browner range of color; external earlobes; present on front flippers in the characteristic "sit": weigh around 600 pounds; go *ook-ook-ook* very loudly; sea lions are natural performers; they are the animals "trained" in marine shows and called "seals," although they aren't.

Seals: grayer range; sleek heads; don't "sit"; much smaller; do not go *ook;* hang out with no desire to extrovert.

Eileen, who works at the Oregon Coast Aquarium, told me that the sea lions are so huge that their performing skills have to be solicited in order for veterinarians to care for them; they are taught to open their mouths, play dead, and follow a ball on a stick to get them through routine medical and dental procedures.

Monday, Monday: I'm thrumming with go-to-work rhythm. As I walk down to the estuary I feel a pull from behind me where the sun makes its demand to be watched as it rises. The meadow with the white sun behind it becomes a sheet of light, each blade of grass holding its rain crystal at the tip. My eyes don't want to take it in. Human families are back in the woods this week, kids home from college until Easter, much wood smoke over the valley, animals gone to ground. It's whale-watching time as well and that brings in a lot of tourists. All of those little shacks in the woods are full of people from Portland or Seattle.

"That's where they pulled the child from the water"—I heard a man say—*"and over there another,"* his friend replies.

"Have you been following the story?" someone asks me.

"No," I say, meaning, "Yes. For millennia." Folk music has a huge category called "murder ballads." I think of one of the most sordid, in which a man pulls a murdered girl from the river and makes fiddle strings of her long yellow hair and tuning pegs of her small finger bones; when he draws a fiddle bow across this gothic instrument, he gives her a voice to cry out the name of her murderer.

On the low piers, the sea lion fathers fight for a space to nap, one pup like another to them. A tourist points to a balcony over the bay. *They lived there, that's where he dropped them in.*

We are all starting to wake up earlier and earlier. My skylight glows opal at 6 a.m. I hear the clatter of an elk harem, the big disorganized animals falling over their own panicky feet, as I hike up the Cascade Head. I am always afraid they will slide down the mountain and fall on me in their urgency to get away. They are rather dim, like the women I saw in the Safeway last night, pushing their carts, trying to get out of there. One of them smacked her two-year-old, who was tormenting the baby: "I'll teach you to hit somebody smaller." The grocery-store ladies damage everything in their way, just by force of thoughtless momentum. Their faces are wizened and cracked from hourly pulls on the cigarette. Their lives are desperately hard.

The cashier coughs and smiles at me, calls me by name as cashiers are taught to do, in case the manager's watching. She has to work until 1 a.m., she won't get home until 3. It's a two-hour drive up the coast road home, she says. "You have a nice day, Miss Reilley." This is not my name, but it's on the credit card, and the credit card people refuse to change it; they say it makes no difference.

"You too, Saundra," I say back, reading her plastic name tag. It's not her real name either, Saundra tells me; she took it off the soaps one day when she and Belle—that's not her real name—were so bored they were just sitting in front of the TV watching the orange and green easterners and picking the polish off their toenails. "Wouldn't you just like to be somebody different?" one of them said, they can't remember whose idea it was. So they got a can of Dr. Pepper and baptized each other.

"Are you watching the Oscars tonight, Saundra?"

"Honey, I won't get home in time. You go and tell me what happens."

"We don't have TV."

"Well, we all got our problems, Miss Reilley."

I woke up this morning missing my children so acutely that tears started from my eyes before I was awake. Kids trick you with their rhythms during the college years. They are gone and not-gone. That whole delicious summer you have them; and it sneaks up on you all unaware that one year not even those three months will be yours. I feel close to them; we talk on the phone, but I suffer acutely from the lack of their physical presence.

Shadow on the floor next to my desk: I look up and come face to face with a deer looking in the window.

Easter

THE PASTOR AT FRIENDS CHURCH WORE A TIE this morning that featured a realistic photomontage of the Passion Week scenario. It was wide and yellow with pale brown bands inscribed with photo-real images of the stations of the cross. I don't think I've ever seen a stranger item in North America, even though I was raised in a religion where nobody thought it odd to picture Jesus and Mary on the wall pointing to their filleted bloody hearts pinned outside their clothes, strangulated with thorns.

I described the sartorial item to Karl who gently inquired, "Was this humor?"

Oh, no. The pastor would think humor on this point to be irreverent. He was just happy that Jesus is up and around again; his voice kept breaking during the sermon. For my part, I started to cry as soon as I started north on Highway 101; the uglier the tie, the uglier the music, the more I know I am there for the right reasons. One of the women who has been kind to me in that church asked me again, "Are your children Christians?"

I thought I was ready for her this time. "I don't know," I replied. "They are religious."

"It's not a question of being religious; do they know the Lord?" she said.

I can't imagine what it would be like to answer her question affirmatively without clicking through a thicket of metaphors so dense I would rattle where I stood. Yet when the pastor, in his unspeakable tie, asks us "if we feel it's right" to repeat the prayer of committing our lives to Jesus, I repeat the words like a raven, a crow, or a parakeet. My hands burn as I hold them open in my lap—no, I do not wave them over my head—yet I feel such longing.

A large white moth flings itself over and over against my window. Being a Celt, I think it might be one of my more unsuccessful relatives. Finally I turn out the lamp, to spare him apoplexy: why do they long for the light so?

Well, this is not a thing I should wonder about.

But you'd think if Creator made a creature nocturnal, holy wisdom would not simultaneously implant such a passionate desire for light. This seems a cruel trick, worthy of God the Teenaged Boy Scientist. This moth had tiny electric dots for eyes: he was keen. Perhaps moths spend so much time looking at the stars that the chance to get into the fire at close range overwhelms their primitive emotional machinery. That's my excuse, anyway.

Meanwhile, in the dark forests that earth still provides, millions of night-flying lepidoptera are born and die without seeing any more light than the moon or the Southern Cross, without having a close-up of what it is they long for. Here on the edge, at the kitchen window, we commune with the martyrs and visionaries, the übermenchen of moth.

This is what I learned from Brad Mattson: If you put a sea sponge into a blender, it breaks up, but recombines and reforms—rises again—as it were. If you put two sponges in the blender, each will recombine only with *itself*; it won't get mixed up with the other. The sponge's contribution to evolution is what later went on the marquee at Delphi: *know thyself.* Once the sponge recombines with itself, all its cells will start to communicate with each other to plan their specializations in order to meet the needs of the organism.

(This is a process difficult for the average English department.)
And, as the Beatles put it, *La la how the life goes on.*

Each organism in the evolutionary chain learns to do something
new and important, Brad explains: repel invaders, sing Puccini arias.
Life keeps trying things out—but Mary wonders *why? What's the
telos?* Does the process even have a goal? And why are these organ-
isms so beautiful, when they could just as well look like bat guano?
And does Life communicate with other parts of itself *"Wow! I just
learned to make silicate structures shaped like tiny jacks!"* Does Life in
another corner yell back, *"Nah nah nah, I can digest shrimp larvae!"?*
These questions are going to be on God's final exam.

We talk about such things at our weekly potlucks at Sitka
Center. Brad has been working on a series of videos for PBS about
how life experiments with different kinds of consciousness throughout
the evolutionary process: the consciousness that senses a shrimp
nearby, or Bambi's "Man is in the forest!" or some eruption of Teresa
of Avila in ecstasy. Meanwhile, Karl (I think) and I (I know) preoc-
cupy our little brains with *beauty:* color, rhythm, harmony of parts.
Beauty is the greatest mystery of all. Even if something looks ugly
when you put your face up to it, given physical or historic distance,
the most gruesome battle scene resolves into planes of line and
color, the crimson blood a necessary accent.

We have a new member in our little arts colony: the lithographer
Julia DeMario. Karl is very excited about learning from her. I envy
the collaboration that visual artists enjoy. Also, it must be great to
look at the world without words relentlessly forming. *Forming:* making something happen, instead of receiving. My residency is now
half over; I'm glad I hit the ground running, to the extent I run at
all. When the landscape is new to you, you see it more acutely and
you have the most to say. Karl says this is true for him as well, and
he's grateful for Julia's new energy. For my part, nose to the woods,
I've written about eight hundred pages. Karl says bragging in that
vein would be like his bragging about how many ounces of paint he
has put on canvas.

I dug out some notes from one of poet Mark Doty's craft talks. Doty cautions writers against stopping too soon, refusing to take apart the seams of their work and face complexity. I'm going to rip into my poems with that advice in mind. Karl says the same is true of visual artists; they have to overcome the fear of disturbing what feels tentatively "finished." On the other hand, am I here to "finish" anything?—here in Oregon, here in my life? I am here to be Creation's best audience, God's own blotting paper. Excuse me for taking so many notes. A more enlightened being would just breathe it in and applaud. At least I am sufficiently sick of myself to walk barefoot on the beach at Pacific City without a single thought that is not about the gray ocean or the black-and-tan, long-legged sky disappearing west, an audition for satori.

But then I remember, a little queasily, that a fisherman found a woman's hand on the beach last week, soft parts gone down the crabs no doubt, crabs into gulls. The old ballad relied on the violin-maker to peg her bones into telling the tale; nowadays we have DNA analysis, so the police know who she is and how she got there. And that other parts of her are tossing in the surf.

Yesterday, at the Great Beach Clean-up in Newport, a dead baby was found in a shallow grave. Twelve people, the radio said, have been murdered on the Oregon coast since September, seven or eight of them children.

Oh yes. I'm not only here to flex the muscles of my negative capability. I'm here to learn how to live lovingly in a world that scatters the weak, and even the strong, like bread crumbs on the path of some monstrous, innocent Hansel and Gretel.

A different landscape: each week when I drive north to the little town of Netarts and the Friends church, barreling along to tapes of Sacred Harp music, I stop to following the progress of the bird life at Cape Meares Light. Peregrine falcons are nesting there. Waterbirds are getting ready to fledge. They do this, I've learned, by precipitately —as it were, intuitively—jumping into the water. Some, like common murres, have to leap off cliffs, which exercise kills many of them. How can they call them "common"? They should be renamed the Extraordinary Murres, Demian Murres. Young murres can be seen walking along the cliffs for days in advance of the first jump—one might say, pacing. What goes on in the brain to induce it to that first—or last—flight? For a long time, it seems, the bird can't. It cannot overcome its fear, and then it can. *"And must my trembling spirit fly unto a world unknown?"* I sing along with the tape.

When I get to Netarts Bay, the tide is out; it looks like a broad prairie of sand. When the tide is in, it makes me think of Gerard Manley Hopkins's poem "Heaven/Haven":

Where the green swell is in the havens dumb
And out of the swing of the sea.

Many years ago, I decided against that particular piece of real estate. I would not choose to live on the bay, but on the wild ocean.

"I spread my wings, I mount, I fly . . ." the singers commence their spontaneous combustion.

To enter that church is to enter a place where something could happen, a rift could open. I've learned to respect such places, marvel over them as phenomena, be they in the high country of Guatemala, or the Minnesota River Valley, or western Australia. I don't believe a word of the doctrine here, but I have a clear sense of what it would be like if it were true. Or what the truth is that's represented by what the words cannot say.

Thus, I suppose, in some convoluted way, I believe it hook, line, and sinker.

I wonder if animals have a gear for ecstasy? They must, if ecstasy is a kind of neurological incident, a crashing of gears brought on by some endorphin surge. They must, if ecstasy spins out of the grace-fed, mystical realization that you are connected nerve and bone to every other crystalline structure in the crystalline universe.

What does the peregrine falcon worship, then? Or the deer Karl saw yesterday, swimming straight west into the ocean, pursued, he thought, hag-ridden or unglued? Why would a deer head into the breakers toward the setting sun?

> *I mount, I fly! O grave where is thy victory?*
> *O death where is thy sting?*

Credo

I DON'T BELIEVE IN GOD—not in any way I can reconcile with the
Friends church—but I wake up every morning praying. Before I am
conscious, love words start rolling out of my heart like the words of
a woman who forgets she's been divorced for twenty-five years,
words of seduction and harmless quarrelling about dropped socks
and belly scratching. I don't believe in anything after death except
perhaps an explosion of consciousness into some other, differently
annoyed brain, such as that of the fledgling seabird pacing along its
cliff, knowing it has to get into the water before long.

And this morning, I am already angry with God—whom I don't
believe in—and with the whole green world. One thing you learn,
living alone in the beautiful woods, is that the vexations you
thought came from other people, politics, or snow, are in fact just
manifestations of the *self*. Creator arranges some species in packs, I
guess, because they are the sort who need someone to blame.

I like to talk to Brad, who does not believe in a different God
than I do not believe in. Brad professes to have no time at all for
religion. He says that Christianity introduced shame and guilt into
what would otherwise have been a perfect world.

Contrariwise, I assert over potluck, guilt is good for us. It lets us
know we have standards. Before the Hawaiian islanders got
Christianity and muumuus, they didn't have a standard about
throwing girls into volcanoes, for example. Shame—which is not
quite the same thing as guilt—feels worse and does more damage on
the psychosocial level, but it too serves a function. Sexual shame—
for example—helps us to limit our population. The French invented

the diaphragm, the English, primogeniture, and the Irish, shame. After the Great Famine, most historians agree, subsistence farming made it almost impossible for the Irish to marry and have children; an out-of-wedlock pregnancy was a disaster in a world where a wedded pregnancy was not exactly a blessed event.

When I write about my conversations with Brad, I always give myself nice, long speeches.

But anyway, shame, as a way of controlling overpopulation, is a rational advance over infanticide and the sacrifice of virgins in volcanoes. Now that shame has gone out of fashion, Gaia protects herself with gang warfare, drugs, and an exploding population of incarcerated males. And with war. Someone quoted to me recently the aphorism, "I tremble when I think that God is just."

Not to worry. God is not just. But look out for Gaia. She is merciless. She requires a few million of us. Mess with her and you'll wish you had God the Father to kick around again.

Yesterday I began to grow restless and bored and annoyed with the mountains, the ocean, the drama of it all. I grow homesick for the soft hills and farms of southern Minnesota. The sky around Northfield is all the sky I can stand to think about for the moment. I can't seem to settle down in this new spring ecosystem. I keep demanding that something happen in my life or poetry or spiritual experience that is on a scale with the landscape. I felt more in harmony with Oregon when it rained all the time, when the mystery was vested in decorum.

Adding to my restlessness, I am flummoxed by the change to daylight saving time. I lay awake a long time in the night, somehow went into another sleep cycle, and was wakened by a call from Peter at 8 a.m.

Hello: where am I?

I am crying on the phone to Peter about not being saved, about being too small against this landscape, about wanting something to happen, about not knowing what verse from Ephesians Luther was worrying about in the outhouse, or was it Philippians? And how can anybody entertain the idea that Jesus arose from the dead?

"Be quiet," Peter says. "The physical resurrection of Jesus is not important; *holy presence* in the world is important."

Okay, I'm awake.

"Everything else is speculation," Peter continues. "The idea of resurrection is speculation; the idea that Jesus's body was eaten by coyotes in a garbage pit—which is popular with some contemporary theologians—is speculation. *Holy presence is real.* You are good at small, low-key revelations, so leave the big ones alone. Anyway, a person can be *overly saved.*"

He tells me how, when he was young man, he felt his call to ministry so urgently that he tried to jump over the intermediate steps.

"Oh, like *Sparky's Magic Piano,*" I say. This was a record my parents gave me when I was about six years old. It tells the story of a little boy, Sparky, who's taking piano lessons. He hates to practice, but one day when he is sitting miserably at the piano, it begins to speak to him . . .

Peter snorts. "Don't tell me you had that record when you were a kid? No wonder we're both so fucked up."

"*Spa-a-a-rky* . . ." I croon into Peter's ear. Peter threatens to hang up.

The magic piano, under Sparky's hands, plays all the great classics of piano repertoire—that was the selling point to our parents, Peter's and mine. Sparky grows more and more famous as a boy wonder and finally winds up in Carnegie Hall. Just as he sits down to astonish the world, the magic piano quits on him. It says, in effect, "Schmuck, go home and practice."

Peter says, "Yes, this is what will happen if you take Jesus Christ for your Lord and Savior."

I went down to the estuary at low tide and sat on a rock. Everything stinks like pig manure. Why does this beach stink like pig manure? This is so remarkable. Then slowly it dawns on me that I am sitting very close to something dead, which is disquieting, considering the body count on our local beaches of late. So I look around and discover a rug of skin caught in the root cavity of a stump of old-growth Sitka, along with a fan of wedge-shaped bones. I assume it is the deer Karl says leapt into the surf.

But later I will discover that I have fallen for one of those logical fallacies, the one where you expect to see a particular thing and, therefore, when phenomena arise, you name them what you expected to see.

Is the story of Jesus's resurrection something like this?

Karl will tell me that this skin belongs to a sea lion. The deer event was more recent and could not have taken such a toll on the carcass.

"Good, I want to think the deer escaped."

"Me, too," said Karl. "I want to think that."

The Wager on Rebirth

THIS MORNING IT HAPPENED AGAIN, though I had made a firm
resolution that it *not* happen, this turning my nose toward Friends
church and starting to cry with fifty miles yet to drive. Such a
tenderness comes over me. It's as though a space inside me opens
up and mercy flows into it, but there is always more space and
more mercy.

To say it that way is, of course, to use too many words.

Maybe the excess of tearful tenderness I feel in these middle
years is simply proportional to the depth of sorrow anyone carries. I
have not lived a sad or difficult life. If a normal life can be so
confounded, what overflowing love must be needed to inundate the
world of real suffering? No wonder they thought up the idea of the
Son of God.

Julia Kristeva observed that "love is the wager on rebirth." She
talks about writing as an act of forgiveness, in fact, a transcendent
act which makes time stand still, makes the clock stop running on
the victimizer. She said, "In religion . . . forgiveness is understood to
be the suspension of judgment. It is the act by which one forbids
judging and stops time, which proceeds toward vengeance, and
allows the person who committed the reprehensible act to begin
anew, to take up another life and another activity."

Rain, falling relentlessly at my north window, has inscribed a
series of rivulets down the glass, distorting vision just enough to
make the green hillside look like a landscape rolling itself up into
the corrugations of an Impressionist painting. Rain at the other
windows is more spotty and irregular as it glides off the different

240

surfaces of light and shingles and spruce needles. At the north window it sleets down unimpeded, leaving its regularly spaced fingerprints.

With spring on the calendar—time for me to go home—it's suddenly colder than it was all February. We are washed daily. The rain becomes a presence, a god, as the snow becomes at home.

On Saturday, Amy, from the Sitka office, and her husband, Tim, found me hiking along the road. They picked me up and took me along to see a dead gray whale that had washed ashore at the north end of Neskowin Beach—poor huge animal—its baleen drifting over the immense tongue. He looked like he had a mouth full of corset stays—for which the baleen was prized by nineteenth-century ladies. An odd transmigration, when the body of the creature becomes less comprehensible than the product the body is made into. But few people remember corset stays anymore, and so baleen will be baleen again, a unique adaptation to the great creature's food gathering. And the creature will remain incomprehensible.

You can find carrion by looking for carrion birds. In the case of a dead whale, one will see hundreds of gulls. However when we arrive at the body, the gulls haven't made much headway. They have managed to pull back sections of black skin and expose the layer of blood-rich tissue underneath. The apostrophe-shaped eye socket is covered by its thick membrane of lid, as though the animal could not bear to watch what's going on.

Bear, Amy's dog, bounds along the beach and skids sideways, hackles up, eyes down as he gets within four feet of the great death. What sight or scent had spoken confusion to his dog brain? Land animals do not understand sea animals very well.

The kind of racing love the ocean's good at pulled the whale to shore and revealed a black form that seemed to come out of a dream we don't remember sleeping through.

A dream, a conundrum.

Perhaps we humans are the only creatures who experience ephemerality. I know that this is my last week alone in this woods, and that—when I go and pick up Robin at the train station—the difficult condition of solitude will change for the difficult condition of companionship. Have I learned anything, or have I just ridden around on the great wheel?

Kristeva again: "Even if the writer's story turns in circles, writing is nonetheless a way of coming out of the trauma, of forgiving oneself or the other and translating it for someone else. This constitutes a distancing from the place of the crime through sharing."

Even better, she says, "By . . . reflecting on them through music, affects, sensations, metaphors, etc., you will not efface these places of suffering but attenuate them, allowing them a certain luminosity, a certain laugh."

A certain laugh. She is right about that.

Is spring always a surprise to the deer? Does she know when autumn is coming and mating season, fawns, and hunters? She knows in a kind of bone way. Our brains give us perhaps too much dailiness, too much information, distract us from the great turns the deer knows. We experience, therefore, multiple subdivisions of anxiety and ecstasy, rather than the long, slow licks of change the animal feels. No wonder the deer come to my windows to watch me on deer TV. I am living, in their eyes, a frenetic life, like those overstimulating cartoon characters human children line up in front of on Saturday mornings. Pity, the deer must feel, and horror—

How does my old dog, Shep, experience my absence? The maternal shape withdrew on schedule, but this time did not return. Perhaps a sadness ensued, from which her heart was distracted by the kindness of her new caregiver. Perhaps the low note of memory endures below present joys. When I come back, she will be happy, surprised. A color returned to the vast shapes that inhabit her world. Dogs literally do not sweat the small stuff, and it's literally all small stuff to them.

"I am going home," I wrote yesterday on one of the yellow prayer cards in the pew at Friends church. "My mother is ill and my sister and I are going to try to take care of her. I can't imagine how to do that . . ."

During the service, as the pastor spoke gently about lambs and sheep and I started to cry routinely in my pew, he finished up by saying, "I feel there are people here who want to come to the front of the church and pray with us, so I'll just suggest everyone else leave . . ."

I felt a strong motion to go forward and pray, but once on my knees at the front of the church, words left me. A kind woman put her arm around me and said, "What do you want to pray about?"

Of course I had no idea. I felt like a jackass. I said, "I don't know what to do with this longing I feel."

She asked me if I had ever prayed for Jesus to come into my heart. I said I had, but it didn't make any difference. Babbling, I tried to explain that I did not believe. Then why am I on my knees?

What a long way up it was, off the floor. But worth the trip.

This morning I went back to the beach to see the dead whale, but the sea had taken her back. No great comma in the sand remembers the lash of her tail. Did we know her at all? This huge problem or vast titanic grace we thought for a moment we saw? A tourist in bright yellow shorts came along and asked about a dead whale. I pretended not to know anything about it.

I am taking the whale back to a room in the brain, protecting a vision I thought I had.

I point with an oblique shrug to the clean sand and a long hungry wedge of gulls facing into the wind.

To wager on rebirth, I am coming to understand, is to believe that after a lot of careful work on the past—or an explosion of grace—we can reenter the world, periodically, intact, ready to live.

Recessional

LAST NIGHT I DREAMT ABOUT PAMPA, TEXAS, where I was born: light brown plains, the B-52s with their dangerous bellies, June Allyson waving her hat, exuding a single photogenic tear as she calls, "Happy landing, flyboy!" I dream, I guess, the movies Dad took us to, in our pajamas, at the outdoor theater; or I watch the collective unconscious.

Flybaby: all my dad's lessons about percussion, lift, and Bernouilli's principle were pretty well wasted on me. Truly sympathetic to what we now think of as "women's issues," Dad encouraged me to be an engineer or a physicist, but I was too stupid. Good parents put wonderful opportunities before their children, but there is no guarantee the children will be wired for the task. I was a frustration to my dad; similarly, my children had little interest in the music lessons I offered them. Parental fantasies aside, children learn what they need to know.

What did the Air Force teach me? To sleep in the daylight; we were always traveling. I learned the instincts of a third-shift worker. I learned to stay awake in the dark, when the tedious highway or flyway became mysterious. The dark is, after all, worth watching. It spreads itself over the landscape looking for home. Look at it, there at the end of runway behind June Allyson, waiting to have its say when the time comes, if the time comes, if there is any such thing as time and you can find it in Texas.

Perhaps it's the wide vistas of sky on the Oregon coast that have carried me back to the mental spaces of early childhood, those vast prairies.

Human consciousness has so much room for *landscape*. Can we know anything at all without knowing its *terra:* landscape of the sublime, the terrible, the holy? The particular holiness—to settle on that word—of the coastal landscape has to do with the emptiness and openness of the sky, the way *brightness falls*. Space is always waiting for us, hidden down some logging road or tucked in a curve of the coast. Immensity leaks and you enter it, grateful or afraid.

Does my perception matter? Does the landscape in any sense need *me?*

After some months in an unfamiliar place, one loses the ability to see with newborn eyes. If it needed me awhile, this country doesn't need me any longer. After three months at Sitka, I began to get sick of the coastal drama, to long for the fleshpots of Minnesota winter.

In the night, somebody's belt of stars comes off over my western skylight, the constellations divesting, Orion taking Dawn to bed. I lie here thinking of home, a land still quiescent in snowdrifts and struggling to make it through alive. Perhaps because I have lost the ability to hear my life, quotidian and stable, I begin to dream it over from the beginning.

I fall back asleep and find myself in the choir loft of our old church in Roseville. I am looking down at pink spots in the granite floor, trying to get up the nerve to go downstairs to receive Communion in the main body of the church. In the dream I am lost, trekking through the classrooms attached to the church, fluttering in my brown silk dress, trying to find my way.

There is no logic to this dream. There was, in reality, nowhere to get lost on that journey. I was not going to miss a step and end up in the boys' lavatory or grade one. There were, however, a lot of steps between the choir loft and the Communion rail. Maybe it was one of the mornings when I hadn't wanted to go to mass because my hair was limp; perhaps I hated my body for one of its many reasons. The long climb down to Communion could be too much for a fourteen-year-old girl, all the boys staring, the pretty girls whispering behind their hymnals. You could slip—at least in my dream it seemed

possible to slip—and wheel over the balcony railing onto the suburban moms and dads and the thirteen red-haired O'Leary children, a
meteorite from the choir loft, badly dressed.

I knelt, instead, in the pew beside the organ, which, at fourteen,
I wanted very much to learn to play, and I watched Mrs. Delahanty's
feet pedal-out the recessional. The organist was a fastidious, tailored
woman whom my dad had remarked, with one of his strongest
affirmations, to be "a perfect size ten." Her expensive shoes sat next
to the organ bench. I had heard my dad call that color of leather
some fancy name for the blood of an animal. How uncharacteristic
that she would—and she alone *could*—remove her shoes in church,
the fashionable Mrs. Delahanty. Her small feet in their nylon stockings
sped left and right on the floorboards of the organ with a subversive
life of their own, as though the top half of her, primly bloused and
jacketed, had a separate life from the bottom half. She remained
upright and haughty, like a woman riding a terrible horse only she
could control. She would not break a sweat, nor roll her eyes when
Mrs. Polski, the aging soprano soloist, flatted her high note with an
astonishing vibrato.

When I think about the *Titanic* striking its iceberg—which the
Catholic church of the fifties was certainly doing at the moment,
downstairs at the altar where I did not want to go—I think of Mrs.
Delahanty riding that organ down.

Awake finally to Oregon, I got out of bed, had a cup of tea, and
hiked to the top of Cascade Head. It took me four hours to climb a
thousand feet. A bald eagle was soaring below me, carrying its heavy
white body between two black planes of wing. He flew up, finally, to
check me out and we hovered eye-to-eye for a minute.

Elderberry in bloom smells like sweetgrass. Skunk cabbage smells
like skunk. What really hates you up there are the cliff swallows,
unused to company, who screech and dive-bomb the interloper, as if

I were going to shinny down a cliff face and disturb their nests. Nature is full of stupid anxieties: why should I be immune?

Yesterday I drove all the way to Yachats to buy a necklace of purplish-black baroque pearls to wear to my son's wedding. I saw them in the window of a craft shop a month or so ago, and they reminded me of my life: odd, luminescent beads reflecting gray, green, and pink, knotted onto that all-important string. It's common wisdom in the oyster beds that every mollusk should make pearls out of what annoys and tries her—for my part, I make black pearls, not very expensive, funky.

"Sometimes I don't know whether I'm dreaming my dreams or my mother's"—says a very old woman who has brought me some of her writing to look at.

This seems to me to be a profound insight about a certain kind of writing process. "I feel that way, too," I respond, newly aware of it. "I think it's a good way for a writer to feel."

Like so many women of her generation, schooled in humility, this woman feels shy about composing in the genre of memoir. "Who am I to say?" she wants to know.

"We're just taking dictation from our race," I tell her. Under the skin of every human being is a star map of the human condition. When people read what I write, I want them to feel a momentary dislocation, so that perhaps the reader pencils in the margin (as I found in a copy of Eva Figues' *Ghosts* last night as I read myself to sleep): "*Me!*" I want to give the reader the effect of seeing through scrims of dream and memory, so that for a moment of disorientation she doesn't quite know whether she's reading my dreams or hers or her mother's. The other day, standing by the ocean in Depoe Bay, I felt a suitable tremor, like the skip of film in a movie house. Not an earthquake proper, but a little shake, that puts reality on notice and then gives it back.

Going Coyote

BUT WHO AM I TO HAVE my mother's dreams? My mother would have *been* June Allyson, no watcher from the sidelines, she.

Just now, my sister and I are trying to leave from our various star systems on journeys that will end at my son's wedding in the North Cascades. Our mother is being as obstructive as she can be. My Native American friend, Larry Cloud Morgan, used to call her kind of behavior "going coyote," a pattern of irrational conduct that seems to have some tricky purpose to it. Our mother has taken against the upcoming marriage and refuses to attend.

At the last minute, as my sister is ready to leave town, the cleaning woman has found Mom sitting on the floor.

"She didn't exactly fall," Peggy tells me on the phone. "But, suddenly, neither can she walk. Or will she. I don't know which." Gone coyote.

We are perplexed. This is our mom, who used to feign psychotic episodes and then—one of our social workers diagnosed the pattern—feign that she had feigned them because she didn't want anyone to know that she had momentarily lost control. More than anything she fears being locked up like her own mother.

"What I actually think," said my sister, "is that she stopped moving for a few days and then stiffened up. Now she *can't* move." Later my mother herself would confirm this diagnosis. "I went on a little sit-down strike. That wasn't very smart of me."

We don't know why she wants to stop the wedding. Coyote reasons. Should I fly home? Should Peggy stay with her? Finally we decide to hire a nursing service to take care of her for the week of the wedding. This solution will make us feel sad and guilty, emotions that pickled us in utero until we achieved a degree of immunity. But only a degree.

Peg and I spend a lot of time on the phone trying to lay out a plan to care for our mother at home when I return. Far away in the mists of Oregon, I am able to imagine a time of forgiveness and peace among us. I will rub Mom's feet while we listen to a Mozart quartet. I will pray with her and tuck her into bed.

"The house is so full of cigarette smoke, you can't breathe," Peggy, the realist, tells me. "She lets the dog bite the nurses. The TV is turned up loud. She says very, very mean things."

"I know. She hung up the phone on me yesterday."

It is by no means certain that any given mother will love any given child. This is one of the more difficult lessons of being human. This is graduate school. Most animals never get it. They will always return to an inhospitable den. But we humans are capable of getting it—"This is how families operate," Brad laughs when I tell him about Mom's pranks.

It's difficult, though. Yesterday in Friends church they were singing some moony song to Jesus that went, "Listen to me, Love, let me look into your eyes," and I started to snivel. Some vague maternal figure interposed itself between me and the poor cornered savior. Were these songs all made up by people with difficult mothers?

Mom sits home in fury. For the moment, I have to put her out of my mind and throw myself into the joy of the wedding.

In fact I will dance all night.

Robin and I, both unmothered, confess to each other that we can get into a dark space where we feel there is not enough love to go around. Weddings, by contrast, celebrate the hypothesis that there is plenty, abundance, mercy running over the bowl and down the legs of the table. Jude and Leslee have created and re-created this potential in their friendships and affiliations and, above all, in their love for each other. And there was Julian, simply shining; there was my dear Peter, who pastored the ceremony, so tender. When that darling bride put her arms around me and said, "Mama," I thought my heart would crack with joy, Jude glowing neon, with a borrowed ring on his hand. They want to be married forever, they want not to be ephemeral. What a gift they gave us all.

Would things have gone better for Mother if she had been able to eat that bridal meal, I wonder later.

"She would have completely and utterly ruined it," says my practical sister. I like to think I inhabit a Shakespearian comedy, when, at the moment I'm trapped in *King Lear*. My parents didn't produce enough daughters to cast Cordelia.

After the wedding, Robin and I drove back to Sitka to pack and participate in the closing ceremonies of the residency. Nature is on the side of marriage and procreation at the moment. We see few animals. They have withdrawn deep into the forest to bear their young. But, just as we are carrying our suitcases out to the car, four mule deer come up the road.

I nudge Robin, "I think they're boys."

"Do they exhibit superior logic and spacial reasoning?"

"They have small horns."

"That, too."

Driving home to Minnesota, we stopped overnight in Theodore Roosevelt National Park. From there we phoned my sister, who had flown home three weeks earlier. She has just managed to negotiate another crisis and gotten our mother into a "transitional care facility." There, Mom is scheduled to have therapy and rehabilitation, none of which will materialize in any coherent way.

Robin and I sit in the car, eating sandwiches, and he calls my attention to a vision in the rearview mirror, some fifty buffalo cows with their calves, slowly and with utter calmness, retreating behind us into the mist, a sight for which, he tells me, he has a deep feeling but no words.

We don't know why we find the presence of animals so quieting. I am about to embark on the craziest three months of my life, and I know it. The huge silent beasts, inexorably plodding, pass into my consciousness, a last gift of the wilderness. We could not turn and look directly at them. We needed to see them in a mirror, slantwise. They needed to exist as promise and potential, ancient and earthly, a steadiness beyond the facile credos of daily life. Under our car, the dirt road shook rhythmically.

PART FIVE

The Red Plush Heart

The Door to the Ocean

AFTER MY MOTHER DIED, I couldn't pray for over a year. I couldn't write, either. As my mind shut down, my joints stiffened, as though our mother, who suffered rheumatoid arthritis her whole life, had dropped it on me like a cloak falling from her shoulders. I can smile now, and say, that's the kind of trick she would pull: *see what it's like to be me.* Because, though imagination is my strong suit, I can't imagine what it was like to be her.

This is what I do know: until you forgive someone as close as a mother, you are at war with yourself, you continue to gnaw that leg of yours caught in a trap. Why are you at war with yourself? I think because to hold a grudge against another person you have to recognize in them a quality that you yourself possess but can't admit to.

Forgiveness takes a while, and you can't help suffering because you're in the millrace of change. The process won't speed up because you think it might be nice to get back in connection with the human race. When you come to the place where you can forgive, you are a different person than you were at the beginning of the journey. The person who can forgive is different from the person who could not forgive. You have to shed millions of cells and regrow them all.

It helped me to look at my feelings systematically, in the way that Thich Nhat Hanh taught, like "older sister taking care of younger sister": "Breathing in, I know that I am feeling anger. Breathing out, I see the deep causes of my anger . . ."

I do not yet, as I write this, see the deep causes, but I know that my mother and I were locked in a struggle that replicated my mother's struggle with her own mother. Is there a way in which the child shapes the parent, as much or more than the parent shapes the child? My own children have molded me to the good that's in them—we've been entrained in a positive feedback cycle that began with breast-feeding. But what if parent and child lock into a negative cycle, as did my mother and I? I think that, in her youth and neediness, she didn't want a rival for Dad's affection, and she felt I effaced her from the moment I was born.

Walking by Siletz Bay one afternoon, I came upon part of an old doorframe, its antique knob and hook in place, floating at the tide line. It wasn't easy to haul it up and get it in the car, but who can resist *the door to the ocean?* There are seals, cavorting in the surf, wanting, I know, to knock. What mystery might come through this door, what alien form of unconscious life, trailing its hair of golden dulse? During our time at Sitka, both Karl Pilato and I had been working, in our separate studios, with concepts of liminal, threshold space, worlds between worlds, clearings, the sky holes these huge trees keep open: while on all sides of us, the landscape kept coming on.

I don't know the deep causes of my feelings, but I honor the door through which *anyone, anything* may arrive.

After my mother died, I couldn't pray and I stopped dreaming almost entirely. Stuck in the everyday world, all the usual sources of transcendence dry, I hung out with my old dog until she, too, passed on, and with my crazy, affectionate young dog, Star.

Then, when a year had passed, I tried to write about my mother's death. Immediately, Mom called me on the phone at 4 a.m. She told me in crisp, businesslike tones that she was being held prisoner in a fancy hotel and I had better get busy liberating her. I doubted anybody would believe this story, so I desperately recorded the call on my answering machine. I tried to go back to sleep, but the phone kept ringing. I was somebody's wrong number. Malevolent female voices whispered about tangled plots involving my mother. Two of them, at least, were trying to damage each other; cagily, I managed to splice the phone wires and put them in contact. They confronted each other and combusted with terrible screams, which woke me again. I was going to play you the taped evidence of this but—there is no phone in my bedroom, no answering machine and no tape recorder.

I couldn't pray, but I put in my time. I uttered words and watched them fall with a tinkle a few feet from my body. Peter told me, "You think nothing is happening but you and your mother are locked in conversation still. It will go on and on until you are both healed. When you love somebody you sit by their deathbed year after year."

"I *don't* love her."

"You do."

"I don't."

Transitional Care

AFTER OUR ENCOUNTER WITH THE BISON, Robin and I drove straight through to home and headed for the care facility where my mother was temporarily an inmate. I had expected to feel my usual repressed annoyance with her, but her condition roused in me a shock of compassion. She had shrunk to ninety pounds, her feet were ulcerated and causing her great pain. I found her curtained against an uncongenial roommate who played talk radio, and she seemed to be at the mercy of a cadre of social workers and administrators, all with silly names like "Peaches" and "Muffy," girls my nuns would have taken into the janitor's closet and soundly baptized "Mary Margaret."

Mother used to tell us about her English bulldog, Mickey, who hated cats. Old and blind and sick, Mickey was finally carted away in the Humane Society truck—I guess they made house calls back then—and the truck was full of cats. Looking at Mother among her pert young tormentors, I remembered Mickey.

"Mom's not working very hard, are you, Mom?" said one of the Peaches as I came in.

I practiced my own bulldog stare and the young woman left us alone.

Mother was sitting up in bed when I got there, so I sat beside her and rubbed her back. She turned her head into me—I can only say, like an animal—like that great blue heron who died on my shoulder. "Oh, it feels so good when you touch me."

This is the most personal, kindest thing she has ever said to me and it lifted my heart. I have not touched my mother in years, beyond a cursory peck on the cheek. She was not a cuddler, and, for my part, I began to shrink from her at a young age. Civility was the best we could produce, whatever we might have wanted from each other. But illness has altered her. For one thing, her voice has become melodious. The shrillness that always assaulted me is gone.

"Please take me home," she says in her new contralto.

"Let's see."

Peaches bounces back in. "We're going to have a care conference next week." She makes it sound like a party.

"What's the agenda?"

"To get Mom working."

"I'm retired," snaps my mother. She hasn't lost any edge.

"In what way is she not working?" I carefully inquire.

"She won't feed or toilet herself, or get out of bed."

"Why should I?" Mother reasonably asks. I feel like a parent called to the principal's office to deal with a sulking teen.

I demand of Peaches: "Do you realize that she's legally blind, her hands are very crippled, and—why have you got that diaper on her?"

"They won't answer my call button," my mother pipes up. "They won't take me to the bathroom. I don't know where the bathroom is. They put this diaper on me and told me not to bother getting up."

"Who are *they?*" I want to know.

"The aides."

"We're a little understaffed on the weekend," Peaches responds.

This is a rehabilitation facility, but no rehabilitation is going on. I have a talk with Peaches in the hall about how to shape desirable behavior versus how to reinforce dependency. I'm a teacher and this is the kind of thing I know about. I ask politely if they have any utensil-gripping devices to help her feed herself. Have they set up a schedule to walk her to the bathroom? Peaches alludes again to the upcoming care conference.

"If she doesn't start working," Peaches snaps, "she's going to be terminated."

"Huh? *Excuse me?*" I am green and inexperienced, but I've seen friends go through the managed-care hoops, among them, two disabled young people. If a managed-care plan sends a patient to rehabilitation, then he or she has to show progress within a certain length of time or they will alter the patient's status to "chronic." If the patient is on rehabilitative status, insurance picks up the tab, if the patient is "chronic," he or she—with any financial resources— becomes "private pay." Once you have spent down your estate, medicare takes over. It is, of course, to the benefit of your insurer to get you out of rehabilitation and into a nursing home; then they no longer have to pay for you.

To accomplish this heist with the least resistance, I theorize, the Peaches and the Muffies must first drive a wedge between patient and family. Had I not accompanied others on this journey with a dependent family member I would not have heard before this provocative phrase—*"She's not working, she's not trying"*—and I might have fallen for it.

Instead, my sister and I will repeatedly remind the hospital administrators that our mother was taking care of her own house three weeks ago. "We hope to bring her back there," we assert over and over.

"Oh, we wouldn't be comfortable with that," Peaches replies. "Your mother needs to be in a nursing home. It happens we have an opening in our facility."

The blatant venality of this advertisement astonishes us. They propose to change the patient's status, wheel her down the hall, and convert a liability into an asset.

Not only is Peaches "not comfortable" with our suggestion about taking Mom home, she reminds us that she has an obligation to call in Adult Protective Services if the social workers don't agree to our plan.

Protecting her autonomy, Mom has refused to go to the doctor for twenty years. Peggy and I had to trick her into the brief office visit that got her into "rehabilitation"—a maneuver that, necessary as it seemed at the time, still makes us feel sad. Now her fears have been justified. She has lost control of her life. We are in the millrace, for sure.

Care Conference

THEY WILL BE SORRY THEY MESSED with my sister and me. We will become the daughters from Peaches's nightmare. We research rehabilitative equipment on the Web and try to charm the staff into using it. We butt into the physical therapy sessions, which usually consist of lining up old people in wheelchairs, who don't know where they are, and saying, "Want to walk today, ladies? No? Well, back to bed then." We bring bags of potato chips and lure Mother into walking a few steps. But they keep raising the bar on her. The administrators get to define "progress" and hers is never enough.

"They're setting her up to fail, right?" I ask a young physical therapist. Too green and good to lie, he sighs, "Yes."

One of us, my sister or I, is almost always with her, and, when we are not, we are at home in Roseville cleaning. We rip out the carpet and wash walls that run with nicotine. We paint and patch tile, hang lace curtains. If there is a chance of installing her at home with a health aide, we are going to go for it. Although we soon discover that home health care has its own scams. "If she can't get into a wheelchair without assistance, our rules require two aides on duty at all times." This will cost about a hundred dollars an hour. It would be cheaper, and tempting, to install her in the St. Paul Hotel.

We explain all this to our mother. "My house is perfectly fine," she tells us. "Will you drive me over?"

"Let's see."

The care conference is held in a violently air-conditioned, square room attached to the transitional facility. It's the kind of room, like certain legal offices, designed to intimidate, but my sister and I have enough graduate degrees between us to know how to put the chairs in a circle. Peaches comes in and rearranges the furniture "so that we can accommodate your mother's wheelchair."

My sister and I exchange a panicky glance. We hadn't counted on Mom, terrified and angry, being present at this discussion. "She's at lunch."

"Our protocol is to have the patient present."

We understand the rationale behind this, but we know it will work to our mother's disadvantage. The staff does not know who our mother is; certainly they are ignorant of her history of anxiety and her pathological fear of hospitals. The care conference is starting to feel like a parole hearing.

Our mother is wheeled in, disoriented, shivering in the cold room, her lunch tray propped crazily on her lap. Because of her poor vision and difficulty with utensils she dislikes eating in front of people. She has managed to spill applesauce all over the place. Her hair is uncombed, and I know she can't see who the hell is interrogating her. Like Mickey among the cats, she has gone into her characteristic defense of shutting out the opposition as though it does not exist.

We are surprised when the green, young male therapist begins the conference with a guardedly optimistic report. He has been working hard with Mom and knows she is clear-headed and straining to overcome her situation. He notes the speed with which disability has come upon her, and how much her shock and disorientation figure into what looks like a reluctance to cooperate.

"I think she's making good progress, considering," he ventures.

Peaches is clearly not prepared for his positive assessment. "What plan do we have in place?" she demands to know.

My sister and I are ready for this question. We paint with bright strokes our intention to get her walking and feeding herself—if we could have some modified utensils, please—

One of the junior Peaches swings in with a mental assessment that finds Mother deficient in math skills and unable to track times and dates. She has suffered from this dyscalculia all her life and dismissed it with an English major's, "Silly me."

Peaches suddenly raises her voice and turns to Mother in an aggressive way. "What have we been talking about, Honey?" she yells. Peaches sounds like a grade school teacher trying to catch an unprepared pupil.

Mom jumps and spills her coffee. Clearly she has not been listening. One of her life-long defenses has been to shut out any realities that do not please her.

Peaches crosses her arms and faces us. "What are we going to do when rehabilitation fails?"

Not *if* but *when*.

My sister has warned me not to mouth off and to keep "them" on our side, so I do not raise the obvious question: *has rehabilitation started yet?*

Later in a long letter to Peaches, which Peggy doesn't let me send, I instruct the social workers about how to treat people. As a teacher with thirty years' experience, I tell Peaches, for free, that I would never have a motivational chat with a student that turned on the phrase, "But what if you fail?" I simply do not want the student to visit that imaginative terrain. I want the student's mind to be filled with pictures of success and competence. Before talking about grades, I work the conversation around to what I know she or he is good at, like basketball or playing the piano.

But my sister will tell me not to throw pearls before swine or even swine before pearls. She is a nurse, she knows the system. "They'll have a good laugh," she tells me.

Even knowing the system, we are baffled by the fact that our mother has been required to appear at a conference at which the staffers act as if she isn't there. We gently draw their attention to this point. Peaches responds that "She isn't tracking." Mercilessly, they start to converse across her wheelchair about nursing home placement. This is our mother's worst fear: incarceration, loss of autonomy. She is shivering by now, from cold and terror.

"Listen, we have to take her out of this room," my sister says. "It's freezing in here." Although she has been charged with inattention,

Mother says as we wheel her down the hall, "They've given up on me. Why should I try?"

"Well, trying is to your advantage," my sister explains. This is the kind of conversation we are used to having with our mother. Over the years, she has developed a habit of reverting to some teenaged space of arrested development. She was eighteen when her father died, and her conversation with authority figures gets stuck in this groove.

That evening she will have a terrible panic attack and my sister will have to go out and spend most of the night calming her down.

The morning after the care conference, Peaches leaves the astonishing message on my answering machine that our mother will be released at 3 p.m. and we should be ready to pick her up. It turns out, after we have raced around for a day and made countless unreturned phone calls, that they have confused Mother with some other patient and some other care plan. Probably, though, they say, she will be released at the end of the week. Again the suggestion from Peaches: we could just wheel her down the hall to the nursing home. That vacancy won't last forever.

I'm not the kind of person who usually calls up talk radio shows, but the other day I started dialing when someone who advocates for the elderly cooed about the "help line" that will assist you to figure out what resources are available to you, and other soothing fibs. It must seem as though my sister and I were foolish, unprepared tenderfoots caught in the machine of eldercare, but this is not true. Within the constraints of our mother's refusal to discuss the future, we had long ago consulted the available help lines, established a bulging file of resources, chosen an assisted care facility that catered to elderly teachers, negotiated powers of attorney, interviewed congenial physicians—done, in fact, all that could be done to assure a reasonable transition when the inevitable time arrived. We had a friend, a mole in the bureaucracy, who could advise us at any time. We had contacts in congressional offices.

What do people who are *really* unprepared do? Honey, there is a help line you can call.

What we hadn't planned for was the venality and cruelty of a system indifferent to human suffering. I think it was this recognition of what I can only call *deep systemic evil* that for a year kept me from praying and dreaming. *Wake up, the world is a thousand times more vicious than you have imagined.* Again and again, the koans of my life reveal this truth to me, but I try to cling to some rosy vision instead. Every time I get it, I have to hide out for a year among the animals, trying to get my poise and courage back, and my capacity to love the world anyway.

My sister and I are now determined to transfer Mother to a private-pay assisted living facility up the road from my sister's house, a hotel-like, potpourri-scented environment of chintz-covered sofas and little white private apartments. Let's call it Sunnybank. I spend several days painting delicate pieces of wicker furniture and arranging plants, as though for a child going off to college. The nurse from Sunnybank visits Mother, tests her intellectual functioning, and reviews her medical record—which, by the way, still contains no diagnosis. The nurse approves transfer to Sunnybank, and we hand over a huge nonrefundable entrance fee, "kind of like you'd pay to a condominium association," smiles the director, whom we'll never see again.

But Peaches—my sister calls me at midday—has suddenly put up a roadblock. "There's no way I can release your mother to Sunnybank. She's cognitively impaired," she told Peggy. "I evaluated her right in front of your sister."

"It never happened," I respond. "They've confused her with somebody else again."

"They can't do two-person transfers at Sunnybank"—Peaches is now yelling into a conference call.

"Of course we can," says Lad, the social worker from Sunnybank, "and you know it, Peaches. Why are you lying?"

Two facilities are now fighting over our mother.

Nausea

MY FATHER BOUGHT A REVOLVER, sometime back in 1958, in case bombs started to fall and our neighbors wanted to get into our fallout shelter, which he had hollowed out of the basement and filled with iron bunk beds, a battery-operated radio, freeze-dried food, and the kind of reading material he liked, history books about World War II and romantic poetry. On the wall he hung a white glow-in-the-dark crucifix.

Some of the Catholic magazines that came to our house, like the Jesuit publication *America*, were running articles on the moral implications of shooting your neighbors at the door of your bomb shelter. I began to study these treatises earnestly— an eighth grader by then. It was the first practical use I had found for philosophy: to relieve the aching nausea that cramped me when my dad reviewed protocols for shooting the neighbors. Later that summer I would discover Marcus Aurelius and stoicism. Dad had bought us a set of the *Great Books of the Western World*, which I had started to read obsessively. Hiding out in the rec room with Marcus Aurelius saved me from the 1950s. Fortunately, I found the intellectual route out of family dissonance rather than getting pregnant or having a nervous breakdown.

The whole subdivision in which my poor parents had invested their veterans' housing allowance was built on a swamp. The fallout shelter quickly degenerated into a filthy sinkhole, pumped out now and again when Dad was alive. Mom's approach to it had been her usual, "Pretend it's not there."

Now my sister and I have to sell the house to keep Mother in Sunnybank. She has no liquid assets. We crawl behind the broken canning jars and slime to negotiate an unlighted stairway descending into muck and blackness. "Who in hell is going to buy this house?" we ask each other.

Perhaps a militant survivalist.

I slosh in my farm boots across the underground crypt through two feet of standing water and bring out the white plastic crucifix. "This is *mine*. I got it for selling five dollars worth of Holy Childhood Christmas Seals."

"Those things are painted with some kind of radioactive glaze," my sister tells me. "It probably would have killed us before the bombs."

By now, Lad of Sunnybank, who has been our rock of opposition to Peaches, has reevaluated the situation and decided that the assisted care facility near my sister's house is too understaffed to handle mother, and she will have to be wheeled down the hall to the nursing home unit of the rehabilitation facility until he can find another placement. Funnily enough, this has always been Peaches's preferred solution: how has she brought this about? It will cost around seven hundred dollars a day.

I thank Lad and tell him that, since we have signed a contract with Sunnybank, we presume he will be taking on the financial responsibility for this little ride down the corridor.

Immediately after this conversation, as though orchestrated by Walt Disney, a place opens in a different Sunnybank "campus" across the street from Mom's transitional care facility. We are furious about Lad's treachery because our plan for our mother's comfort has depended upon her being a few blocks from my sister and her children. I imagine—indeed I see plenty of evidence—that these social workers, like defense and prosecuting attorneys on the same case, socialize at night, fraternize, and date. But at least we have a "placement," and Mother will regain her coveted privacy. One July afternoon, we wrap two sheets around her—it's pouring rain—and wheel her across the freeway. We don't bother to return the sheets. No wonder care for the elderly is so expensive.

Ensconcing our mother in that little white room at Sunnybank West, we allow ourself a moment of relief before the true horror dawns on us. "Heartsick" is a real, not a metaphorical, condition.

"Will I be here a week?" she asks, staring into the white space of her incarceration, no cigarettes, no dog. "I can't stand it for a week." She will be desperately alone and her life will crash in on her. My white wicker tables and potted ivy are no solace.

"Life without parole," is the assessment of an elderly man at the dinner table, when we wheel Mom in to try to get her to eat and socialize. "They dropped me off here"—he indicates his steak with contempt—really, the food is excellent—"and I never saw them again. What have I done, I ask you?"

I am not able to say. It's common for people to feel they are being punished out of all proportion to any wrong they have ever committed; this is a recurring trope in spiritual direction. Mother is blind, barely able to speak, unable to feed herself, too weak to push a wheel of her chair. She can't even handle the remote control of her little TV. And worst of all, she is imprisoned in her rage.

But, "Mama good lady," says one of the African aides, a kind woman who prides herself on making our mother smile. "You girls love Mama lots."

We do not want to upset the metaphysics of creation by denying this, but it is not *love* that brings us to visit our mother daily and work so hard for her good. No. Nor is it guilt. I remember my friend Richard changing Joe's diapers and denying he loved him. If that puzzled me at the time, now I can take him at his word. If I name it anything, this quality of mind that coexists with heartsickness, I call it *integrity*. Perhaps *order*. These are our bulwarks against the horror that *nothing we do means anything, that there is nothing we can do*. Against the horror of those sentences.

Being-With

ALL WE CAN DO FOR OUR MOTHER NOW is sit with her. My old dog, Shep, is good at this kind of duty. She has to be where her people are. She drags her arthritic bones up and down the stairs over and over because we, unlike dogs, seldom want to stay still and commit to one floor or another.

As a child I was ill for several months and confined to bed. My grandfather, during this time, was a rock of security. He would come and sit by my bed with his hands in his lap and do absolutely nothing. As soon as he came in I could relax and be at peace. Other relatives, by contrast, flitted in and out, fretting and crying. I could hardly breathe, stifled by their anxiety.

Peter's mother, Margaret Crysdale, now in her nineties, taught me about being-with. She had two difficult children, with whom communication was sometimes impossible. She knitted the most beautiful socks for them, out of lightweight baby yarn on the tiniest needles you can buy. No store-bought sock would ever fit like that, wear like that. These socks were a kind of sacrament, an outward sign of an inward spiritual reality. If Margaret herself could not be-with, the socks would stand in. Margaret had to live through the terrible crisis of her daughter's death from breast cancer. She sat by the bed, day after day, and quietly knitted.

Many of us suffer from the feeling that we cannot do enough or say enough to those in pain. But the people who feel themselves to be the most wordless and short on therapeutic strategies are often the best at being-with. It's good to have communication skills and healing gifts or a Master's in Social Work, but often these contributions come with a hook: you'd better follow my plan, *you'd better get well, you'd better get over it.*

There's another kind of person who can simply bear witness: the spouse who curls around you in bed and holds you till you sleep, the midwife who sits through the long hours of early labor when there is nothing much to do and no drama to star in. To keep a vigil, to watch and pray—these are old religious impulses dating from a time when we knew far less about therapy or birth or what is sociologized as "death and dying." Or far more.

I had excellent training in the ministry of being-with, but I could not companion my mother. I could only sit there in dumb horror, which is not the same.

After a week at Sunnybank West, Mother came down with pneumonia and refused, predictably, to go to the hospital. Therefore she was put on hospice service. The hospice nurses—who come from a different managed-care system—explained that this designation would last for some three months, then be reevaluated. They are now diagnosing congestive heart failure. It seems to be a surprise to Mom: "They tell me I'm going to die."

Some months ago, Robin and I drove through Dickeyville, Wisconsin, where we came upon an astonishing monument to obsessive-compulsive religious passion. A certain Father Mathias Wernerus, one day in 1918, decided to build a little backyard shrine to Mary at his church. One thing led to another. Soon he found himself embarked on creating a castellated undersea kind of structure embedded with shells and costume jewelry, a geologists' treasure trove of fancy crystals. He kept going. There had to be a grotto honoring the Blessed Sacrament, decked with bits of crockery, children's tea sets, dolls' heads, hundreds of stone caps from old gear-shift levers. He went on to build a place for the Sacred Heart, Abraham Lincoln. Abraham Lincoln? Where would it end? Father Wernerus died young.

At what is now called the Dickeyville Grotto, I bought a little plastic paperweight with a model of the main structure inside, the kind you shake and the snow flies. I love things like that. The Dickeyville paperweight goes nicely with the beer-can opener decorated with the head of Pope John Paul, which my daughter Julian brought me from Rome. Religious dogma seldom makes the slightest sense to me, but I love the crazy superstitious objects of Catholicism with their carnival mix of magic and mercantile exploitation. If it glows in the dark, I must have it.

I appreciate as well the formulaic mantras of pre-Vatican II religion: rosaries, novenas "never known to fail," devotions to saints who specialize in selling houses or finding lost objects. For example, I am going to bury this little statue of St. Joseph upside down—he hates that and really goes to work for you—and out of nowhere will materialize a buyer for our mother's house. Someone who wants to make a wine cellar out of the bomb shelter. Burying St. Joseph will work, ask any voodoo practioner. Folklorists call these "apotropaic prophylactic gestures."

"What is prayer," asks one of my atheist friends, "but a way to align our private purposes with those of the universe?" St. Anthony, who specializes in finding lost objects, always gets back my stuff, which is fortunate because things slither and slide through my fingers—sweaters, wallets, reading glasses, heirlooms, lovers. It's as though our individual intention needs to meet cosmic drift at some physical location. We are hardwired for sacramentality.

From Dickeyville, I also brought back a prayer card with a special novena to St. Therese, the sentimental Carmelite saint who died at twenty-four and promised to let fall from heaven "a shower of roses." You say five Our Fathers, five Hail Marys, and five Glory-Bes for five days, with some extra mumbo jumbo on the fifth day.

Now I am making a novena to St. Therese that my mother will die easily and soon. I know that Therese will understand, if nobody else will, the complex intentions of this prayer. The little Carmelite herself died horribly, of tuberculosis of the bone. What was infinitely worse, she died in a mental state characterized by utter deprivation of religious comfort, faith, or love. If anybody could understand the suffering my mother is going through, it's Therese.

Like every scholarly person I have ever known, I regress in times of stress to my ethnic grounding. Irish people habitually pray each other over the bridge to death. "I pray for the Lord to take her," Grandma Rose used to say, apropos of anyone suffering.

I make this intercession for my mother, because it's been over 99 degrees for two weeks, yet she is freezing; because her hands and feet are swollen to the size of cantaloupes and ready to ulcerate again; because she's not too far gone to be furious with caregivers who call her "Honey." Because she simply cannot stand it.

Sitting by the bedside, I'm reading a book about farming in the nineteenth century. I have to look up the word *harrow*: a spiked bar drawn over a field in the spring to break up clods of earth. When I was a child, the old farmer next door would harrow and plow with a team of horses in the spring. It seems, in my memory, like a picture from another age, framed in that trendy window of which our mother, who liked to know what the whole world was up to, was so proud. *Harrowing: a psychological process akin to having a chain of spikes drawn over the mind . . .*

. . . *to break up the clods.* Thus I finish the definition.

Last night I dreamed I had been given the task of strangling a lamb. "It's the fastest and kindest way to kill it," says a voice in the dream. But the lamb wouldn't die. The physical reality of the dream was horrible. I wanted to release my hands, but I knew that if I did I would only have to begin again and cause the poor animal more pain.

I drive back and forth to Sunnybank in a car full of bags of Mom's clothes, which I am trying to find time to drop off at the Goodwill. It seems such a betrayal to give them away while she remains alive and begging to come home, but we are trying to get the house ready to sell. We need to pay the bills at Sunnybank, and St. Joseph is head over heels in the garden.

Day five: I have fouled up my novena to St. Therese by forgetting to say it before 11 a.m. This is one of the rules. Now I will have to start again on Monday. It's like a job. Robin can't understand this at all. "I thought grace was free," he ventures.

"Sweetheart, that's only for Lutherans."

This puzzles him immensely.

"Catholics," I say, "have to put out."

At least Irish Catholics do. In penal times, Catholics got a good dose of Jansenism when all the seminaries were shut down and the pious young men had to go to France to study for the priesthood. The French contributed a lot of odd threads to the fabric of Irish Catholicism, including the cult of Therese, to whom I am developing what Grandma Rose would have called a full-fledged "devotion." Lots of girls in my youth had a fixation on the coy saint. Back then, I found Therese beneath contempt. I went in, myself, for the more adventurous male saints.

Later I read Ida Goerres' biography of Therese, *The Hidden Face*, which told me how much of her writing had been bowdlerized by her remaining family and fellow nuns to fit the contemporary image of piety. Therese was, certainly, a spoiled, sentimental daughter of the bourgeoisie, the kind of innocent fool who would have been pilloried by her contemporary, Émile Zola. He would have pictured her with a brioche in hand and butter running down her chin, while the masses surged outside. She was a Barbie doll; the true miracle is that grace got hold of her, as it can get hold of anyone.

The narrative—the real story, not the pious embroidery—of her last days, her physical suffering and sense of abandonment by God, horrifies me. Poor child, she was like a poodle stranded on an ice floe. Yet she hung on. I'm sure that in whatever transcendent place or state Therese now abides, she thinks this stupid novena I'm making to her is a hoot. And she knows it's my nature to put out.

On the fifth day of my screwed-up novena, I bounded into Mother's room at Sunnybank to find her being bathed and counseled by a hospice nurse who is strange to me. "Do you feel safe here, Honey?" I hear the nurse asking.

One of my male friends calls this question a "ponderous therapeutic feminist cant phrase." Mom tries to process it on her own terms. "Has there been a burglary?"

The nurse goes on, "I just don't think the staff here is very responsive to you."

We have been involved with Sunnybank for three weeks, since they won the custody fight for Mom. She's warming up to Henri, who answers her call light within three minutes, and to Gloria, who gently tickles her ribs when she changes the diaper, the one who croons, "I can make Mama laugh." She's made friends with another retired teacher who scolds her for not eating. Even in her terrible condition, Mom demands to be wheeled into the current-events quiz each morning, where she is establishing herself as a formidable competitor. So I'm astonished to hear the hospice nurse seeming to undermine her confidence in the fragile refuge she has come to.

I introduce myself to the nurse and remind her to check Mom's bedsore. Mom has to go to the bathroom. I ring for the aide, who chooses this occasion not to show up. The hospice nurse gets on the phone to complain to her supply depot about the lack of a certain kind of bandage. I visit with Mom for a few minutes, and then, since I haven't eaten or peed since breakfast, I break for the ladies' room. When I come back, the hospice nurse is having this conversation with Mom, which I think I can put down verbatim, because shock has engraved it on my mind:

"You're very tired, Honey, and you're not eating. Sometimes our bodies know something we don't know about us . . ."

"I'm not tired," Mom says. "Please help me to go to the bathroom and put me in my wheelchair."

". . . so I'm wondering how you want to spend your time and where you want to be until . . . um . . . and how much time until um . . ."

Ever the drama teacher, Mom hates poor delivery. "What are you talking about?"

"When do you think you will pass?"

"I don't want to *pass*. I want to go to lunch. Is lunch over?" Gloria comes in just then, with some fruit and a milkshake from the dining room.

The hospice nurse is inexorable. "It's just that you seem so lonely here, Honey. Where would you like to spend your final days?" The nurse keeps punctuating her astonishing speeches with the phrase, "Of course I've never met you before and I don't know your story, but . . ."

"Shut up then," I long to shout from the attached bathroom, but I want to see where the nurse is going with this.

Here's where she's going: "I know a wonderful place called The Pines where there are only ten rooms and you could have very individualized care . . ."

I don't feel angry, just stunned. I draw the nurse away from my mother, like a killdeer protecting its nest, by beginning a little side conversation with her. "You see, our mother has had a series of difficult moves. She's just beginning to get settled in here. Her own house is uninhabitable. My sister and I are trying to get it in shape. Just yesterday we arranged for a bank loan. She has no assets . . ." I am babbling. My long, stupid habit of respecting authority and assuming that medical people have one's good at heart makes me humble and diffident.

(Later I call The Pines, which happens to have an opening for three thousand dollars more a month than even Sunnybank charges, and, with a flush of horror, I think I understand: they must be paying the nurse a bounty.)

The hospice nurse says haughtily, "Well, if money is a problem, there is always the Good Counsel Home."

If she means that as an insult, I don't take it, because my father died at that hospice, run by the Dominican Sisters. "But they only take cancer patients," I respond patiently. "My mother has conges-tive heart failure."

"Oh, I thought she had cancer," the nurse says. She exits so quickly, without saying good-bye, that I wonder if she is heeding a sudden call of nature. I expect her to return, but it soon becomes clear she's fled the scene of her *faux pas*.

Mom and I laugh about this, on what will be her last clear day. "Imagine a hospice nurse who can't talk about death," Mother marvels.

"She was probably just feeling her way into your vocabulary."

I have tried to do that myself, with no success. Just now, Mother is not planning to die. She is planning to have lunch. "How do you feel about being in hospice care?" I ask her.

"Nervous. I've never done anything like this before."

"Some would say"—I go on like Barbara Walters—"that everyone we have ever loved will come to help us when we die. Maybe Dad will come. What do you think?" Saying these words, I feel like a complete fool.

"I doubt it," says Mom, definitively. These will be, in effect, her last words. She slips into a kind of twilight sleep.

For ten more days we will climb the mountain of her death. The nurses, good-hearted but bad actors every one, keep trying to prepare us. "You see," says Laney, who smiles all the time no matter what crisis she is talking us through, "how labored her breathing is, how slow. She's very tired and losing her interest in life."

"That's because you're giving her too much morphine," snaps my sister, on the tenth day.

"We could cut back if you think it's right."

Peggy shrugs. "I just don't know."

"Well, let's watch her and keep in touch," I say. As we walk out, my sister says, "I'm a midwife. We don't believe in drugging people. I just don't know what's going on here."

What's going on, I think, is that the hospice protocols are slowly easing our mother out of life, and, to the extent we understand this, we agree to this course of action.

If there is deep love in a family and a loved one is suffering physically, it's easier to sit with such a process. But our family life is based on denial and courtesy, and our mother's pain is more psychological than physical. Sedation, then, becomes slightly problematic—not problematic enough to provoke us to outrage. Nobody knows better than we do the extent of our mother's psychological suffering. Yesterday we sought two outside opinions validating what seems to us the odd strategy of sedating a patient suffering from pleural effusion. It's a therapy that delicately eases her breathing and delicately erodes simultaneously. In classic moral theology, this is the famous Double Effect: if the effect you desire is the relief of suffering, you are not bound to avoid the second effect, the death of the sufferer.

But this moral syllogism demands extraordinary clarity of focus. The clerics who devised it also believed that a man could have sexual intercourse with no intention but the procreation of children; they taught that it was legitimate to kill an enemy in battle so long as you didn't get *angry*. I am incapable of such clarity. I am confused, *harrowed*.

Suppose I let my scruples overwhelm me and demand that they call our mother back from the dream she is in, her feet moving a little as a dog's do in sleep, call her back from where she is walking, no doubt happily at last, toward her death—how cruel would that be? Why would I do this? Out of some hope that she might reach enlightenment, conscious dying, all that new age stuff? Are we back to the Mozart quartets?

Awake in the night, I pray about this sedation issue. I have a word with Jesus and with Buddha, whoever's on call. I go to sleep and then awaken to the sound of a great sigh, as though the whole neighborhood were releasing its breath.

She died around 4 a.m.

The House of Dreams

THERE WAS A DRAWING IN MY Baltimore Catechism of souls leaving their bodies. They looked like disembodied nightgowns with heads and faces. As I dig through each layer of my family home in Roseville, it seems I release spirits like that. A nightgown flies out of the box of Christmas ornaments, a fetal form slides from under the lid of the cedar chest. Looking into the chest where it sits on the basement floor, damp on the bottom and a little rotten, I remember the yellow silk dress my mother and I put away in here, one summer day in the kitchen of the Case Street house.

"I don't think we should sell this chest," I tell Peggy. "I'll take it if nobody wants it."

"Ella wants it. I think it should go to somebody young, don't you?"

"Sure." Ella needs a hope chest. She is going to be the next to marry. It's the yellow dress I want to find. It was lined with silk from Dad's parachute, the one he bailed out with when his plane caught fire. I remember Mom folding it away here. But it's gone. No doubt I opened the lid and it flew out, glad to be out of the basement. Where the cedar chest sat, the mummified skin and tail of a dead mouse are barely discernible on the floor. I have to use a shovel to scrape it away, trying to keep the picture from entering my mind.

Consciousness, like the old chest, like the closets and the photograph album, is a repository for images, partial holograms, half-burnt letters, torn photos, and slides projected on the skull's white screen. All night they flit and trouble me.

We have moved through our childhood house from the attic cupboards to the surreal, dripping cave of the bomb shelter. I retrieve:

278

the black knit suit I wore on my first day of teaching, the high-waisted flower print I sewed for my sister's wedding, when I was a few months pregnant with Jude. In the master bedroom, I discover my niece, trying on my bridal veil, delicate tulle with an edging of fine lace, so Jackie Kennedy. "Take it if you want."

The nut grinder, the cookie press. I can't put price tags on them, but I have to because our houses won't hold all this stuff and we are getting ready for a garage sale. I take the cookie press home, push dough through the fierce little extruding device, and take the results to the faculty autumn potluck. Usually I shuffle through with pita bread and tabbouleh.

"Those look like quite the project," says one of my amazed colleagues.

"You are going to see more of this from me," I promise rashly.

The French critic Gaston Bachelard writes about *the oneiric house*, the house of dreams. He says that the architecture of one's family home bestows upon the growing child a kind of template for consciousness: the basement is a repository of ancient secrets, the public rooms resound with family life, and so on. Of course he was thinking about the old Norman fortresses of his native landscape. He didn't have much time for nineteenth-century Parisian apartment buildings. I wonder what he would make of our suburban boxes?

I follow the smell of cigarette smoke to the kitchen of Mom's house, where she is sitting over a cup of coffee and the paper, her red hair all fluffy and neat. A great feeling of warmth and friendliness radiates from her.

"Mom, you're smoking again!" I'm almost proud of her. What a feisty woman. I throw my arms around her and she returns my hug with great affection. "It was not an option for me to continue in that Puritan establishment!"

I keep crying and embracing her. "I'm so glad you could come home."

"I'm glad, too." She is soft and tender and stable, as never in life. When the dead come to us in dreams, they are always *improving*, which is such a blessing. Whatever liminal space they inhabit—as the nuns said of purgatory—is a place of learning and growth, where it's never too late to change.

I had not expected to grieve so much for my mother. There are, of course, many forms of grief. When Robin's mother died, he mourned, he told me, the possibility of ever having a relationship with her.

Some writers on grief say the loss of an ambivalent and vexed relationship is "worse," but who is giving grades? It has its downside. I fret that, had I been a better person, I could have made a bridge between us. Or, if life were not so relentlessly uncontrollable, both she and I would have found the love we needed. Mourning, then, becomes mourning for one's own failures or for the human condition. That's a complicated and dangerous terrain. One is at risk of falling into an abyss of depression or that terrible existential nausea.

What both torments me and saves me is what we may as well call *pity*. Those old photos of Mother, her actressy, uptilted, beautiful face shining with possibility. How could she come to saying in the last weeks of her life that—the phrase itself even a bit dramatic— "all my life has been a waste."

The critic Suzanne Raitt writes, of the protagonist of a Virginia Woolf novel, that she "is increasingly taken over by intuitions of her own disintegration, the woman she previously appeared to be is gradually exposed as—or comes to seem—an empty illusion." I associate this phenomenon of dissolution with grief, my mother's and my own. When she repudiated her life, perhaps my mother was feeling what I feel now, an abrupt withdrawal of the tide of illusion, leaving only the naked bone on the beach. The bone may have done its work in the world, but it is not half the bone we thought it was.

Grief then, is not only about loss of the other. It precipitates loss of the self. When my husband left, I felt myself, in some sense, pulled limb from limb. But in retrospect, that pain had to do with losing the sense of oneself as a certain kind of person, summed up in all the associations of "wife."

Beyond this grieving process I sense a larger world of possibility, something like a larger self, out beyond ideas of right and wrong. The bone is not its household.

Perhaps this will be my last dream about the Roseville house: Jude and I are working in the yard, when suddenly I see that the sky has become black. A tornado is approaching, as, indeed, they used to approach across the wetland when I was a child. Jude and I have to get into Grandma's house, into the basement, to safety! I feel the familiar confusion and smothering sensation of dream-panic. My feet are all tangled up in a garden hose or a nest of snakes.

Finally we make it to the back door, but I don't have a key. Never mind, there is a key in the door, an old-fashioned skeleton key. I turn it and stumble in, leading my son. There is a flicker of candle-light coming from the direction of the living room.

We have made a terrible mistake! Mom would never light candles. Omigod. We don't live here any more. I'm caught between fear of the tornado outside and the wrath of those whose house we have invaded. We don't live here any more.

Phases of the Moon

WHEN I'M ANGRY AT GOD, I resist the moon. I ignore her phases. If she awakens me off guard, bright and full, I pull the bedcovers over my head: *shine if you want to. You'll have to do that all by yourself. I don't care if you're waxing or waning.*

In my environmental writing classes, I always teach my students about lunar phases. "Hold up your hands toward the moon," I tell them, "thumbs together. If her curve fits into your right hand, she's waxing; if left, she's waning. Both the dark of the moon and the left hand are associated with sinister forces. You can remember that, can't you?" One of my former students recently wrote that when she catches sight of the moon she often thinks of me. This may be my best shot at immortality.

When I'm mad at God, I resist this wet dusting of snow that encases each tree, each bush, each red rose hip in white fur, which in the moonlight looks—*go away, I shut my eyes to you.*

Since my mother died, I have only been going through the motions of spiritual practice, which, I am now convinced, I only bother with because my smart dog, Star, so immensely enjoys sitting on the zafu. I ring the bell, she's there, flinging herself before the altar, nose to the floor. I can resist God, but not my relentless border collie.

The queer sense of having failed some test of life, not having been able to save my mother, haunts me. Or of not being clever enough, beautiful enough, tender enough to have attracted the little butterfly feet of her attention. I don't know why my mother's death has dropped me onto this night road where the moon has no changes. It may be the familiar territory that John of the Cross called *Dark Night of the Soul*, refusing, for his part, to take the moon in his hands. Being of an intense temperament—or holy—John suffered from God's darkness. With my peevish disposition, I treat God like any other lover: *fine, be like that*. Don't think I give a shit. Don't even think I'm looking at your display of moonlight on furry branches.

In high school I asked one of the nuns how you could distinguish between Dark Night of the Soul and plain old depression. She said, "It depends on your self-concept." Only a vain girl, my teacher implied, would presume to have a spiritual experience described by saints and mystics. Nowadays, I think my old mentor spoke in error. The Dark Night experience is more democratic, and it is nothing like depression, though it may coincide with a lowering of spirits. This, even, is not the case with me. The rhythm of my life is buoyant. I have enough leisure, enough love, music and craft, a sufficient number of dogs, thank you. It's just that I refuse the moon.

And I've completely stopped dreaming, or remembering my dreams, at least. I go to bed, I hear snowplows roaring somewhere, great machines that take over the world when I relax my vigilance. Then it's morning and I jump up ready for a lovely pot of tea. Shake my fist at the government. Life is on course again.

But I cannot, for the moment, abide spiritual practice. If it were worth anything, my mother would not have died alone at 4 a.m., unreconciled either to life or to leaving it. But "prayer and love are learned when prayer has become impossible and the heart has turned to stone." The best work comes of being stuck and stymied this way. It allows a space for grace to enter. Things happen that we can't use to swell the ego, because we are too shut down to take credit for them. You can't pray, in any way you used to know how to do, through the Dark Night experience, because your whole worldview is on the line. Who or what, in that condition, would you possibly pray to?

Lately I have been ranging through photographs of my mother, her face always avid for life. She wears, inevitably, the happy expression of a dog who wants to play ball. How could so much energy and loveliness have fallen into the adamancy and corrosive fury that characterized her last years? She was not mentally ill for one moment. Not demented. She could still charm the staff at Sunnybank. She was, at eighty, authoritative and beautiful, angry and unforgiving. She despised my Quaker beliefs; pacifism, as a philosophical position, seemed to negate the war experience that had given my parents their most intense and meaningful moments.

Some time ago, a young American girl stood in front of a bull-dozer trying to stop Israelis from leveling an Arab settlement in Gaza, which has seen it all, and the bulldozer crushed her.

Every wisdom tradition has told us to be gentle, kind, creative, and relentless before the bulldozers of tyranny, but why? "The only heroism," wrote Romain Roland, "is to see reality as it is and love it."

I have failed. I repeat my mother's words. Much of my failure has derived from strategic misapprehension about the depth of the darkness, the magnitude of the task, and my own weakness compared to the resilience of those who are less sensitive.

When I tell friends, experimentally, that I have failed, they rush to comfort me, which is not what I'm looking for at all. It doesn't make me sad that I've failed. If anything, it makes me smile ruefully at our collective folly. My mother is dead and all over the world—turn on the news—we are preparing to kill each other again. I cannot stand *reality as it is.*

Glare ice on the spring roads, a dark day. I'm going outside to plant things in the garden, heirloom morning glories, edible nasturtiums. I'm going to go out and plant something in case the seeds might be needed. Perhaps these flowers will be the last things we have to show for our race. Pierre Teilhard de Chardin taught that even if we manage to blow up this shining planet, consciousness will fly to the farthest end of the galaxy and start itself up again. These days I think *consciousness, let it rest in peace:* scatter sunflower seeds or arugula. Something for the rabbits to bed under.

Selling

YESTERDAY, CRUISING AN ESTATE SALE, I was overcome with anxiety and revulsion. This was, by far, the most hyperorganized Lutheran sale I had ever been through, run by the two daughters of a dead woman, each wearing a little gold cross around her neck. Everything was meticulously washed and laid out in plastic containers: their mother's half-used lipsticks, dabs of moisturizer, powder puffs, make-up sponges, her heavy brassieres and her polished old lady shoes. "We managed to price everything in three days," I hear one daughter say.

I felt overwhelmed by a recollection of my mother's unhappy face, hanging above her wheelchair. We had to get her stuff out quickly—yes, someone came along and bought the house within ten minutes of our starting to mow the grass outside—and mostly we just shoveled everything into the garage and let antique pickers come and snap things up for fifty cents here and there. I still run into items in the shops along Grand Avenue that belonged in my childhood bedroom— the torn curtain with the Robinson Crusoe pictures, that awful stuffed fish (they want a hundred fifty dollars for it). Not for a moment do I think we sold stuff too cheaply, I wish we had set fire to it.

How can these serene women so meticulously price their mother's lacy underthings?

At the Lutheran ladies' sale I bought, for four dollars, a red polyester coat with fake-leopard fur lining and a big fake-leopard collar. It offends the taste and sensibilities of everyone I meet, especially my dogs. Shep regards it with weary patience, as yet another obstacle in her daily journey from nap station to food bowl. Young Star stalks it. Robin hates it also.

Last night we went out for dinner.

"How many are you?" asked the hostess.

"Three," Robin replied. "Me, my companion, and The Coat."

"Maybe it would like a booth of its own," the hostess said.

I enjoy wearing The Coat to Quaker meeting where, when I open my eyes for a moment, I see wave after wave of beige and khaki. It's spring. A month ago, I would have seen black, gray, and indigo. I love these people. But I cannot mourn my mother and the endless war in beige. I have to wrap myself in the ugliest items America can produce. I have to shroud myself in polyester and plush with fake leopard spots. This is my attempt to engage *reality as it is*.

I sit there meditating on the words, "Happy are they who mourn, for they shall be comforted. Happy are the meek, for they shall possess the earth."

My dogs possess the earth. The powerful never see landscape because they are trying to get hold of more landscape. They are always looking over the next hill: *option to buy adjoining acres*. The dogs just walk on over. A Korean friend of mine says she is always spooked by the rustling of wildlife in the deep darkness along the demilitarized zone (DMZ), hares and flying squirrels easily traversing the dreadful boundary.

I suppose the meek could be shot. Jesus was inattentive to details like that. No doubt he had his own blind spots about accepting reality-as-it-is.

I am, on the whole, comforted. When I wrap myself up in red polyester plush, I feel that I am making an appropriate address to a world more absurd and comic than I had previously imagined. In my youth, I mourned war. Like all young people, I thought highly of myself and my analysis. I believed that if I worked hard, war would go away. Every time violence broke out again, I took it as a personal affront.

Of course, there's always something new to hear about and mourn. When I stop wailing altogether, I will have accepted reality with my whole red plush heart.

Sitting in Meeting, I check in on my life like a student monitoring the clock on her final exam. There seem to be more problems than I can possibly cover in the time allotted.

PART SIX

Controlled Burn

Writing the Wolf

DRIVING HIGHWAY 1 FROM ELY to Isabella, Minnesota, I watched a dark space in my peripheral vision begin to move, as though a piece of the wilderness jigsaw puzzle had detached itself and stalked into my visual field. A moose looks more like a two-dimensional cutout than a living animal, and whatever woods he comes out of seems like the wrong woods. Here on Highway 1, a vivid young patch of aspen and beech delivers what looks like an ungainly cartoon creature drawn by a talented child. When deer emerge from the woods, they look—if one is to make judgments about such things—as though they have a right to be there; wolves, though I sight them more rarely, act like they own the place. Moose alone seem computer generated, superimposed on a bucolic scene.

Moose, the overgrown knobby-wristed boy at the senior prom, looks perpetually out of place in spring landscape. He might work better in Oregon, with its ancient primordial woods. Once, however, I took off in a small Cesna from Isle Royale and saw a cow and two calves wading in a slough next to the great lake. The perspective, in that landscape, was exactly right. Moose are meant to be seen from fifty feet in the air, with something as big as Lake Superior defining the space behind them, creatures on the edge of time.

For all that, a moose will walk right into your car and smash it to pieces, at great cost to both of you.

The moose is never going to step into your poem, at least not in anything like the romantic lead. These huge creatures seem made for a comic role—as humans construct nature at least; how nature actually *is* being harder, perhaps impossible, to know. But local wisdom around here is that if you come upon a moose in the woods, mating, or fighting or, especially, calf-tending, you'd better climb a tree fast. A week or so ago, an experienced forest ranger surprised a cow and calf on the trail she was tending. The cow struck out viciously and broke the ranger's fibula. The ranger shot up a tree anyway, and had to stay there several hours. Then she got herself home and sat in the sauna for a while, till she figured out the swelling in her leg wasn't going to go down. This is what life is like in the woods between Ely and Isabella, Minnesota. You are as far north as you can go and still be an American. Something in me responds to this landscape, these people, as to nowhere else I have lived.

I have not come to the woods to get over my mother's death, and it will surprise me that this healing comes about, that the woods do their ancient work despite the fact that I have come here to work and work hard teaching a summer course in environmental writing at a place called Wolf Ridge Environmental Learning Center.

Most of us teachers are stationed in primitive cabins in the Superior National Forest near Isabella, midway down Highway 1 between the Boundary Waters Canoe Area and Wolf Ridge, which is near Finland, Minnesota. I drive fifteen miles north for groceries and fifteen miles south for work, and all the day long I meet my classes or attend lectures or go on field trips. Here I am in the wilderness telling you about my *daily commute*. But this is how most twenty-first century humans experience nature, from the car window. Some environmentalists think that's a good thing. Stay out of the woods, go to the zoo: you represent a lethal mutation, to use Noam Chomsky's phrase.

Returning home at night to my two dogs, I am often the only one in camp—for the first few weeks at least. Other teachers come and go. There is no radio, TV, or telephone. In the off-hours, we take old-dog walks and young-dog walks. Shep can barely make it, panting, down the hill to Lake Gegoka. She pads along diffidently, as though her paws were treading a hot griddle. Star gets in her young-dog run, tearing in and out of the woods with a black lab who has befriended her.

Shep has been in poor condition for a few weeks. She had an allergic reaction to some arthritis medication and got three spots of infection on her head and paws. Two hundred dollars later, she had new medication, one of those plastic lampshades on her head, and a lethal case of doggy depression. Finally, I cured her by putting tea tree oil on the wounds, mildly antispeptic and revolting for her to lick.

Everything this spring smells of bone, blood, and fur.

The day I saw my first moose was my mother's birthday. She would have been eighty-one. That month, last year, she had entered the rehabilitation center, reluctantly, on her own two feet. By her birthday she was in a wheelchair. One of the aides had tied a balloon to it for our disconsolate celebration. She had a month and a half to live.

God should send us a letter. This business of not knowing the day or the hour is destabilizing. Or perhaps the problem is half-knowing. Shep breathes happily on the floor, getting up and down with patience and pain, but innocent of what that portends for her eighteenth year of being a dog. She guards her privileges, spreads her arthritic legs over her food dish lest Star get a whiff. She is as happy as she has ever been.

But Mother was in utter misery. All her life she had tamped down the big feelings, exchanged passion for sentiment, anger for bickering, terror for anxiety. At the last, what she could say about death was it made her nervous. She was trapped in her wheelchair. She couldn't read. Television no longer interested her, no friends visited, and her little dog was dead. Strangers—aides and hospice visitors badgered her—I badgered her, trying to make it better, perhaps only for myself.

Henry David Thoreau wanted to drive life into a corner and publish whatever he found, the grandeur or the meanness. But what if he had found it mean? Would he have written the journal? Yet that is the diary of many lives, a hand drawing back the curtain, a frightened glance, the letting-fall. This is reality, kiss up to it.

It takes so little to scare us right out of our lives if we are sensitive. Going to war at nineteen must have overpowered my mother's soul: the soul, that delicate discerning instrument, fragile and luminous as stained glass spun from the maker's pipe, still molten, unsure of its form. My parents, and Robin's mother, Cynthia Fox, lived much the same lives of avoidance.

Yet here is a lovely story about Cynthia Fox that I want to remember.

"Robin," I asked one day, "how did you come to know so much about ornithology?"

"My mother taught me. She was a life-lister. It was one of the safe subjects we could always return to."

"And who taught her?"

"That's a funny story. During the war, she volunteered as an enemy-plane spotter. She had the early shift in a bunker in Princeton, and the man who shared it with her was a famous ornithologist from the university. Every morning he would teach her the birds and she would teach me."

My father taught me the silhouettes of enemy planes from those little kits the soldiers were issued. Cynthia Fox's time was better spent. This young Quaker bride, with dark braids wrapped around her head, celebrated her engagement (Robin told me), making love in the woods near the eighteenth-century Quaker cemetery where we laid her ashes two years ago. She told Robin that scandalous tale, and she gave him the names for *pine sisken, cerulean warbler,* and he gave them to me. Not a bad legacy. I want to pull these golden threads out of the wreckage and dreck of any life, to retrieve its promise and buoyancy, also real.

The forest service here in Isabella creates periodic conflagrations to burn out the undergrowth and windfall. Writing the personal essay is, like that, a controlled burn.

Nosing my old car into the parking lot at Wolf Ridge and getting out, I notice a doe's track, and beside it, the nickel-sized mark of her very small fawn. Do they come here at night to inhabit "staff parking" with a full sense of entitlement? Wolf Ridge is, with respect to the surrounding wilderness, like the DMZ, where many kinds of living creatures come to regard each other in a state of truce. For the humans, it offers up a world of possibility, physical, spiritual, emotional, moral. In the past, I have taught school in the city and fled to the woods for reprieve; it's a very different thing to bring school into the woods. It calls into question the importance of everything I usually teach in an environmental writing course. It shrugs aside all the data our minds are so full of. There's a lot I could say about Edwin Way Teale or Edwin Muir, Thoreau or Whitman, but it seems more important to let my mind take in the mark of the doe's hoof and the fawn's small brand. These have to find a place in the syllabus; these *are* the syllabus.

We always begin class with the ring of a Tibetan bell and enjoy five minutes of quiet centering. I'm aware, in this time, of a deep tiredness, and at the edge of it, an agitation for change. I've liked being on the road, a new feeling for me, the homebody. I've liked taking off in my car, wanting to put on miles like a teenager, wanting to venture, like a boy. It's taken me such a long time not to count the cost, in gas, in wear-and-tear on the vehicle, in larking away from some responsible thing I could be doing.

What might that be?

In the wilderness, I sleep more, eat less, read more, stare into spaces that were there before but didn't open. I feel on the edge of a bursting happiness, even a triumph. Although my balance is shot and my joints hurt, a vision seems to rise: *I could learn this*—all the fascinating things the naturalists at Wolf Ridge write on the blackboards, orienteering, for example. Since last we met, my students have hiked ten miles into the national forest, learned to identify twenty new species of flora, turned over their kayaks on command, swum below a waterfall, and—Miranda speaks out of the silence—"I learned the

Latin name of the biggest spider I ever saw." Another student comments, "Wolf Ridge seems like a place where anything is possible."

Last night I dreamed I had inherited a house full of terrible junk, brightly colored mechanical things that would cost a lot to haul away. Voices in the dream are urging me to keep things, be concerned, be responsible. I tell the Voices about *controlled burns*.

As teachers so often are, I'm led by my students. The fact that I'm here at all is because two of my writing students, Michelle and Lindsey, recommended it. Listen, I'm not one of those women who runs with the wolves. I'm a woman who runs from the wood ticks. There are Wendell Berry naturalists and there are Gary Snyder naturalists. Wendell Berry naturalists, like me, are comfortable on farms. We like to talk about sustainable agriculture. We're up for any bloody-minded farm task—here let me castrate that for you—but, in my family at least, canoeing and hiking were thought of as "recreational" and therefore not quite righteous. Canoeing, like tennis, was for people who didn't know how to do a job-a-work. Why climb a rock face if you can climb a windmill and fix the motor while you're up there?

I love to watch my students being changed by the wilderness experience—this is the great joy of teaching out here on the edge. But a peculiar tension and joy comes into the learning process when the teacher, as well, enters the rapids, upsets her own canoe. In most higher education, by nature of its traditional boundaries, little is at stake. Case studies and inquiry-based learning may simulate real issues, but the teacher rarely cedes control. At Wolf Ridge, by contrast, I may find myself tomorrow stalled, frozen with terror on a granite cliff, with a twenty-year-old to talk me down.

After lunch, I wander into a classroom where a naturalist is lecturing. "Do you think I could do the ropes course?" I ask the young staffer. "It's mostly mental," he assures me. I start to collect brochures about winter camping, snowshoeing, and chasing around behind a dog team.

It's mostly mental.

Driving Meditation

LONG-DISTANCE DRIVING INDUCES ALL that most of us know of the contemplative state. Perhaps this is why so many people go on solitary long-distance road trips in much the same spirit as medieval monks used to go on pilgrimage. Medieval Irish monastics would abandon themselves to boats without oars, fetching up wherever God and the waves willed. I have a goal in mind when I drive from Isabella to Finland every morning, but I seem to ride off the grid as soon as I hit Highway 1 and its misty plate of space.

Yet I can tell you, two white-tailed deer stood a long time by the road, then suddenly skittered into the alder thicket, trading their food for fear at the very last minute. I can tell you an SUV going ten miles over the speed limit gained on me steadily and finally passed, doing me a great service: he can look out for moose, now, and I can just listen to Yo-Yo Ma on the car stereo. Watchfulness is one of the essential trials of life on earth, for two-legged and for four-legged.

When we can release our watchfulness—and our high school driving instructors may not have encouraged this practice behind the wheel—a space opens into which new knowledge and understanding can enter. My students at Wolf Ridge are very clever and suspicious. They mistrust everything the books tell them, question every statement I make. And this is a good intellectual habit: Cartesian, as Simone Weil observed. For my part, though, I am becoming more and more comfortable with the spaciousness beyond words. It may be a developmental pattern, if things are on track. I have gotten comfortable with the slash between the words *true* and *untrue*. My grandparents and old aunts and uncles were comfortable to be with when they fell into this space. It's a space children inhabit out of naïveté and old people out of experience, which perhaps explains the rapport between these age groups. The young inhabit a middle world, and this is the source of their peculiar suffering. It's why I feel so much concern for and interest in the young without, thank God, sharing their perspective any more.

One's attention is changed, not taken, I have to say to my high school driving instructor. Spruce, jack pine, alder, ahead of me a bank of cumulus clouds building.

Here by the road, I saw a moose carcass three days ago, a gaping wound in its shoulder and the gay red headlight of an SUV next to it. I watched the moose progressively cede itself to the wilderness. Yesterday its legs were gone. This morning the chest bones are starting to look flayed, starting out of their case of black leather. The head is gone now. Not very much says *moose*, here; he could be a lost biker.

Then I make out the low shadow of wolf, the first I have seen in the wild, if a rural highway can be called wild. Wolves are opportunistic hunters, able to eat five times their weight at a sitting. They have made short work of this carcass.

The road keeps developing itself out of a bath of mist. I remember an eccentric translation of Rilke's poem, "On an Archaic Torso of Apollo": "Art is looking at you / you must change."

"Why," the deer inquires, "*art?* I am looking at you; you better brake at least."

I am looking, but nothing will change for me. The sky will change, but not for me. The deer will change, but not for me.

First light. Scouts used to talk about "first light" in the novels of James Fenimore Cooper, or maybe it was in the movies of the novels of James Fenimore Cooper, starring the likes of Daniel

Day-Lewis, his muscles rippling across some rock face he was climbing at first light. First light at my place could also be called "first yip." I have locked Star out of my bedroom because she is afraid of storms and crashes around under my bed all night if there's even a whisper of rain in the woods. I have locked Shep in the bathroom because she has become completely incontinent. I refuse to get her those expensive doggy diapers; I buy Pampers and cut out a hole for her tail.

Yip. It's 4 a.m. I get up, pet some dogs, let some dogs out, go back to sleep. Second light. Full woof. It's 6 a.m. Dogs out, tea water on. Dogs in.

I decide to take them for a quick hike around McDougal Lake, to give them a run before I head out on the road. It was hiking to hike we were doing, not hiking to smell the roses or investigate species or have a good look at the landscape. On this particular trail, the forest service has placed benches at beautiful spots so the sojourner can sit and view, in the same spirit as the Japanese create moonhouses to contemplate cycles of beauty and dash off the occasional haiku.

No haiku for Star. She's always on a mission. Get in, get out. So was I, just then, having a class to teach. Sometimes the hike is about hiking. Cover the ground, get a general sense of the terrain, get on to the business of the day. I don't have much respect for the quick-coverage model so popular with western educators. I like to subvert school situations by plopping myself, figuratively, on the bench and taking in a long breath of pine-scented air. But the dogs are always teaching me new ways of being in the world. Even creaky old Shep wants to keep moving.

She has had a wonderful time up here, walking a mile or so every day with a big smile on her face, more ground than she has covered in two years. Yet I know her lungs and heart and kidneys are failing; she faints, or stands for an hour, staring at nothing, forgetting to lie down. Sympathetic friends keep saying, "Don't you think a dog lets you know when it's ready to go?"

Maybe. The trouble with Shep is she tells me every day that she's happy to be here and might like a hamburger for lunch, if it's all the same to you . . .

But the day finally comes when she can keep nothing, even baby food, in her stomach. Then another series of fainting spells and something in both of us surrenders.

I took her to the vet in Ely. I've never met a vet I didn't fall in love with, and this soft-spoken, grandfatherly man was no exception. He stroked her white muzzle. "Boy, she's old. She has had some innings.

"She has that look," he went on. "The way I think about it, we can save them the worst week of their lives." So I sat on the floor with Shep while he gave her a tranquilizing shot and then the euthanasia fluid. Somehow, it was easier to do it up here on the borderland where she has been so happy.

A moment later I blundered down the wrong corridor and came upon the vet carrying Shep in his arms, wrapped up in an old green bedspread. The look on his face was gentle and sad, though he was all by himself in the corridor and didn't know I was watching him.

Little Marais

OUT ON THE CRAGS OVERLOOKING Lake Superior, my young border collie, Star, tries out her claws and courage. She slides across a bed of orange lichen that tickles her city pads. She herds whitecaps out to the place where rock drops off into freezing boreal—*heat*—I could tell her. She's no swimmer, but for my part, I love the weird sensation of diving into the fifty degree water and feeling my skin seared by hot blood as the circulation revs up and tries to protect life's tender machine. Well, okay, it's cold *at first*. Reluctantly, Star follows me into the tide's Platonic slap. You can't get into this water and not be changed. Out of the lake we exit—pretty rapidly—shaking our mortal hairs into a semblance of something unkillable, smiling our animal smiles . . .

The lake, vast as an ocean as the mind's eye measures distance: how would we know, without taking its blood or wine on the lips, whether it's salt or sweet? Just where (today) a white margin of water touches white sky, a bank of islands rises. Tomorrow the sky may be blue, or the islands misted over. At my feet, seven mallard chicks spin around their mother, learning to feed and swim. What all of us know and forget and recall. The sun is beginning to burn a slit in the white air. Star and I enter the landscape, actors arriving late at an improvisation that began long before we walked down to the lake.

Over and over, the rock releases its little river, and whether we are there to see it or not, the mist walks like Jesus over the lake and takes over. The dog and I lie in a little cave on the rim of things, a space as indistinct as the margin between sleep and waking, or, though I have not been there yet, life and death.

It's Sunday morning, and I am reading only this bible of small stones, harebells making it out of the fundament, birds drifting two by two along their chosen edge. I prefer, like any small mammal, the transparent petal to stained glass. The angels are too large in the books written by men: what did the virgin report, really, back to someone safe as an aunt, about the sun making it through her personal mist?

Here at my feet, a bee enters the ovary of a flower, stumbling as if he were drunk with light, or just, maybe, doing his job in the world.

Works Cited

p. 5   Lao Tsu, *Tao Te Ching,* trans. Gia-Fu Feng and Jane English (New York: Random House, 1972).

p. 15   Abraham Joshua Heschel, *I Asked For Wonder* (New York: Crossroads, 2000), 56.

p. 18   Henry David Thoreau, "Solitude," *Walden and Civil Disobedience* (New York: Penguin, 1983), 178.

p. 19   Katherine Anne Porter, "The Grave," *The Leaning Tower and Other Stories* (New York: NAL, 1969), 55.

p. 20   Parker Palmer, *The Active Life* (New York: Harper and Row, 1990), 4.

p. 21   Georges Poulet, *Studies in Human Time,* 97-104, quoted by Thomas Merton, Woods, Desert, Shore (Santa Fe: Museum of New Mexico Press, 1982), 40.

p. 35   See Angela Bourke, *The Burning of Bridget Cleary* (New York: Penguin, 1999).

p. 37   Elizabeth Bowen, *The Heat of the Day* (New York: Penguin, 1976), 263.

p. 47   Mary Caroline Richards, *Centering* (Middletown, Conn.: Wesleyan University, 1964), 19.

p. 50   "Sacred Throne," *The Sacred Harp: The Best Collection of Sacred Songs, Hymns, Odes, and Anthems Ever Offered the Singing Public for General Use,* ed. Hugh McGraw et al. (Bremen, Ga.: Sacred Harp Publishing Company, 1991), 569.

p. 51   Julie Landsman, *Basic Needs* (Minneapolis: Milkweed Editions, 1993), 162.

p. 52   Thoreau, *Walden,* 257.

p. 53 Thomas Merton, *Dancing in the Waters of Life: The Journals 1963–1965)*, ed. Robert E. Daggy (San Francisco: Harper, 1997), 291.

p. 53 "Restoration," *The Sacred Harp*, 312.

p. 55 "Villulia," *The Sacred Harp*, 56.

p. 56 Merton, *Dancing*, 162.

p. 59 Leonard Woolf, *Downhill All the Way* (New York: Harcourt, 1967), 74.

p. 69 Hafiz, "A Cushion for Your Head," *The Gift*, trans. Daniel Ladinsky (New York: Penguin Arkana, 1999), 183.

p. 71 Simone Weil, "Spiritual Autobiography," *Waiting for God*, trans. Emma Craufurd, (New York: Harper Colophon, 1973), 73.

p. 82 Merton, *Dancing*, 160.

p. 82 E. M. Forster, *Howards End* (New York: Vintage, 1921), 195.

p. 83 Forster, *Howards End*, 73.

p. 92 Rita Nakashima Brock and Rebecca Parker, *Proverbs of Ashes* (Boston: Beacon, 2001), 36.

p. 97 Rainer Maria Rilke, "Sonnets to Orpheus" 1, 4, trans. Stephen Mitchell, in *Into the Garden: A Wedding Anthology*, ed. Robert Hass and Stephen Mitchell (New York: Harper Perennial, 1993), 102.

p. 97 Mark Doty, "Migratory," *Atlantis* (New York: Harper, 1995), 74.

p. 100 Rainer Maria Rilke, *Letters to a Young Poet*, trans. Stephen Mitchell (New York: Random House, 1986), xii.

p. 102 Gretel Ehrlich, *A Match to the Heart* (New York: Pantheon, 1994), 41, 150, 199.

p. 103 Parker Palmer, *Let Your Life Speak: Listening for the Voice of Vocation* (San Francisco: Jossey-Bass, 1999), 38.

p. 105 Alvin Greenberg, *Why We Live With Animals* (Minneapolis: Coffee House Press, 1990), 36.

p. 114 Rod MacIver, "Frederick Franck: Ink Painter, Writer, Sculptor, Draftsman," *Heron Dance*, no. 20 (Winter 1998), http://www.herondance.org/Frederick_Franck_W20.cfm.

p. 115 Gerard Manley Hopkins, *Poems and Prose* (London: Penguin, 1968), 51.

p. 118 Thomas Keating, O.C.D., *Open Mind, Open Heart* (Rockport, Mass: Element, 1986), 94.

p. 120 Pema Chodron, *Start Where You Are: A Guide to Compassionate Living* (Boston: Shambhala, 1994), 47–48.

p. 131 Parker, *Proverbs*, 43.

p. 132 Parker, *Proverbs*, 43.

p. 136 Joseph Conrad, *Lord Jim* (London: Collected Edition, 1946), 214.

p. 137 Richard Hibberthorne, quoted in Ernest Taylor, *Richard Hibberthorne: Soldier and Preacher*, Friends Ancient and Modern # 16 (Friends Tract Society, 1911), 53.

p. 139 Luce Irigaray, "Belief Itself," *Sexes and Genealogies* (New York: Columbia University Press, 1993), 53.

p. 140 Robert Karen, *The Forgiving Self* (New York: Doubleday, 2001), 33.

p. 142 Dorothy Day, *The Long Loneliness* (New York: Harper & Row, 1981), 148.

p. 143 Anne Carson, *Eros, the Bittersweet* (Princeton, N.J.: Princeton University Press, 1998), 26.

p. 144 Emit Gowin, quoted by Thomas Merton, *Wood, Shore, Desert*, xi.

p. 152 Galway Kinnell, "There Are Things I Tell No One," *Mortal Acts Mortal Words* (Boston: Houghton Mifflin, 1980), 59.

p. 153 Willa Cather, *Death Comes for the Archbishop* (Lincoln: University of Nebraska Press, 1999), 54.

p. 156 Rumi, "A Great Wagon," *The Essential Rumi*, trans. Coleman Barks (San Francisco: HarperSanFrancisco, 1995), 36.

p. 157 Lalla (Laldyada), *Naked Song*, trans. Coleman Barks (Athens, Ga.: Maypop, 1992), 29.

p. 157 "Infinite Day," *The Sacred Harp*, 446.

p. 164 Thomas Merton, *New Seeds of Contemplation* (New York: New Directions, 1962), 21–22.

p. 168 William Butler Yeats, "A Voice," *The Soul Is Here for Its Own Joy: Sacred Poems from Many Cultures*, trans. and ed. Robert Bly (Hopewell, N.J.: Echo), 14.

p. 168 Thomas Merton, *The Seven Storey Mountain* (New York: Harcourt Brace Jovanovich, 1976), 37.

p. 168 Reshad Feild, *The Last Barrier: A Journey Through the World of Sufi Teaching* (New York: Harper & Row, 1976), 104.

p. 168 Merton, *The Seven Storey Mountain*, 325.

p. 170 Thoreau, *Walden*, 50.

p. 175 Merton, *New Seeds*, 8.

p. 175 William Stafford, *The Darkness Around Us Is Deep: Selected Poems of William Stafford*, ed. Robert Bly (New York: HarperPerennial, 1993).

p. 175 Merton, *New Seeds*, 13.

p. 176 Hugh Prather, *A Book of Games* (New York: Doubleday, 1975), 60.

p. 179 Rainer Maria Rilke, "I Have Many Brothers in the South," *Risking Everything*, ed. Roger Housden, trans. Robert Bly (New York: Harmony, 2003), 31.

p. 183 Shunryu Suzuki, *Zen Mind, Beginner's Mind* (New York: Weatherhill, 1973), 21.

p. 200 Rumi, "Say Yes Quickly," *The Soul is Here for Its Own Joy*, ed. Robert Bly, trans. Coleman Barks (San Francisco: Ecco, 1995), 157.

p. 202 Chris Maser and James R. Sedell, *From the Forest to the Sea: The Ecology of Wood in Streams and Oceans* (Delray Beach, Fla.: St. Lucie Press, 1994).

p. 203 Maser, et al., *From the Forest*, 57.

p. 204 Maser, et al., *From the Forest*, 4.

p. 205 Rumi, "Who Says Words With My Mouth?" *The Soul Is Here for Its Own Joy*, 162.

p. 212 Rumi, "Longing for the Birds of Solomon," *The Soul Is Here for Its Own Joy*, 176.

p. 222 Daniel Matthews, *Olympic Natural History: a Trailside Reference* (Portland, Oreg.: Raven, 1988), 355.

p. 224 Hafez, "The Garden," *The Soul Is Here for Its Own Joy*, 240

p. 234 "Idumea," *The Sacred Harp*, 47.

p. 234 Gerard Manley Hopkins, *Poems and Prose*, 5.

p. 235 "Claremont," *The Sacred Harp*, 245.

p. 240 Julia Kristeva, "Forgiveness, an Interview," quoted by Allison Rice, *PMLA*, 117, no. 2 (March 2002), 281.

p. 242 Kristeva, "Forgiveness, an Interview," 287.

p. 280 Suzanne Raitt, "Virginia Woolf's Early Novels," *The Cambridge Companion to Virginia Woolf*, ed. Sue Roe and Susan Sellers (Cambridge: Cambridge University Press, 2000), 38.

Acknowledgments

I'm grateful to all who have let their lives be woven with mine, in real life and in this narrative; I acknowledge their guidance and forbearance in checking the facts as they appear here. Thanks are due in particular to John Geisheker, to whom I was married for fifteen years, and to whom I'm indebted forever, especially for his funny and profoundly loving comments on the first draft. Robin Fox, companion of my life these last twenty years, reined in, with his passion for accuracy, any metaphors of mine that threatened to break away. Peter Crysdale, as ever, bothered me on the phone. My children, Jude and Julian O'Reilley, and my sister, Margaret Plumbo, read early versions with a keen eye for the details of households we had in common. I express my deepest thanks to those who have let their lives nudge mine at times of special vulnerability for them, Mary Beth Young in particular, and the man who appears in this book simply as "Richard." Many writers in the genre of personal essay, for very good reasons, fictionalize events in the service of craft, but I try not to do that, except in rare instances where I've shaded the contours of someone's identity, or changed a name, to preserve their privacy. I apologize for any instance in which I've mistaken the details of someone else's story, or inadvertently caused them pain.

My deceased parents and grandparents, whose stories are the bedrock of this narrative, could not give their permission for me to ponder their lives in public. I know they would have seen many things differently. I can only acknowledge my presumption in speculating about matters on which they kept silent; that's a survivor's burden.

Writers are, in most respects, only as good as their editors, and this book was blessed with two of the finest: Emilie Buchwald and H. Emerson Blake. As ever, I'm grateful to the entire staff at Milkweed Editions, but want to thank, in particular, Hilary Reeves and James Cihlar, who worked so hard with me in the final boarding stages, and Jennifer Shepard, copyeditor, for her astute suggestions.

The University of St. Thomas's University Scholars Grant provided reassigned time for me during the writing of this book, and the Sitka Center for Arts and Ecology let me sit in their woods as artist-in-residence. My fellow artists, Brad Mattson and Karl Pilato, were a great inspiration during that residency, living their own lives and vocations with a spirit and joy that inspired me daily.

ABOUT THE AUTHOR

Mary Rose O'Reilley teaches English at the University of St. Thomas, St. Paul, Minnesota. Her prose works include *The Peaceable Classroom*, *Radical Presence*, *The Garden at Night* (Heinemann), and *The Barn at the End of the World* (Milkweed Editions).

Recent awards include a contemplative studies grant from the American Council of Learned Societies, a Bush Artists Grant, and the McKnight Award of Distinction.

O'Reilley's first book of poetry, *Half Wild*, was recently announced the winner of the 2005 Walt Whitman Prize of the Academy of American Poets, selected by Mary Oliver. It will be published by Louisiana State University Press in 2006.

MORE BOOKS ON THE WORLD AS HOME
FROM MILKWEED EDITIONS

To order books or for more information, contact Milkweed at
(800) 520-6455
or visit our Web site (www.milkweed.org).

Toward the Livable City
Edited by Emilie Buchwald

Wild Earth:
Wild Ideas for a World Out of Balance
Edited by Tom Butler

The Book of the Everglades
Edited by Susan Cerulean

Swimming with Giants:
My Encounters with Whales, Dolphins, and Seals
Anne Collet

The Prairie in Her Eyes
Ann Daum

The Colors of Nature:
Culture, Identity, and the Natural World
Edited by Alison H. Deming and Lauret E. Savoy

Boundary Waters:
The Grace of the Wild
Paul Gruchow

Grass Roots:
The Universe of Home
Paul Gruchow

The Necessity of Empty Places
Paul Gruchow

A Sense of the Morning:
Field Notes of a Born Observer
David Brendan Hopes

Bird Songs of the Mesozoic:
A Day Hiker's Guide to the Nearby Wild
David Brendan Hopes

Arctic Refuge:
A Circle of Testimony
Compiled by Hank Lentfer and Carolyn Servid

This Incomparable Land:
A Guide to American Nature Writing
Thomas J. Lyon

A Wing in the Door:
Life with a Red-Tailed Hawk
Peri Phillips McQuay

The Pine Island Paradox
Kathleen Dean Moore

The Barn at the End of the World:
The Apprenticeship of a Quaker, Buddhist Shepherd
Mary Rose O'Reilley

North to Katahdin:
What Hikers Seek on the Trail
Eric Pinder

Ecology of a Cracker Childhood
Janisse Ray

Wild Card Quilt:
The Ecology of Home
Janisse Ray

Back Under Sail:
Recovering the Spirit of Adventure
Migael Scherer

Of Landscape and Longing:
Finding a Home at the Water's Edge
Carolyn Servid

The Book of the Tongass
Edited by Carolyn Servid and Donald Snow

Homestead
Annick Smith

Testimony:
Writers of the West Speak On Behalf of Utah Wilderness
Compiled by Stephen Trimble and Terry Tempest Williams

THE CREDO SERIES

Brown Dog of the Yaak:
Essays on Art and Activism
Rick Bass

At the End of Ridge Road
Joseph Bruchac

Winter Creek:
One Writer's Natural History
John Daniel

Writing the Sacred into the Real
Alison Hawthorne Deming

The Frog Run:
Words and Wildness in the Vermont Woods
John Elder

Taking Care:
Thoughts on Storytelling and Belief
William Kittredge

Cross-Pollinations:
The Marriage of Science and Poetry
Gary Paul Nabhan

An American Child Supreme:
The Education of a Liberation Ecologist
John Nichols

Walking the High Ridge:
Life As Field Trip
Robert Michael Pyle

The Dream of the Marsh Wren:
Writing As Reciprocal Creation
Pattiann Rogers

The Country of Language
Scott Russell Sanders

Shaped by Wind and Water:
Reflections of a Naturalist
Ann Haymond Zwinger

THE WORLD AS HOME

The World As Home, a publishing program of Milkweed Editions, is dedicated to exploring and expanding our relationship with the natural world. These books are a forum for distinctive writing that alerts the reader to vital issues and offers personal testimonies to living harmoniously with the world around us. Learn more about the World As Home at www.milkweed.org/worldashome.

MILKWEED EDITIONS

Founded in 1979, Milkweed Editions is the largest independent, nonprofit literary publisher in the United States. Milkweed publishes with the intention of making a humane impact on society, in the belief that good writing can transform the human heart and spirit. Within this mission, Milkweed publishes in five areas: fiction, nonfiction, poetry, children's literature for middle-grade readers, and the World As Home—books about our relationship with the natural world.